S0-ARO-472

Bipolar **Identity**

'A monarchy conducted with infinite wisdom and infinite benevolence is the most perfect of all possible governments.'

EZRA STILES
American academic and educator (1727–1795) ·

Bipolar **Identity**

Region, Nation, and the
Kannada Language Film

M.K. RAGHAVENDRA

OXFORD
UNIVERSITY PRESS

OXFORD
UNIVERSITY PRESS

Oxford University Press is a department of the University of Oxford.
It furthers the University's objective of excellence in research, scholarship,
and education by publishing worldwide. Oxford is a registered trademark of
Oxford University Press in the UK and in certain other countries

Published in India
by Oxford University Press
YMCA Library Building, Jai Singh Road, New Delhi 110 001, India

© Oxford University Press 2011

The moral rights of the author have been asserted

First published in 2011

All rights reserved. No part of this publication may be reproduced, stored in
a retrieval system, or transmitted, in any form or by any means, without the
prior permission in writing of Oxford University Press, or as expressly permitted
by law, by licence, or under terms agreed with the appropriate reprographics
rights organization. Enquiries concerning reproduction outside the scope of the
above should be sent to the Rights Department, Oxford University Press, at the
address above

You must not circulate this book in any other form
and you must impose this same condition on any acquirer

ISBN-13: 978-0-19-807158-7
ISBN-10: 0-19-807158-2

Typeset in Trump Mediaeval LT STD 9.5/12.6
by Sai Graphic Design, New Delhi 110 055
Printed in India at Rakmo Press, New Delhi 110 020

For

Usha KR,
the kind of attentive reader
that most writers might dream about

Contents

Acknowledgements   ix

Acronyms   x

Introduction: Mysore, Cinema, and Language   xi

1. The Kannada Nation: 1957–69   1

2. The Distance from Delhi: 1970–9   40

3. Vestiges of Mysore: 1980–9   73

4. Provisional Communities: 1990–9   99

5. The Curse of Bangalore: 2000–8   130

Conclusion   161

Notes   169

Bibliography   192

Film Index   201

General Index   205

Acknowledgements

This book would not have been possible without the assistance of the people who helped me in ways that are too difficult to enumerate: Usha K.R., Narendar Pani, B.Y. Krishnamurthy, Maya Chandra, Sushma Veerappa, K.V. Akshara, S. Raghunandana, and the editors of Oxford University Press, who have been deeply understanding, sympathetic, and prompt. The book also owes a debt of gratitude to the comments of the anonymous readers who made helpful suggestions, most of which I implemented. Last but not least, this book would not have been written if I had not been initiated into the career of a film scholar by the Homi Bhabha Fellowships Council which awarded me a fellowship in 2000–01.

Acronyms

AIADMK	All India Anna Dravida Munnetra Kazhagam
AICC	All India Congress Committee
BATF	Bangalore Agenda Task Force
DMK	Dravida Munnetra Kazhagam
FFC	Film Finance Corporation
FRCS	Fellow of the Royal College of Surgeons
I&B	Information and Broadcasting
IGP	Inspector General of Police
IISc	Indian Institute of Science
INC	Indian National Congress
KFCC	Karnataka Film Chamber of Commerce
KPCC	Karnataka Provincial Congress Committee
NFDC	National Film Development Corporation
TDP	Telugu Desam Party
FTII	Film and Television Institute of India
COFEPOSA	Conservation of Foreign Exchange and Prevention of Smuggling Activities Act
BCID	Bradford Centre for International Development

Introduction

Mysore, Cinema, and Language

The Cinemas of India and the Regional Language Film

The 'cinemas of India' is perhaps a more appropriate term to describe the cinema produced in India than 'Indian cinema'. The categories once acknowledged within 'Indian cinema' were only two, 'popular' cinema and 'art' cinema—with 'middle' cinema as a compromise. To distinguish between the two (perhaps antiquated) categories, it can be argued that 'art' cinema (in Hindi and the regional languages) is a by-product of modern Indian literature and the novel,[1] while the varieties of popular cinema inherit the characteristics of the oral tradition.[2] The differences between the Indian popular cinema and Indian art cinema can perhaps be traced to these origins because where the myths deal with typical/archetypal situations and characters, the novel attempts to deal with individuals.

The different categories in popular cinema have themselves risen out of different impetuses and address different constituencies. This may perhaps be more pronounced after 1947, but mainstream Hindi film is the closest we have to a 'national cinema' because it addresses wide audiences within the boundaries of the nation and is deliberately tailored to play this role.[3] After the linguistic reorganization of the states, the different regional language cinemas have had people from the states associated with the respective languages as their constituencies. Tamil and Malayalam cinema cater to people from Tamil Nadu and Kerala respectively, and Kannada cinema caters to those from Karnataka. Since each of these languages has its own diaspora, their respective cinema includes within its constituency those from the diaspora, which often stretches beyond the nation. Tamil cinema, for instance, is popular in Malaysia while cinema in the Bhojpuri dialect is enthusiastically consumed in Mauritius. However, primarily because there is no significant Kannada language diaspora, Kannada cinema is apparently a local cinema addressing people only within Karnataka state.

The Aim of the Inquiry

This is an inquiry into how local/regional identity is addressed in regional language cinema and also whether regional identity can conflict with the national identity/other identities. Kannada (popular) cinema may provide an instance of cinema addressing a local identity with its discourse not influenced from without by a diaspora—since it is consumed almost entirely within a definite political space demarcated by language. Although Kannada art cinema, which commenced around 1970, was seen locally, later day art films, from the late 1970s onwards, are closer to the pan-Indian art film created by the policy associated with the Film Finance Corporation (FFC)[4] and promoted by the National Film Development Corporation (NFDC). This cinema is artistically significant but has had little local appeal. Most of the art cinema in Kannada may, therefore, not be pertinent if our interest is in how the Kannada film addresses local identity.

The inquiry must also take into account various other related factors. Each popular cinema has its constituency and my interest is in how cinema addresses its constituency through narrative. Since the same audience often consumes cinemas in different languages, film texts may address different identities concurrently. Film convention in mainstream Hindi and some of the regional language cinemas appear similar, but the differences will be more significant when our interest is in identities other than the national one.

This book is primarily a work of film interpretation but different kinds of meaning can be made of cinema. A film's meaning to the audience which consumes it locally is not the meaning that a national film jury would ascribe to it, and an academic studying it would construct a third kind of meaning. The meaning I am concerned with is the 'local meaning' of the cinema to the audiences it is intended for, but this is not apparent and may need to be excavated. Taking these factors into consideration, the inquiry proceeds from the following propositions:

1. It is now a truism to say that media texts are not only authored by their creators but also 'co-authored' by audiences.[5] If one supposes that there is a 'natural selection' of patterns and motifs in the popular cinema of any period depending on their pertinence,[6] the role of the consumer co-author is made more significant and this places a greater value upon popular cinema. One could therefore interpret a cinema to understand how the concerns of its constituency are narrativized.

2. Unlike mainstream Hindi cinema which largely addresses the national identity, regional language cinemas are more complex in their address and may appeal to different identities concurrently—for example, the local identity determined by language/region and also the national one. As an example, Mani Rathnam's Tamil film *Roja* (1992) addresses national identity through the male protagonist and concurrently appeals to the identity determined by region/language through the film's heroine.[7]

3. Many of the regional popular cinemas in India operate roughly with the same codes that mainstream Hindi cinema operates and there is also a large overlap of audiences between the two. Our understanding of form and convention in the mainstream Hindi film[8] can therefore be adapted to understand/interpret Kannada popular cinema, although it is the identification of the differences that will be crucial.

4. Interpreting popular cinema in India has tended to be 'theory down', that is, hermeneutics favours the cultural theories (or 'Theory') developed in the West under historically specific circumstances and assumes that Indian cinema is only an

instance in a generality. But an inquiry relying on the larger theories (post-Marxist or psycho-analytical) may not be the most reliable way to interpret local phenomena.[9] If we were to inquire into Kannada cinema's response to Bangalore city, for instance, we may find more clues in the development of Bangalore's industrial climate and the demographic transformation of the city—which have owed to local processes.

5. Karnataka is the state where Kannada is spoken and Kannada cinema consumed. But the state is composed of different Kannada-speaking areas brought together in 1956,[10] in line with the policy of linguistic reorganization of Indian states, and comprises of: (a) former princely Mysore state, (b) a part of the princely state of Hyderabad formerly ruled by the Nizam, (c) a part of the erstwhile Bombay Presidency, (d) a part of the erstwhile Madras Presidency, and (e) Coorg (or Kodagu), which had once been under a British chief commissioner. Since Kannada cinema before 1956 was produced from the area corresponding to the princely state of Mysore,[11] the concerns of the cinema of this era are specific to this region. It may, therefore, be possible to locate the significance of its earliest conventions in this cinema—specifically, in those conventions that depart from the mainstream Hindi film.

The meaning of the term 'local' is always a relative one and depends on the location from where the cinema is viewed. Mainstream Hindi cinema has a 'local' meaning if one is interested in the intricate ways in which it has sustained the nation by narrativizing its social history,[12] and a 'global' meaning if one looks at the way it addresses the diaspora. In the 'local' context in which I propose to examine Kannada cinema, Hindi cinema is 'non-local' and 'national'. This inquiry into Kannada language cinema will examine the changing motifs and narrative turns dominating it between 1956 and the new millennium, and, given that 'identity' is historically constructed, tries to locate them in the social history of the period. Since Kannada language cinema is also an Indian cinema, the inquiry will also explore the possibility of local and national identity coming into conflict at moments of crisis, and how this has been registered—if not in

Kannada cinema, at least in the differences between it and mainstream Hindi cinema. Hindi cinema has a hegemonic presence in Indian cinema that is impossible to ignore. At the same time, its discourse has also a basis in the subsuming characteristics of nationhood and national identity.[13] An inquiry into regional language cinema (as instantiated by Kannada cinema) could reveal some areas of resistance to the subsumption. The 'national' cinema represented by the mainstream Hindi film is a bland category because of its desire to cause as little annoyance as possible,[14] but regional language cinema—Kannada, Telugu, and Tamil cinema in particular—does not hesitate to cross the boundaries of 'good taste' and give offense. This 'aggressiveness' on the part of regional language cinema suggests that its study could also reveal local tensions. Kannada cinema comes out of Karnataka, which—in contrast to Tamil Nadu and perhaps Andhra Pradesh—has had less of a history of conflict with the centre[15] and the general findings can perhaps be extended to other Indian cinemas. An important step in interpreting Kannada language cinema usefully would be to arrive at some conclusions pertaining to its narrative conventions. But we first need to examine the milieu in which these conventions were created, because many of them are culturally specific to Kannada cinema.

Understanding the Milieu: The Logic of Indirect Rule

Hindi cinema is intended to appeal to a wide cross-section across an enormous territory and therefore attempts to use a 'non-local' idiom, but the Kannada popular film began by addressing only the citizens of princely Mysore. Therefore, the socio-political milieu in princely Mysore has a large role to play in our understanding of Kannada film conventions (if not form, which appears to be similar to the mainstream Hindi film). That Hindi, Tamil, Telugu, and Kannada films are frequently dubbed into other languages implies that the films cannot be formally very apart, because they must be understood by audiences from other regions just as they would their own cinema. Needless to add, the information provided here on the milieu in princely Mysore can only be contextual. Since systematic work on the politics of Mysore before 1947 is limited, I have relied largely on two works of historical scholarship that conclude with the creation of Greater Mysore in 1956.[16]

The key factor to realize about princely Mysore was that it was under indirect rule by the British before 1947. After the break-up of the Vijayanagar Empire (1336–1646) and before the rise of Hyder Ali in the 1760s, the area that came to be known as Mysore state was ruled by a network of 'little kingdoms' over which the chieftains who claimed to rule had only a loose suzerainty.[17] The Wadeyar family, the ancestors of the maharaja of Mysore ruled over Mysore, but it was only under Hyder Ali and his son Tipu Sultan that any genuine consolidation of the little kingdoms under one authority took place. After Tipu's defeat in 1799 the British needed suitable rulers for the dominions that they did not wish to administer themselves and reinstated the Wadeyars—although they ruled indirectly through the *dewan* (minister), who was (in the initial period) an official from the Madras Presidency.

When the maharaja resumed power he was required to raise resources for the British while also restoring the splendour befitting a royal court, and the peasantry therefore had grievances. The Wadeyars, being regarded as only one of the numerous chieftains, were also resented by many others and they were unable to contain the north-west region (Nagar province) when the Mysore Insurrection of 1830 took place.[18] The British forces assisted in restoring order but they also superseded the princely government in 1831. The British commissioners ruled thereafter until 1881 when the princely house won reinstatement. The rulers were now sensitive to the crucial nature of British approval and also the need to avoid confrontations with the powerful local elements whose dissatisfaction had seen them deposed. Then there was also the issue of caste. The Wadeyars were Arasus, who were only a few,[19] while the most powerful castes/sects in the region were the Vokkaligas and the Veerashaivas/Lingayats who constituted the local elite and could not be turned into staunch loyalists. It has been argued that these factors contributed to the political climate in princely Mysore and its differences with that of the British-ruled presidencies of Bombay and Madras—though the maharaja was presented with an administrative structure based on the Bombay and Madras models. The British had also installed an Indian official as the dewan with the centralization of power in his hands. These chosen officials were usually of the highest calibre and Mysore state soon earned the reputation of being one of the best administered native states in India. Since caste will be of some importance in this inquiry it may be necessary to note that while Brahmins constituted a small minority in princely Mysore,[20] of the thirteen dewans of Mysore between 1881 and 1947, nine were Brahmins, most of them from the Madras Presidency.

Mysore state was exceedingly fertile and blessed with two rivers, as a consequence of which cheap hydroelectric power could be produced. The state was therefore able to bring off several impressive entrepreneurial schemes. Its performance in areas like industry and education were so impressive that the Government of India rarely interfered in governance either formally or informally. Huge sums were spent to transform Bangalore and Mysore into two of the most elegant cities in South Asia, and Bangalore had electric lights before Bombay, Calcutta, or Madras. Mysore was also the first princely state to have its own university. This progressive image of Mysore state also made the maharaja and the dewan heroes in the eyes of the nationalists and examples of how Indians could rule. The maharaja had also been contributing to the Indian National Congress (INC) from as early as the 1880s. Overall, it may be surmised that Mysore state was a prosperous state, with several contrasts with the rest of India. It was not unaffected by nationalism, but nationalism still remained an abstract sentiment because of the way its space was insulated from colonial encounter by the relative autonomy it enjoyed—a consequence of indirect rule.

Since the thrust of this inquiry will partly depend on the differences between Kannada and Hindi cinema, it is also necessary to acknowledge that Mysore was a Hindu kingdom which was ruled autocratically. Hinduism was more orthodox and the position of the Brahmin caste and the priests more elevated although Veerashaivism developed here as a system of protest against Brahmin domination. It is also to be noted that the fact of the state being governed by Muslim rulers from 1761 to 1799 did not change this Hindu characteristic as far as structure was concerned—although in terms of personnel Brahmins and Veerashaivas were largely replaced by Muslims in this period.[21] The fact that the Mysore regime was virtually created by the colonial power does not mean that it did not strive for autonomy. In fact the struggle for autonomy became the dominant interest of the Mysore Government and the maharaja even designated his country as a 'nation within a nation'.[22] It has even been noted that when the threat to autonomy came, it came from the Congress rather than the British.[23]

Administration, Social Composition, and Conflict

The administrative structure mirrored the one in British India, with each district presided over by a deputy commissioner. Under him, at the taluk level was the *amuldar*, usually an educated young man from one of the towns/cities. These two officials were representatives of the centralized power but the small size of the police made it difficult for the amuldar to extend his influence at the local level. Under the amuldar was the *sheikdar*, usually a person of low education, not part of the gazetted cadres of government service and poorly paid. Given the fact that the rulers were unable to exert influence at the local level, the amuldar was also powerless to prevent the sheikdar from arriving at arrangements locally and this naturally led to high degree of corruption at the lowest official level.[24]

The local board policy in Mysore was devised to follow the example of the Madras Presidency. Since the boards did not exercise significant power and officials were able to maintain strict control over the boards, there was little interest among non-officials even to contest elections. A representative assembly had been created quite early by the rulers but although a provision was made for the election of members in 1891, the position prevailing in the boards also prevailed here. The assembly was given the right to pass resolutions on the general principles of all legislation (including taxation), but none of the resolutions were binding on the government. In 1907, a legislative council was also created with limited powers to vote on proposed legislation submitted to it by the government but the council contained an overwhelming majority of government officials and nominees. Mysore state was governed autocratically—a benevolent autocracy, perhaps—with the rulers ruling largely through their *personal authority* and declining to share power through institutions. At the same time, their reluctance to intrude upon the traditional prerogatives of the dominant elements of the land meant that outside the cities this power was restricted.

As indicated earlier the dominant groups in Mysore were the Vokkaligas (20.4 per cent in 1931) and the Veerashaivas/Lingayats

(12 per cent in 1931).[25] They were, by and large, the landowning groups in the rural areas although the division of land was not as unequal as in other parts of India and individual landholdings never as large. According to a later estimate, compared to the all India average of 18 per cent landless cultivators (28 per cent in Madras), Mysore had a much lower level of landless cultivators (9.7 per cent).[26] If the Vokkaligas and Lingayats had relatively modest landholdings they were still more substantial than that of their neighbours, giving them wealth that could be used productively in other areas like trade, money-lending, small industry, etc. More importantly, the two dominant groups (spread evenly across the state) held the hereditary position of village headships that made them influential. The Brahmins, on the other hand, were few in number (3.8 per cent) and had little or no influence in the rural areas—holding only the hereditary post of village accountant. This lack of influence in the rural areas was compounded by Brahmins migrating to the cities—but this was also paralleled by their increasing affluence in the cities. In 1941, 87 per cent of the Brahmins were literate as against 32.6 per cent of Veerashaivas and 15.2 per cent of Vokkaligas.[27] The Brahmin caste therefore dominated the administrative services of the Mysore government. Sixty-five per cent of the gazetted appointments were held by Brahmins, while Veerashaivas and Vokkaligas had less than 2 per cent each.[28]

Caste/sect being a crucial way in which ties were created and maintained, the largest arena within which sustained social interaction occurred was the area across which people from one caste group or sect had established marriage alliances with other families. The endogamous marriage networks extended over a radius of ten to thirty miles—not more that a day's journey away. Being of the same caste/sect was not enough and families sought out links with families of comparable status, some of these ties reinforced by second and third generation alliances. The marriage networks overlapped with one another so that over a range of eighty or hundred miles an entire endogamous unit would be knitted together. At the state level, the dominant groups later formed associations through the efforts of those from the city, like merchants and civil servants, belonging to the particular caste or sect. While class status—and other factors—were important in contacting marriage ties with other families from the same caste group, people of the same caste/sect could still band together across class barriers through the state level associations.[29]

Although the earliest kind of group conflict witnessed in Mysore after the fall of Tipu Sultan was between the 'Madrasis'— those Brahmins brought in from the Madras Presidency and considered more sophisticated and capable by the British—and those Brahmins who were from Mysore, this conflict was entirely within the administration.[30] The first Mysorean dewan was P.N. Krishnamurthi (1901–6) and the next one was Sir M. Visveswaraiya (1912–18), who was perhaps the greatest of the dewans. A wider conflict—which eventually led to Visveswaraiya's resignation— was the one between the Brahmins and the non-Brahmins for representation in the administration. The 'non-Brahmin movement' was perhaps inspired by the similar movement in the Madras Presidency. As a consequence of this movement, a non-Brahmin dewan (the maharaja's own uncle) was installed in 1919 and a committee under a British jurist, Sir Leslie Miller, was instituted to look into the issue of a quota for non-Brahmins in the administration. The enquiry produced a report that called for a quota-system to favour non-Brahmins in the civil service. The dissatisfaction of the non-Brahmins found itself reflected in the creation and the growth of the Praja Mitra Mandali, a political party that (renamed later as the People's Federation) merged with the Congress prior to Independence. The Praja Mitra Mandali was dominated by Veerashaivas and Muslims (then classified as 'non-Brahmins') with the Vokkaligas becoming more powerful after 1927. As regards the possible conflict between the dominant communities—the Veerashaivas and the Vokkaligas—there is no evidence of it before 1947.[31] While it is difficult to assert that these socio-political factors are all pertinent, some of them appear to influence Kannada cinema's conventions—those that set it apart from the Hindi film.

Form and Convention in Kannada Cinema

Film convention and form are not static but actually change in cinema; still, it is necessary to examine the earliest available Kannada films to understand how the later conventions come about. The prints of only a handful of films from the 1940s and early 1950s are still in existence, and the films chosen here are

R. Nagendra Rao's *Harishchandra* (1943) and H.L.N. Simha's *Gunasagari* (1953). The films are separated by ten years and common to them may be features generally characteristic of early Kannada cinema. Another early film Ramaiyer and Shirur's *Vasanthasena* (1941) will also be touched upon.

Formally, Kannada language cinema of the 1940s and 1950s is akin to the Hindi cinema of the same period. The differences, when they arise, are largely in the areas of motifs and generic conventions. To reiterate what was said earlier, I will try to establish the form/conventions in the early Kannada film through a comparison with those of mainstream Hindi cinema, which have been studied.[32] While Hindi cinema has employed them to narrativize the historical experience of the nation, my purpose here is to examine Kannada cinema's codes and conventions in order to understand how Kannada cinema deals with two overlapping narratives, a local one pertaining to the immediate milieu and another pertaining to the nation—or, rather, attempts to negotiate the space between them. The use of the term 'code' may lead the reader to expect a semiotic study but my reliance is less on visual 'signs' than on the larger units of narration such as standard plot devices.

As in mainstream Hindi cinema, space is not continuous but each separate space is a narrative abstraction defined in terms of its 'qualities'. *Harishchandra* is a version of the popular myth about the truthful king who is tested by the gods but who willingly gives up his kingdom, sells his wife and child to a rich Brahmin—and even himself to the keeper of the cremation ground to honour his commitment to the sage Vishwamitra. The action in the film takes place in separate spaces corresponding to 'palace', 'forest', 'rich Brahmin's house', 'sage's hermitage', 'cremation ground', and 'market place'. Each space has its own signifiers and it is impossible, for instance, to confuse 'palace' with any other kind of dwelling. A distinction is for the doors in the palace to have ornate arches while the doors of rich houses have square tops. Brahmin's are denoted by tonsured heads and tufts and their dwelling is easily identified by their presence. Also used to identify the rich Brahmin's household in *Harishchandra* are the tethered cows. The 'forest' is an abstraction because the film uses footage including all kinds of beasts—tigers, lions, and even apes. Most of the habited spaces are designed sets and there is no likelihood of the viewer confusing one space for another. 'Heaven' is recognizable through the clearly identifiable gods.

The representation of time is also as in the Hindi cinema of the period although *Gunasagari* may appear to depart a little. To elaborate, the films do not specify duration, that is, the time interval lapsing between the first and last event in the story. *Gunasagari* is about the virtuous wife of a rich merchant whose brother-in-law begins to make his desire for her evident. Her husband sets off on a long journey that is to last several months but is stopped nearby, by a river in spate. Being thus halted, he returns home briefly but leaves the next morning after a night of togetherness. A month later the virtuous wife is pregnant but is unable to explain it because the husband's brief return was not made known. Her brother-in-law takes advantage of it to cast aspersions on her character and she is sent off to the forest. Her husband returns a little after the nine-month period of her pregnancy and this nine-month period can pass for 'duration'. However, this interval is crucial to the plot, and the period prior to the pregnancy remains undefined.

As in mainstream Hindi cinema, the only context provided is the family and the film, too, concludes with a family reunion. It is only the appearance of Lord Shiva (as a bear) to protect the heroine in the forest that underplays the 'social' side of *Gunasagari*, bringing it closer to the mythological. At the same time, the furniture and household décor are from a more contemporary milieu. The film neither suggests that it is dealing with an identifiable past nor that it is contemporary, but the general sense is that it is dealing with contemporary 'issues' in a pertinent way.

The narratives of both films chosen here—*Harishchandra* and *Gunasagari*—are similar in their causal linking to the mainstream Hindi film. Both films are episodic which means that while the events respect a chronology, they are not held together by a chain of causes and effects. Instead, both narratives emerge from a key 'first cause' with each subsequent event invoking it.

As observed about mainstream Hindi cinema, the Kannada film subscribes to the 'aesthetics of identity':

Hindi film aesthetics, as has now been sufficiently demonstrated, is based not on cognition but on recognition.... The fan knows what to expect.... Thus the Hindi film is a particular product of 'the aesthetics of identity', which J.M. Lotman (*Die Structur Literarischer Texte*,

Munchen, 1972) opposes to the 'aesthetics of opposition'. A typical also trivial product of the latter is the detective story, which functions, as a rule, on the basis of the reader's ignorance of 'whodunit'.[33]

Two other attendant characteristics are that Kannada cinema disallows 'point-of-view' and it is the passive voice that is favoured in narration. The absence of point-of-view has other consequences and one of them is that the viewer is presented with the 'facts' and the possibilities for suspense and surprise are persistently disregarded. Second, the omniscient eye seems most appropriate for a mode of narration that incorporates the mythological—because divine intervention can hardly allow for 'subjectivity'.

The employment of the passive voice means that psychological motivation cannot play a part. Even wicked or unbecoming thoughts have to be placed in people's heads by external agencies. In *Harishchandra*, for instance, it is the celestial mischief-maker Narada who plants scepticism about the king in the sage Vishwamitra to spark off a difference of opinion with another sage—over the king's adherence to dharma and his capacity to honour the code.

The Message of Dharma

In writing about the mainstream Hindi cinema, M. Madhava Prasad contrasts its relay of meaning to Hollywood, allowing the meaning to be produced in the mind of the viewer.[34] The cited Kannada films are not different from their Hindi counterparts; the messages they relay pertain to virtue/honour that does not stray from the path of dharma, and this is ensured by making the protagonist exemplary.

The unambiguous relay of the pre-existent message means that characters and situations must be typical/archetypal and present in their essence. I earlier proposed that the difference between the popular film and the 'art' film could lie in the former being a product of the oral tradition and the latter a product of the modern Indian novel. While epic characters are larger-than-life, heroic, and emptied of psychology, novels have depended largely on psychology and psychological motivation. The difference between a character as 'type' and 'individual' is illustrated by Devdas, who can either be shown as an indecisive/weak individual (as played by Dilip Kumar in Bimal Roy's 1955 film) or epitomizing weakness and indecision (as played by K.L. Saigal in P.C. Barua's 1935 film). The difference between the two is as allegory is to the novel.

Before the advent of the novel 'the fundamental thing was not men but humanity, not the individual but the species'.[35] The allegory is a 'fable of abstractions', just as the novel is a 'fable of individuals'. Devdas as an individual is a character out of a novel but if he represents the weakness of the Indian feudal class during British rule, he is the subject of an allegory. At the most obvious level, both the Kannada films cited are allegories about dharma[36] in which virtues take the shape of human beings. The conduct of the eponymous protagonists is therefore intended to be instructive. This is supported by the suffering inflicted upon the protagonists not making the viewer fear for them. In *Harishchandra* the periodic return of the story to the wager helps reassure the viewer because it means that the protagonists are being watched over. In *Gunasagari*, divine intervention happens only at a key moment in the forest but, as in the Hindi film, there are earlier scenes involving the protagonist's devotion before lifelike statues of god, which convey the same comfort because of the sense that god is being attentive.

The messages of both films also exclude the possibility of 'motivated action' being meaningful. When people are placed in difficult situations, the films seem to propose, the best way of coming through is to stick to one's dharma. The wives in both films are placed in trouble due to the decisions of their husbands, but they are both certain that in the next incarnation their only wish is to have the same husband. In *Harishchandra*, Vishwamitra sends his assistant Nakshatrika to the king's family with the brief that he should persuade the queen and the prince to rebel against their lot, but the two bear the situation with equanimity and the young prince retorts with the wisdom of an adult.

The Domestic Melodrama and Mythological Film

Like Hindi cinema, Kannada films were, without exception, melodramas in the earlier years, but they also incorporated large chunks of mythology. The mythological in Indian cinema has been understood as an element in the agenda of anti-colonial nationalism. As Partha Chatterjee proposes, anti-colonial nationalism created its own domain of sovereignty within colonial society long before it began its political battle with the imperial power—credited in history text books with the founding of the INC in 1885. Anti-colonial nationalism did this by dividing the world of social institutions and practices into two domains—the material and the spiritual. The material is the domain of the 'outside', of the economy and of statecraft, of science and technology, a domain where the West had proven its superiority. In this domain, western superiority had to be acknowledged and its accomplishments studied and replicated. The 'spiritual' on the other hand, was an 'inner' domain bearing the essence of cultural identity. If in the first phase of social reform, Indian reformers looked to state action to reform traditional institutions and customs, the second phase was different. In the second phase of social reform, which was nationalist, there was already a strong resistance to allow the colonial state to intervene in matters affecting 'national culture'.[37] This finds substantiation in D.G. Phalke's films because Phalke was preoccupied both with replicating 'western' technology and with bringing Indian belief to life. In fact, Phalke used technology to give 'manifestation to the spiritual'. It has been argued that his mythological films were akin to the paintings of Ravi Verma and were a symbol of *swadeshi*; they were intended to bring what was traditionally sacred into the space of the modern, with the 'modern' mediated by colonialism.[38]

Phalke was inspired by a film entitled *The Life of Christ* and became preoccupied with providing Indian spectators with a manifestation of their own beliefs.[39] The mythological in Hindi/ Marathi cinema—at least after the early Phalke era—took the shape of the saint film. It has been argued that the quasi-biographical material pertaining to the lives of saints was used as part of the agenda of nationalism to light the way to social justice. The need to publish new editions of the bhakti poets was emphasized as early as the nineteenth century, and in the 1930s leaders like Gandhi were making the message of spiritual and consequently social equality part of their campaign. Hence, when V. Shantaram made a film about Sant Eknath entitled *Dharmatma* (1935) the film meant to propagate among other things the 'message of non-violence, truth, and national consensus'.[40]

The mythological in Kannada cinema is different from the saint film of the 1930s and appears closer to Phalke's films which are also retold Puranic stories. At the same time they remained popular until the 1980s, and this indicates that they cannot be understood in terms of 'anti-colonial nationalism' but serve a different purpose. While Phalke's films are perhaps too primitive for us to take them as completely realized intent, there is a later Hindi film also based on the Harishchandra legend, V. Shantaram's *Ayodhya Ka Raja* (1932), that may be helpful in our understanding the Kannada *Harishchandra* as a mythological film.

One difference between the two Harishchandra films is that the Hindi film appears much more lavish, with its emphasis on the princely life sacrificed by the protagonist. A closer look at both films shows that while *Ayodhya Ka Raja* uses the long shot even in the palace sequences to convey a sense of indoor space—commensurate with the life of a great king—the medium shot dominates in Nagendra Rao's Kannada film. While Shantaram's film may only be following the precedent followed by Raja Ravi Verma who painted scenes of splendour from the puranas as an expression of nationalist pride, the Kannada *Harishchandra* is only preoccupied with conveying a pertinent message—the devotion of the queen and the prince to the king, and the king conducting himself in accordance with dharma to deserve it. This is supported by scenes of domesticity in the household into which the queen and prince are sold, and which are filmed as in a 'social'—as domestic melodrama. While *Ayodhya Ka Raja* never loses sight of the grandeur of the legend, *Harishchandra* is less intended to 'bring alive the legend' than to deliver a contemporary message. When we examine *Gunasagari*, which came ten years later, we are struck by its similarity to *Harishchandra*—a social which incorporates mythological elements[41] with a message valorizing the wife's loyalty and steadfastness to her husband in the face of great hardship.

The third film I invoked earlier—Ramaiyer and Shirur's *Vasanthasena* (1941)—may now be useful in helping us understand the motif of the noble husband and constant wife in early Kannada cinema. This film is an adaptation of Sudraka's Sanskrit classic *Mricchakatika* purported to have been written around the second century BC. The play is about a young Brahmin merchant named Charudatta and his love for Vasanthasena, a rich courtesan. The love affair is complicated by the king's brother-in-law, who is also attracted to Vasanthasena. Full of romance, eroticism, political intrigue, and comedy, it has numerous twists and turns. The plot is complicated by thieves and mistaken identities, thus also making it comical. Charudatta is poor because of his past generosity but he cannot take his mind away from Vasanthasena. Here he is being vocal on his condition when he is with Vasanthasena:

Let the storm rage for a hundred years. Let the rain fall and the lightening flash incessantly, for now I enjoy the embraces of my beloved and the pleasures that are rarely known by men like me. Happy is the life of the man whose mistress comes to him, and who may warm with his limbs her limbs that are drenched and chilled by the water of the clouds.[42]

The Kannada film seems faithful to the play but turns the erotic relationship between Charudatta and Vasathasena into a one-sided infatuation on her part. When the courtesan paints Charudatta's portrait and clings to it, he is pictured looking upwards as if at heaven and with a halo around his head—to suggest his 'divine' status. Charudatta's house, which is a huge space with pillars and almost like a palace, also has a mural showing the sage Vishwamitra turning away from Menaka who is confronting him with their child. According to the legend, Menaka was sent by (the god) Indra to interrupt Vishwamitra in his penance but fell in love with him thereafter. Vishwamitra declined to follow the life of a householder after he learnt about the child. This mural pertains to the sage's regret and its presence in Charudatta's house after his meeting with Vasanthasena indicates that his feelings are not lustful. The 'erotic' scene between the two in the garden in the rain is also undercut by Charudatta patting her shoulder indulgently—though there is a romantic song indoors that follows.

The relationship changes again later with Vasanthasena behaving like an affectionate mother towards Charudatta's son. After several twists and turns—Charudatta being tried and found guilty for Vasanthasena's 'murder', his being sentenced to death, his young son offering to take his father's place, an insurrection deposing the king, Vasanthasena appearing to prevent Charudatta's execution, and his wife's imminent self-immolation—Charudatta is reunited with the two devoted women and his son. In the final frame, the happy women are both firm in their devotion to him. In this film as in the others the relayed message pertains to the father/husband following his dharma without demur and being the object of extraordinary loyalty to his women and to his son.

Vasanthasena is not a 'lover' now but occupies the position of a devoted wife and mother to his son.

While the kind of sentiments expressed in the three films may not be entirely foreign to mainstream Hindi cinema—it apparently derives from the *Manusmrti* (or the laws of Manu)—it is difficult to identify individual Hindi films so extreme in their 'husband-as-Lord' rhetoric. Hindi films of the 1930s and 1940s were actually engaged in the issue of women's emancipation—for instance, V. Shantaram's *Duniya Na Mane* (1937), in which the wife rebels against patriarchy. The issue of women's emancipation was a principal one in nineteenth- and early twentieth-century reformism, itself part of the agenda of the Indian nationalists.[43] It can be argued that since Mysore was only under indirect British rule, colonialism did not have the same implications in princely Mysore that it had in places where the colonial encounter was more intense. But this explanation still does not account for the preoccupation with a single motif, which may have an independent significance.

Since mainstream Hindi cinema does not acknowledge history, it responds to socio-political issues through familial motifs and family drama. The relationship between the Indian and the land/ nation is allegorized as the love of a son for his mother (*Anmol Ghadi*, 1946; *Awaara*, 1951). The conflict between India and Pakistan was allegorized in *Upkaar* (1967) as the enmity between two brothers over the division of their land. The nation itself has been represented as a village (*Mother India*, 1957), as a family gathering (*Hum Aapke Hain Koun ...!*, 1994), as a cricket team (*Lagaan*, 2001) and even as a community of non-residents (*Kabhi Alvida Naa Kehna*, 2007). Kannada cinema follows mainstream Hindi cinema's codes and we may look for allegorical significance in the husband following his dharma and getting the absolute loyalty of his family. A clue will perhaps be found in the way the families are represented.

In *Harishchandra*, the protagonist is a king and the others are the king's family. In *Vasanthasena*, the male protagonist is a Brahmin but the film plays down this aspect and simply presents him as of 'noble birth'. In the very first scene we see Charudatta in court, appreciatively watching Vasanthasena dance. He is not presented as an ordinary courtier but someone of equal consequence as the king's brother-in-law. Further, Aryaka, who assassinates the king and is crowned (in the play) is a shepherd and difficult to see as a monarch (in the film). Since there are no other nobles in the film apart from the villain, it would seem that Charudatta has the qualities required of a ruler even if he is not placed on the throne. In *Gunasagari*, the male protagonist is a merchant named Malla Setty but rides a horse, a transport not associated with merchants but with princes in South-Indian cinema, for example, S.S. Vasan's Tamil film *Chandralekha* (1948), and we are perhaps invited to regard Malla Setty in this way.

Based on these observations it would appear that status of 'lord' granted to the husband by the wife is associated with the princely class. Considering that this discourse originated in Mysore one can argue that the 'king-and-consort' relationship within the household allegorizes the one between the monarch and his subjects.[44] The king will follow his dharma, while his subjects will be loyal and obedient. If this is admitted, there is still an important question to be answered which is why *Gunasagari* should contain the discourse when it came after the monarchy had concluded.

It may be useful here to point to the absence of generic differentiation in early Kannada cinema with all films being 'mythological'. Invoking a myth may be a way of appealing to tradition and is a useful way of justifying a practice. Myth, as Roland Barthes proposes, is a kind of communication in which the exigencies of a historical moment are given eternal justification.[45] While the appeal to tradition was perhaps initially a way of justifying autocratic rule, 'husband-as-Lord' rhetoric stayed on after it had lost its allegorical significance. A motif created by historical circumstances often stays on simply because it has tested narrative appeal.[46] In the case of Kannada cinema, it retains its status as a laudable sentiment till much later.

Love and Marriage as Narrative Motifs

As in mainstream Hindi films, the 'traditional-ideal' family is a constant element of narrative construction in the Kannada film. The parental presence also provides the Kannada film with a surrogate context and heterosexual love facilitates the closure. But where romance and love are generally pretexts used by the Hindi film to facilitate closure, the Kannada films discussed above depend on the family reunion. The films noticeably do not provide for 'romance'—the male and female protagonists' meeting and love being reciprocal. Either they are already married—in which case it is marital love that is affirmed—or the union is brought about by an 'arranged marriage' as in *Gunasagari*. The relationship in *Vasanthasena* cannot be called a romance since Charudatta is already married and with a son. Moreover, the gestures he employs towards Vasanthasena do not correspond to those recognizable as 'love' from our knowledge of cinema although Vasanthasena employs a range of gestures understandable as 'lovestruck' that eventually make way for another range recognizable as 'concern' and 'submission'.

Heterosexual relationships in mainstream Hindi cinema take several shapes and romance itself only fulfils the closure imperative. Romance needs to be examined along with the attendant circumstances to yield an interpretation. In *Devdas* (1935), for instance, the love between Devdas and Paro provides the father with an opportunity for tyranny and helps make evident Devdas' failings. In *Anmol Ghadi* (1946), a poor boy abandons his sacrificing mother to pursue a rich girl and this motif merits interpretation. Unlike romances, arranged marriages are an anomaly in later Hindi cinema and need an explanation. In *Hum Aapke Hain Koun ...!* (1994), for instance, an arranged marriage cements the *dosti* between Kailas Nath and S.S. Chowdhury. Kannada cinema, in contrast, treated the arranged marriage as the norm for several decades and romance was the anomaly. In *Gunasagari* we know nothing about the family that the heroine comes from or its relationship with the hero. Her family is not even invoked by the film when she is in trouble. I would like to argue here that the 'arranged marriage' is the standard way of denoting heterosexual relationships because of the prevailing endogamy and marriage networks in Mysore—described earlier. We may infer that arranged marriages are between people of the same caste and class background unless specified and also narrativized as an anomaly. The affirmation of marital love is identical to the 'arranged marriage' in as much as it reflects the same social circumstances created by marriage networks and endogamy and sons continue in the same way as their fathers. But occasionally, there is a mythological motif that appears as in K.P. Bhave's *Chiranjeevi* (1936)—that of the childless couple praying for a child and being blessed by a god. The child, according to this convention, grows up more distant from his family and having thoughts only for god. The motif appears in films set apart by more than a decade (as also in Y.R. Swamy's *Bhakta Kanakadasa* [1960]) and it is perhaps a measure of the aspiration on society's part to move away from the narrow loyalties defined by kinship ties towards a higher social ideal. This notion will come up for discussion once again later in the inquiry.

Signifying Religion and Caste

Hindi cinema—at least until the early-1940s—was an exclusively Hindu cinema in as much as 'Hindu' was merely a euphemism for 'human' and other religious identities were made anomalous. When the question of the Muslim's place in undivided India became important, there were a few 'historical' films about Muslim rule—*Tansen* (1943), *Humayun* (1945), and *Shahjehan* (1946)—in effect affirming the commitment of Muslim rulers to 'Hindustan'. After this period, Hindi cinema has periodically introduced Muslim characters into the narrative but always as bearers of their religious identity, and often to denote the secular credentials of the milieu being portrayed. Muslim characters are usually outsiders in Hindu society and sometimes (*Dhool Ka Phool*, 1959) perform the roles of mediators. At the same time, Hindi cinema also attempts to provide a balance through the 'Muslim social' a domestic melodrama genre with Muslim protagonists/characters—for example, *Mere Mehboob* (1963), *Pakeezah* (1971), and *Nikaah* (1982). In H.S. Rawail's *Mere Mehboob*, a single Hindu character performs the role that Muslims perform in other films.

Kannada cinema in its early years is entirely similar to Hindu cinema, but while mainstream Hindi cinema does not emphasize caste except as an anomaly,[47] early Kannada cinema can be termed a 'non-Brahmin cinema', although this assertion needs substantiation. Of the three films cited here, *Gunasagari* appears to have no place for a Brahmin character, although there are caste indicators and the protagonist's family can be identified as Veerashaivas. In *Vasanthasena*, although Charudatta is a Brahmin the film plays down this aspect—although his comic friend Maithreya is often vocal about being a 'poor Brahmin'.

When the eponymous hero of *Harishchandra* loses his kingdom and is forced to sell his wife and daughter, they are put to work in the house of a wealthy Brahmin. Harishchandra sells himself to the keeper of a cremation ground in order to honour an obligation. What is important here is that at the conclusion, when the king is given back his crown and his kingdom, those who have negative roles in the story—including the snake that bit his son and the keeper of the cremation ground—are shown to be gods playing parts in order to subject the righteous king to his tests. The people conspicuously excluded are the Brahmin and his shrewish wife, who once heaped abuse upon the queen. This means, I would like to argue, that where most of those placing obstacles in the king's path are really 'performing' the roles assigned to them, the Brahmin couple conduct themselves shamefully on their own. Considering that the director of the film R. Nagendra Rao was himself a Brahmin,[48] the wicked or comic Brahmin was perhaps a convention of early Kannada cinema. We can only speculate about how this motif—soon cast off—came about but the caste factors influencing politics in princely Mysore evidently contributed.

At the same time, the Brahmin caste is the only *caste* actually denoted. While we may deduce the castes or sects from given names—for instance the title 'Gowda' is associated with the Vokkaligas, some names (like Malla Setty and Nirguna in *Gunasagari*) belong to Veerashaivas, and other characters have Brahmin names—it will be incorrect to regard the naming as denotation of caste or sect, just as it would be erroneous to deduce that caste is implicated in a Hindi film when someone is given the Brahmin surname 'Sharma'. In Kannada cinema, 'Gowda' is the title given to farmers and landowners in *Anna Thangi* (1958) while the Brahmin name Ranganna is given to the noble head master in B.R. Panthulu's *School Master* (1958). But when someone is denoted as 'Brahmin' as in *Harishchandra*, it is *caste* (and not vocation or station) that is denoted. Since no other caste is denoted so explicitly, it can be argued that the figure of the Brahmin is employed to represent *caste hierarchy* and not simply the priestly caste.

Moral Instruction and Dharma

Kannada films, like mainstream Hindi cinema, have moral instruction for the spectator that is roughly derived from the code of dharma, but Kannada films follow it more rigidly. It is, for instance, difficult to trace the emancipated woman of the 1930s Hindi cinema to the code of dharma. While an elaborate

philosophical investigation of the notion of dharma is not pertinent to our purpose, a Sankrit-English dictionary defines the word
dharma as 'that which is established, law, decree; usage, prescribed
conduct; duty, morality, religious merit; good works; justice'.[49]
According to traditional belief, dharma represents the order that
governs creation. But dharma is more than just a set of laws of
physics; it is a religious and moral order that also binds the individual. It is traditionally believed that it is best to follow *one's
own path* rather than the path of others. Action has two ends and
if dharma is action conforming to universal order, *artha* is action
with its ends in selfish interest. The latter is permissible but the
two are hierarchized in such a way that artha is legitimate only
within the limits set by dharma.[50] Although this aspect is usually
glossed over by apologists for the Hindu system, 'one's own path'
is, in practice, not determined by choice but by birth and lineage.[51]
This justifies the common understanding that Indian ethics are
'relativistic',[52] and that their emphasis is upon 'givens'—birth,
lineage, and caste—as the basis for one's moral vocabulary.

While the code of dharma broadly informs Hindi cinema there
are discourses in it that are evidently departures.[53] These departures of its ethical moral discourses from the code of dharma can be
traced to the impact of colonialism and the consequent movement
of the nineteenth-century reformers to 'Christianize Hinduism'
because of their embarrassment with the 'heathen mythology'
which was their inheritance.[54] It was not accidental that most
of the major reformers—from Raja Ram Mohan Roy to Swami
Vivekananda—came from Bengal because Calcutta was the earliest seat of colonial power. Kannada cinema, coming as it did from
a space relatively insulated from the colonial encounter, placed
its emphasis on an ethic closer to dharma. Second, its reliance on
'birth and lineage as the basis of one's moral vocabulary' can also
be associated with practice of endogamy in princely Mysore. The
moral instruction contained in early Kannada cinema therefore
draws greatly from dharma—if not in its philosophical essence,
in the way the public generally understood it.

Of the three films discussed, two provide for villains who have
to be disposed of to resolve the narrative. While the Brahmin
couple in whose household Harishchandra's queen labours without reward conduct themselves shamefully, they are not 'villains'
in as much as their removal is not necessary for the resolution.

This is not true of the villains in the other two films because the heroine's brother-in-law in *Gunasagari* is bitten to death by a poisonous snake, and the king's brother-in-law in *Vasanthasena*—who wishes to rule but is too governed by lust and self-interest to merit the position—is also removed. Both these villains are characterized by artha triumphing over dharma in their actions. To word it differently, their wickedness seems to arise out of the misuse of their given positions while the wickedness of villains in Hindi films like *Awaara* (1951) comes from their 'evil'. Kannada cinema also appears simpler because it does not accommodate the ambiguity of a character like Judge Raghunath (also from *Awaara*) who resists categorization under these terms. For want of other indicators we will take the conflict between dharma and artha as important in our understanding of the moral discourse in the earlier Kannada cinema.

Devotion

Exhibitions of faith and devotion in Hindi popular cinema are usually a way of reassuring the spectator of divine intervention at the appropriate moment. Since the generic conventions of the domestic melodrama do not allow the gods to actually make an appearance, the Hindi film hits upon the device of lifelike statues to which applications are made at devout moments. The singing or the praying is cut to the face of the statue (as shot-reaction shot) and it is as though an actual exchange between a human being and the divine were in progress.[55] The gods must intervene with human understanding in human stories and this implies that some actual tokens of divinity—like the *lingam* or the stone phallus that represents Shiva—are not employed because they are not adequately reassuring. Since the early Kannada domestic melodramas also incorporate mythological elements and the gods *can make appearances*, this observation is not applicable to them and applications can be made to lingams or crude statues—the kinds that are to be found in actual Hindu temples.

Second, the devout sentiments expressed by popular cinema—both in the north and south—can be taken to broadly derive from the bhakti movement, which introduced the notion of the personal god who participates in the life of his devotees. The bhakti movement was a reaction to the domination of religion by the

Brahmin caste. It was dominated by *Vaishnavism* in the north but also had a significant *Shavaite* influence in the south. The deities to which applications are made in Hindi mainstream cinema are therefore Krishna or Rama—who are the most popular avatars of Vishnu. Even in Raj Kapoor's *Satyam Shivam Sundaram* (1978), which suggests Shaivism in its title, the actual display of devotion is to Radha and Krishna. Early Kannada cinema, on the other hand, appears a largely Shaivite cinema perhaps because of the dominant influence of Veerashaivas in Mysore.

Kannada Cinema after 1947

Interpreting Kannada cinema requires an understanding of the above conventions although how they will manifest themselves needs deeper historical scrutiny. But apart from taking note of the conventions, interpreting Kannada cinema after 1947 cannot ignore the behaviour of the Hindi cinema contemporary to it and dissimilarities will be significant. Mainstream Hindi cinema addresses the Indian identity while Kannada cinema may have, after 1947, addressed an identity constituted by the fact of allegiance to both princely Mysore and the Indian nation. It has been argued by film scholars[56] that the Hindi film played an important role in the 1950s to take up issues like Nehru's modernization project to the people. They have found evidence that Hindi cinema was also engaged in defining 'the nation' on behalf of the state. In examining Indian cinema after 1947, they postulate that the resources of the independent nation state were deployed to define a homogeneous 'Indian' culture and theorize about how cinema became useful. Cinema apparently served political purposes in India because it was already bridging cultural differences and producing a homogeneous mass culture for an undifferentiated audience before Independence. What this means to Hindi cinema after 1947 is the proliferation of motifs like the following:[57]

1. The police and the judiciary—as emblems of the independent state—are treated as sacred institutions, when they could be lampooned before 1947. For instance, surrendering to the police becomes an admission of moral guilt as in *Footpath* (1953). To show that justice is fair, the judge himself stands trial in the courtroom as in *Awaara*.

2. The city—as represented by Bombay—becomes an important locale and an emblem of national optimism because of its association with the modern.

3. The attitude towards the 'modern' is always ambivalent. For instance, good modernity is often represented by the construction engineer and the doctor, and bad modernity by gamblers, the club dancer, and the night club.

4. Land reform and agrarian issues are frequently brought into focus as in *Mother India* (1957).

5. The conflict between tradition and modernity is presented as the conflict between the village and the city as in *Naya Daur* (1957). It is also represented by the love of the club dancer and the village woman for the hero. Alternatively, the conflict could also be between good modernity and bad modernity as in *Baazi* (1951) in which the club dancer and the lady doctor both love the hero.

6. The sacred 'mother' becomes a way of representing the nation or the land.

7. The modern woman (as in *Andaz*) becomes a way of problematizing the issue of modernization.

8. The lawyer becomes a way of representing the ruling class because of many Congressmen being lawyers.

Interpretation of cinema depends largely on the detection of representational anomalies. For instance, the motifs pertaining to the modern nation (courtroom, the city and its attractions/dangers) which also find a place in Tamil films of the 1950s are not seen in Kannada cinema of the same period. *Parasakhti* (1952), the well-known film by Krishnan-Panju, which was an instrument of political propaganda by the Dravida Munnetra Kazagham (DMK) party, includes all the polemical devices such as lampooning of the government in Madras and criticism of religious exploitation. At the conclusion of the film, the hero Gunasekharan is produced in court where he indicts the whole of organized society. But the interesting point to be made here is that everyone accused in court lowers his gaze as if in acknowledgement of his/her guilt in the single place where it cannot be denied—the sacred courtroom.

Although *Parasakhti* is nominally set in the pre-Independence era, it portrays the court as Hindi films portray it after 1947—as a sacred site in which the truth must prevail. The colonial courtroom did not have the moral sanctity of a courtroom in independent India. *Parasakhti* demonstrates that a Tamil film can be both deliberately scornful *and* naturally respectful of the independent nation and its institutions—in a way not true of the Hindi films. Tamil films serving the DMK cause are therefore beset by a contradiction in as much as they affirm the independent nation while promoting clashing local issues (such as the DMK-inspired satirizing of 'Independence' and 'progress' under Congress rule). The fact that Kannada films exhibit none of these motifs can be interpreted as Mysore state being less integrated with the nation than the Madras Presidency because of indirect rule before 1947; Mysore therefore experienced Independence differently.

Mysore State and Independence

To recapitulate what was said earlier, since the Mysore rulers belonged to a minority caste group with few affiliations, they were reluctant to intrude upon the prerogatives of the dominant elements of the land and exercised absolute authority only around the cities and towns. Consequently, there was a discontinuity between the state level political arena and the political arenas at the village and local levels. At the same time the tendency of the British had been to keep the princely states insulated from political change in the British provinces and to allow well-administrated states like Mysore a high degree of autonomy. Consequently, there was another discontinuity between the state-level and the national-level political arenas and it was difficult for local activists to draw upon the resources offered by Indian nationalism from outside the state borders.[58] There was, in effect, a lack of integration between the three political arenas (national, state, and local) because of the twin discontinuities.

Political activity in the name of the Congress developed in Mysore in fits and starts. By the 1930s, the Congress in Mysore found itself dominated by Brahmins from the urban areas while the only other political force in the state was the People's Federation (formerly the Praja Mitra Mandali), an organization founded to give non-Brahmins a voice in the state which also enjoyed the patronage of the landed elite. As late as March 1937, the People's Federation routed the Mysore Congress in the elections to the legislative council and the representative assembly—despite the Mysore Congress fighting the elections with All India Congress

Committee (AICC) support. But later the same year, after correctly reading the political climate and seeing this move as essential in its own interests, the People's Federation decisively merged with the Mysore Congress. This move strengthened the Mysore Congress considerably and the party now hoped to gain further strength through the AICC's support.

But the AICC was decidedly two-faced in its relationship with the Mysore Congress. The difficulty was perhaps its maintaining a good relationship with the rulers in Mysore. One of the strategies of the Congress at the national level was to hold up the better governed of the princely states as evidence that good governance was possible without the British and this tended to strengthen the Congress' relationship with Mysore rulers. Consequently, the Mysore Congress was persuaded by the AICC to restrict itself to a 'constructive work' programme. After the merger of the People's Federation with the Mysore Congress, there was unrest in Bangalore and six persons were killed in police firing. A representative was therefore dispatched to Calcutta to an AICC meeting where a resolution was passed condemning the 'ruthless policy of repression of the Mysore government'. Within a fortnight, however, Gandhi attacked the AICC resolution in an article in the *Harijan* where he reiterated that the Congress in Mysore should restrict itself to 'constructive work' and the Dewan Sir Mirza Ismail had Gandhi's article translated and read out in hundreds of villages. It appeared that the central leaders were not particularly concerned with bringing freedom to Mysore.

These facts may appear extraneous to the subject on hand but it is necessary to understand that political activism in Mysore was far behind what it was in the presidencies ruled directly by the British. When the Quit India movement began in 1942, there was a spontaneous upsurge among students in the cities to Gandhi's call while the Mysore Congress had actually fallen behind, and the Mysore Congress even abstained from the Quit India agitation, which had taken a life of its own without its leadership. It has been generally noted that between 1942 and 1947, the younger nationalists tended to look to the national leadership rather than the leaders of the Mysore Congress whom they did not altogether trust, although the Mysore Congress did eventually take over the reigns of leadership.

The Moment of Independence

While Kannada cinema after 1947 exhibits few of the motifs common to Hindi cinema of the same period, it would be inaccurate to say that Independence is not registered by Kannada cinema because of a curious motif appearing in *Gunasagari*, which may be considered anomalous. In writing about the Hindi cinema coming immediately after Independence, a scholar notes that apart from acknowledging nationhood as an abstract notion, the films of the period appear to even experience it viscerally[59] and they tend to signal this through changes in narrative structure and an uncharacteristic open-endedness.

Independence may be experienced as 'nationhood' but there is another way it can be experienced viscerally and that is as 'freedom'. *Gunasagari* has a strange motif and it is perhaps significant that one or two Hindi films after 1947 also exhibit them, notably Raj Kapoor's *Aag* (1948). As explained earlier, *Gunasagari* is about an 'arranged marriage' between Gunasagari (Pandari Bai) and a prosperous merchant named Malla Setty (Honnappa Bhagwatar), which runs into rough weather because Malla Setty's brother Nirguna (T.S. Balayya) begins to covet his sister-in-law, this becoming the cause of her troubles. What I find intriguing is that Nirguna takes it upon himself to paint his sister-in-law secretly and this act becomes a covert way of 'possessing her'. This aspect of 'possessing' her body is given emphasis when he paints her in full and standing up—instead of only her countenance. Nirguna also inserts a black spot on her upper lip as a way of putting his mark upon her.

It is significant that when the act of painting the woman is undertaken by the man (this is also true of *Aag*), it is not a way of recollecting a beloved but an act of transgression—since the woman cannot be his. But the sense of transgression is much more severe in the Kannada film because the woman is the man's sister-in-law and the tie between brothers is normally sacred. It is for this reason that Nirguna is punished with death although it is a snake (familiar from a mythological like *Harishchandra*) that carries out the punishment. My argument here is that there is a sense of 'freedom' in the film, instanced as freedom to transgress that is anomalous for a cinema in which the codes of social behaviour are so rigidly ordained. Even when early Kannada cinema is dealing with erotic comedy—which is what *Vasanthasena* is intended to be—Kannada cinema finds the means to tone down its mischievous side. The explanation offered for the disconcerting motif in *Gunasagari* is that it came after autocratic rule by a monarch had ended and 'freedom' had a visceral, threatening quality to it.

Mysore in the 1950s and Linguistic Reorganization

Between 1947, which marked the end of monarchy in Mysore, and 1956, when linguistic reorganization created Greater Mysore, the state leadership under the Congress was inclined to squabble. The Congress leadership in Mysore was not brought into prominence through mass mobilization and was therefore largely an elite with its influence founded on group loyalties and patronage. Mass mobilization implies appealing to the lowest level, resulting in competition for the same support base and, therefore, the growth of a multi-party system. The absence of mass mobilization in Mysore meant one-party rule and the party itself was largely constituted as earlier, finding its bases in patronage and group loyalties. This also meant that the single party had no clear ideology or programme to offer but proceeded by trying to offend as few supporters as possible and building a consensus. Also, when dissidence developed due to dissatisfaction, it developed within the Congress rather than as opposition to it. It was because of the squabbling within the party that Nehru visited the state in January 1951 to urge Congressmen to mend their differences. Although huge party enrolments of the Congress brought influential people at the local level in non-urban areas into politics, the lack of integration between the state level and the national level political arenas continued. We may therefore hypothesize that Mysore state was relatively slow in integrating with the national mainstream in the 1950s, although this does not mean the existence of strong regional loyalties to Mysore state.

The other factor of importance here is the relationship between Mysore and other Kannada-speaking areas. The national leadership, as already explained, had been lukewarm to the Mysore Congress because of its own affinity to the princely rulers. This was very different from the situation in the other Kannada-speaking areas. As part of the Kannada-speaking area of India, Mysore had been placed under the jurisdiction of the Karnataka

Provincial Congress Committee (KPCC), centred mainly in the area coming under the Bombay Presidency, an area left undeveloped by the Bombay government because it was a linguistic minority region. During the civil disobedience movements in British India in the 1930s, the KPCC cultivated its contacts in Mysore to obtain money and manpower but did not reciprocate with financial aid to the Congress in Mysore. Not surprisingly, Mysore Congressmen felt they were being used by the Karnataka Congressmen. Relations between the two worsened after 1935 when the KPCC placed itself in the camp of those opposing AICC aid to the nationalist organizations in the princely states.[60] Mysore Congressmen were also more drawn to Madras than to Bombay-Karnataka because popular newspapers bringing news of British India to Mysore came from Madras. Transportation to Madras was better than transportation to Hubli-Dharwar, and Gandhi also tended to be accompanied on his visits to Mysore by leaders from Madras.

Since the Kannada-speaking areas outside Mysore suffered the most because of their linguistic-minority status, it was outside Mysore that the movement for unification of Kannada areas began.[61] The Karnataka Vidyavardhaka Sangh, for instance, was founded in Dharwad in 1890 by R.H. Deshpande, and important personages of the Ekikarana movement like Aluru Venkata Rao came from northern Kannada-speaking regions outside Mysore state. Mysore itself did not stand to gain materially through the unification of the Kannada areas because it was the most prosperous of the regions. When the linguistic reorganization of the states was considered in the 1950s, the government agreed to the creation of Andhra Pradesh because everyone was for it. When it came to the unification of the Kannada-speaking regions, however, the required consensus proved elusive for want of agreement of a majority of the people, including the people of the erstwhile Mysore state. Those opposing the linguistic reorganization of Mysore into a new state felt that their interests, both cultural and administrative, would suffer in the enlarged state.[62] Mysore state had the smallest incidence of landlessness in south India and this was hardly true of other Kannada-speaking regions. Another important consideration was the prospect of demographic realignment. The largest single community—Vokkaliga—would lose its political influence with the integration of Veerashaiva majority regions with Mysore.[63] As a result of the ambivalence in the stand taken by Mysore state, the linguistic reorganization of the Telugu regions into a single Andhra Pradesh was conceded in 1953 after Potti Sriramulu's death in 1952, but that of the Kannada regions was put off once again. The ambivalent position taken by Mysore state with regard to reorganization apparently persisted until the Chief Minister K. Hanumanthiah's statement in late 1953 dispelled the idea that Mysore was not in favour of reorganization.[64] Reorganization was a key issue between 1953 and 1956 with the state gradually reconciling itself to its prospect because of the pressure applied (largely) from outside through agitations and protests.

Kannada Cinema awaits Linguistic Reorganization

A key factor to be considered in interpreting a body of popular cinema is whether certain motifs are repeated at certain times. The popularity of a motif in a short period of two to three years may therefore be a reliable indication of its pertinence and merits interpretation. Interpretation of popular cinema often presumes that films may talk indirectly. If films need to be pertinent even while being fantasies, historical films, or mythologicals, their methods may be allegorical. Three Kannada mythologicals in the period 1954–6 exhibit the same motifs although they do not deal with the same events and this leads us to interpret them as allegories of socio-political developments. The films are H.L.N. Simha's *Bedara Kannappa* (1954), K.R. Seetharama Sastry's *Mahakavi Kalidasa* (1955), and Aroor Pattabhi's *Bhakta Vijaya* (1956). What follows is an examination of these three films and the interpretation of a key motif appearing in them. It is necessary to describe the films briefly in order to identify the common motif.

Bedara Kannappa (1954), which is based on a folk tale involving a tribal saint from Srikalahasti, begins in heaven with a Gandharva (a heavenly being) accidentally killing a peacock and being cursed by the god of wealth Kubera to be reborn on earth as a lowly hunter. The young Gandharva (Rajkumar) appeals to Shiva who regrets his inability to undo the curse, but suggests that the Gandharva make use of the opportunity provided by the curse to bring righteousness to the world. The Gandharva agrees and he and his wife (Pandari Bai) are therefore planted on earth as infants, to be adopted by a tribe of hunters and given the names

Dinna and Neela. The two grow up to adulthood and their marriage is duly solemnized by the tribe. Dinna has however grown up to be an impetuous young man and he soon quarrels with some other tribals and is cast out with Neela by his adoptive father, the tribal chieftain. Dinna, although made to undergo hardship, remains proud and a fierce unbeliever until the god Shiva appears as a mendicant to relieve him of his troubles. Dinna then understands his errors and becomes a devotee. Providing comic relief in the story are a cunning Brahmin (G.V. Iyer), his good-hearted wife, son (Narasimharaju), and two courtesans—a mother and daughter. Much of the story of *Bedara Kannappa* is true to the original legend. Dinna offers meat to the deity and, while he is castigated for it by the Brahmin priest, Shiva recognizes his devotion. Dinna cuts out both his eyes and offers them to the *linga* (sacred stone phallus) when he finds the eyes on it bleeding. Shiva restores his eyesight when he recognizes Dinna's devotion and the story ends happily and he is called Kannappa. The story is fairly true to the original legend but the changes instituted are very significant.

The scheming Brahmin is a characteristic presence in many saint films (for example, *Sant Tukaram*, 1936) because the bhakti movement was itself a reaction to the Brahmin domination of religion. But *Bedara Kannappa* is not a saint film like *Sant Tukaram* because it begins in heaven and the protagonist is a celestial being who takes human shape rather than someone actually from the marginalized class seeking a personal god—as Tukaram is represented. The motif of the villainous/comic Brahmin has therefore the same basis as the motif in *Harishchandra*. But more significantly, the Gandharva in the prologue is dressed like a prince, with Kubera and the other gods as higher ranking kings or princes attending Shiva's court. His 'princely pride' is also carried over when he is reborn although the story is about his losing it. The original legend itself is silent about Kannappa's pride and the film is introducing it with a purpose. Another factor to be noted is that while Dinna is born a tribal, there is no more mention of the tribe once he is cast out of it. His dealings thereafter are entirely with mainstream society, complete with its caste and class hierarchies. Dinna's devotion being acknowledged by the god Shiva at the conclusion sees him neither going back to his tribe nor ascending to heaven. He is simply gathered into society and Dinna and Neela may be said to gain a community. This is given emphasis when the film does not end as popular films in India usually do—with a family reunion or a happy meeting of separated lovers but with the two joining the social mainstream. The Gowda who is nominally the chieftain is not dressed as a prince/king but simply like the way landowners are portrayed in popular films. I propose that this is done because the true stature of Kannappa is that of a prince and having another prince/king in the concluding scenes might have confused the audience. As presented in the film, Kannappa is not the social inferior of the Gowda because he is actually a prince, athough there are 'kings' above him outside the community.

The second film, K.R. Seetharama Sastry's *Mahakavi Kalidasa* (1955), also relies on a legend—the legend of Kalidasa who authored the Sanskrit classic, *Shakuntala*. In the legend, an arrogant princess is tricked into marrying an ignorant rustic by making her believe that he is learned. When the rustic is cast out he seeks the blessings of the goddess who blesses him with great scholarship. In the film, the rustic is actually an aristocratic young man (Honnappa Bhagavatar) who is cursed with ignorance by his guru for showing him disrespect and he becomes a cowherd. Here the princess does not cast out her husband but he forgets her when he is blessed with scholarship by the goddess. The princess nonetheless follows him to the court of Vikramadhitya in Ujjain and both of them eventually become ordinary subjects of King Vikramadhitya. There is also a twist in the story when Kalidasa's father-in-law intends to install him as his own kingly successor, but Kalidasa prefers to remain an ordinary subject in Ujjain to being a king in his own land and the general sense is that it is the community in Ujjain presided over by Vikramadhitya where he and his wife, the princess, rightly belong. The film also includes the familiar motif of scheming Brahmins out to undermine Kalidasa in Vikramadhitya's court.

The third film, *Bhakta Vijaya* (1956) by Aroor Pattabhi, is also about a proud aristocrat cursed with poverty. In this film, Santhoba (Rajkumar) is a landowner who is cursed by a poor tenant's wife when he tries to evict them for remaining behind in their payments. Santhoba also conducts himself arrogantly with the saint Tukaram but understands his errors and gives away his wealth. Thereafter, he is joined by his wife and he becomes a mendicant and undergoes suffering, only to be helped by the god

Pandurang in human form. The film concludes with Pandurang appearing to Santhoba and him joining Tukaram's community of devotees. In this film as well, there is the motif of the self-serving Brahmin with the good-hearted wife who come into contact with Santhoba, although the Brahmin does him no harm. The film has aspects in common with the other two films and one of these is the representation of the proud Santhoba as a princely personage, wearing jewellery, riding on horseback, and living in a palace.

The three films appear to conform to a single pattern. If we were to identify the common motifs in them, we could say they were about an arrogant prince and/or princess who suffer hardship and poverty because of a curse, but overcome it by appealing to the divine. In all three films there is the sense of a community gained, a community not presided over by the protagonists but by a benevolent authority to which the protagonist submits. In *Bedara Kannappa* and *Bhakta Vijaya*, the community is one of devotees and the authority divine, while in *Mahakavi Kalidasa*, the community is in Ujjain and presided over by King Vikramadhitya. In all three films, the wife joins her husband but the films do not achieve closure through the family reunion, as was the case in *Vasanthasena*, *Harishchandra*, and *Gunasagari*. All three of the later films also feature self-serving Brahmins and their presence has already been explained through the caste issues in princely Mysore.

The fact that the stories of at least two of the films have been deliberately altered suggests that the changes are intended to have them fit a model that would make them pertinent to the times. It is significant that the story of Kalidasa was retold as *Kavirathna Kalidas* (1983), with Kalidasa initially being an ignorant rustic and not an aristocrat. As indicated earlier, for a fantasy or a mythological to be made 'pertinent' its approach must be allegorical. It has also been argued[65] that the distinction between the 'public' and the 'private' that characterizes the first world/developed countries has not yet emerged in the newly independent nations of Africa, South America, and Asia, and 'private stories' therefore have public connotations. Since a popular text must have common connotations for the community it is addressing and the community is usually national, the text is a 'national allegory'. In the case of Kannada cinema, which addresses both the regional and the national identity, we may surmise that the allegory pertains to the region and/or the nation. The 'region' at the time the films were made was apparently confined to the area once under princely Mysore.

Coming to the actual interpretation of the common motif identified in the three films, the motif of the prince should perhaps be considered in the light of Mysore being a former princely state and the representational habits cultivated under monarchy may persist for a while. 'King' and 'country' are synonymous to subjects in a monarchy and this suggests the prince's/princess' predicament in the three films has parallels with the predicament of (former) princely Mysore in the period, 1954–6. The fact that the prince and the princess share the suffering substantiates that this is a predicament shared by the king and his subjects rather than the privation forced upon an individual. This is consistent with my earlier reading of wife and husband being in the analogous position of subjects and monarch.

If this interpretation is conceded, the 'curse' of poverty and hardship finds correspondence in the apprehensions of prosperous former princely Mysore when faced with the prospect of integration with areas which were much poorer and relatively undeveloped. The fact that it was a 'curse' with no remedy suggests that the people of former princely Mysore (the constituency addressed by the film) gradually came to realize that they had no option but to submit. The only solace was perhaps that there was a 'higher' benevolent monarch/authority ensuring that the dispensation would not be without recourse. By showing that in the process of dealing with the curse, the prince also gains a larger community, the films seem to appeal to the attractions of an integrated Kannada community. There are two other films in the same period—T.V. Singh Thakur's films *Sodari* (1955) and *Ohileshwara* (1956)—which work with the same theme of the king becoming poor, and it is apparent that the motif carries a strong resonance in the period, 1954–6.

The Tenor of the Inquiry

The arguments offered hitherto include some interpretation but the purpose of this introduction has been to lay a foundation for an inquiry into Kannada cinema after linguistic reorganization. I have tried to hypothesize hitherto on the identity addressed by Kannada cinema in its earliest phase and it would appear from the discourses contained in it that until the linguistic reorganization of the states in 1956 Kannada cinema addressed only the identity of the citizen of (former) princely Mysore. This being the case it is to be seen whether this cinema went about building a 'Kannada nation' after 1956 and the extent of its success. We also need to understand how the experience of being Indian is taken note of by this cinema and the possible crisis moments when the identities marked by former princely Mysore, by the Kannada language, and by the Indian nation came into conflict/contestation. Overall, it can be said that the purpose is to chart out the way Kannada cinema responds to both the region and the nation, or, to phrase it differently, how it negotiates the space between the two. This factor alone makes it more complex than Hindi cinema, which responded traditionally to the nation. The rest of the book is given to examining key motifs in films generally considered important—not for the official accolades heaped upon them but for their public appeal. There has not been much textual analysis of Kannada cinema either in English or Kannada, but there have been informative histories published in Kannada which are factual.[66] Whatever analysis is presented here, which is not fact-based but textual, is founded on an independent viewing of the films. Popular film texts, being 'co-authored' by the audience, are vast mines of information about the social and political discourses of their times and I propose to go ahead with their excavation. This is a diachronic study and the individual chapters are therefore roughly divided according to decades, although, occasionally, a film appearing in a particular decade may be discussed only in a subsequent chapter because of its pertinence at that point. The study—covering significant Kannada films between 1957 and 2008—ends with a brief conclusion in which I will speculate on the future role of Kannada cinema.

1. The Kannada Nation
1957–69

The Process of Integration

Mysore acceded to the Indian Union nearly two months after Independence and it was only on 12 October that Maharaja Jayachamaraja Wadeyar signed away the prerogatives of the princely house of Mysore. This chapter will deal with the decade or so after the linguistic reorganization of the states but we must first briefly examine the years in which the political system of former princely Mysore was integrated with the polity of independent India. While many of the details may not be relevant to understand cinema, they are being provided to give the reader a clearer sense of the political climate prevailing within the milieu.

The Indian political party system in its earlier period was a system dominated by a single party. It was a competitive party system but the competing parties played dissimilar roles in it. In 1947, the Congress, which was a broad-based nationalist party before Independence, transformed itself into the dominant political party of the nation. Although a number of opposition parties came into existence they did not constitute an alternative to the ruling party. Their role was, instead, to constantly pressurize, criticize, exert pressure and influence from outside—if the ruling party strayed too far from public opinion; actual political competition was internalized and carried on within the Congress.[1] Mysore developed even more markedly along the same lines because there were no political parties outside the Congress. The Congress leadership in Mysore had not been brought into prominence through mass mobilization but had relied on patronage, coming into prominence through group loyalties; they were patricians by temperament and aloof from their supporters.

When the first state level cabinet was constituted in October 1947, most of the leaders belonged to an inner circle headed by the Chief Minister K.C. Reddy. This group was also apparently under the influence of a prominent (but illiterate) landowner and money-lender from Mysore city who contrived to place as many as four ministers who were obliged to him[2] in the cabinet. Caste/religious considerations were primary—as may have been expected—and the cabinet attempted to represent all significant caste/religious groups.

Dissidence within the state Congress emerged early and the reasons were these: the aloofness of the leaders towards their supporters and their forming a coterie, the lack of a clear policy laying down the aims of the government, and the delay in decision making. Apart from all this was the 'corruption' in the government. While K.C. Reddy's inner circle did not favour 'spoils politics', the prominent landowner from Mysore was abusing his influence.[3] The fiery youth leader Hanumanthaiah, along with his key associates, also came out against the systematic strengthening of 'dominant caste' people in the party and drew support from several disaffected groups.

The state had made considerable headway by 1952 in becoming politically integrated with the nation. New men were being attracted to the Congress who were unschooled in party politics but with a large appetite for political power, and the aloofness of the leaders did not suit them. The new entrants had to be admitted into power in some way and also made aware of the extent to which authority had to be ceded to the Indian union by the state. As a result of the growth in government expenditure and the extension of the public sector the state government—which under the maharaja had stayed away from the local arenas—began to impinge upon local politics significantly. The tightening of official control over food grain purchase and distribution also had an impact upon rural life. With the increasing use of cash as a measure of wealth and status—partly resulting from entrepreneurship—the hereditary authority of the local leadership also diminished. With the growth of markets beyond the local, there was also a move on the part of many of the families to contract marriage alliances away from the narrow local domain. These alliances strengthened those with ambitions in state politics and many people with influence joined the only supra-local political organization in the state—the Congress party. By March 1952, the Mysore Congress had developed to a stage roughly comparable to that reached by the Congresses in the rest of India on the eve of Indian Independence.[4]

The period between 1952 and just prior to the linguistic reorganization can be said to belong to Kengal Hanumanthaiah. He entered office as chief minister in March 1952 and was quick in taking decisive action to strengthen the party in Mysore. First, he set about getting the loyalty of legislators by giving them control over allotment of government licenses and distribution of funds for development work. Second, he made it clear to the state bureaucracy that it could not be free of official 'interference' and it soon became an agent of the ruling party. The ability of the legislators to extend patronage at the local level built bonds of loyalty that had not existed hitherto.[5]

With the linguistic reorganization of the states in 1956 politicians from former princely Mysore had an obvious advantage over those from the other areas in their efforts to take charge of Greater Mysore. The Kannada speaking politicians who inherited princely Mysore were able to approach linguistic reorganization with a considerable organizational advantage over their colleagues in the Kannada-speaking districts outside the state and they were able to move directly to power.[6] It should be observed here that there was also a caste factor involved in the issue of unification. If the unification movement, coming from areas where the Veerashaivas were greater in number, was dominated by them, the Vokkaligas, because they would be reduced in the enlarged state, did not favour it. The issue of unification partly became a covert power struggle between Vokkaligas and Veerashaivas. Both Nijalingappa and Hanumanthaiah favoured unification although they were rivals. It was however Hanumanthaiah who officially gave his endorsement to unification despite being a Vokkaliga. Consequently,

Nijalingappa came to power with help from Vokkaligas who had been against unification.[7]

Princes and Gods: Continuing with the Mythological

Among the Kannada films coming after 1956 are a few mythological films dealing with the familiar motifs of princes and their dealings with the gods. The actor Rajkumar has a key role to play in these films—as well as in others—but the key actors of this era are only a handful: the comedians Narasimharaju and Balakrishna, the actresses Leelavathi, Pandari Bai, and B. Saroja Devi, and the character-actor Ashwath. If Rajkumar is the male protagonist in most of the films of the 1950s it may also be because—being the most durable of the Kannada actors—the films with Rajkumar have been preserved with more care.   •

Mythological films do not dominate Kannada cinema after 1956 as much because of the appearance of the family melodrama (the 'social') and the historical film but we may begin this examination with two mythological films of the period—K. Shankar's *Bhukailasa* (1958) and B.S. Ranga's *Mahishasura Mardhini* (1959). Another film Hunsur Krishnamurthy's *Sri Krishna Garudi* (1958), dealing with the bickering among the Pandavas for 'portfolios'—after Yudhishtira's installation as king—clearly allegorizes politics in Greater Mysore but the allegorical side of the other two mythological films is less apparent.

The first of the two films was made in Kannada, Telugu, and Tamil simultaneously, and was a remake of an earlier Telugu film.[8] Although the Kannada version was made separately (and not simply dubbed) this makes it difficult to assert that *Bhukailasa* is a strictly Kannada film. Still, the motifs it has in common with *Mahishasura Mardhini* make it appear a specific commentary on the milieu. This becomes much more striking if the motifs are regarded as a continuation of the motifs in *Bedara Kannappa* and *Bhakta Vijaya*.

It is significant that while all four films—the two before 1956 and the two coming afterwards—are about princes and their dealings with gods, the later two films adopt a position that seems a contradiction of the earlier films. It must be emphasized that the stories are all faithful to mythology and there is no wanton distortion of the mythological element in them. Still, it is interesting to look at the differences in the mythological elements selected.

Bedara Kannappa and *Bhakta Vijaya*, it may be recalled, are about princes submitting to poverty in order to devote themselves to god. The relationship between the god in question (usually Shiva) and the protagonist is like that between a benevolent protector and a supplicant—and the relayed message pertains to unconditional submission to the divine. Let us now examine the two films coming after 1956—*Bhukailasa* and *Mahishasura Mardhini*.

Bhukailasa tells a story about Ravana (Rajkumar) who has grown so arrogant with his prowess that he challenges the gods. Ravana in the film embarks upon penance so severe that Shiva has no alternative but to grant him a boon. When Shiva (Ashwath) comes before Ravana to grant him the boon, he appears with his consort Parvati. Ravana is so drunk with the power derived from his penance that he dares to desire Parvati and claim her for his wife. Shiva is aghast but when he pleads with Ravana to reconsider, the arrogant king simply walks away—until Shiva stops him hastily and makes over Parvati to him. The rest of the film is about the subterfuge thought up by Narada to retrieve the goddess and induce King Ravana to marry the Princess Mandodari (B. Saroja Devi), instead of Shiva's consort.

The second film, *Mahishasura Mardhini*, begins with the wrongdoing of the gods. The god is Indra and he has an *asura* (demon)[9] king killed by a crocodile when he is in penance. The Asura's son Rambha is a *brahmachari* but after he procures a magical fruit from the land of the serpents, he decides to take a wife and beget a child. Indra intervenes once again and tricks Rambha into marrying a buffalo. But Rambha nonetheless has a son named Mahishasura who is tutored by Shukracharya, the teacher of the Asuras. Rambha is eventually killed by Indra through more trickery and when Mahishasura (Rajkumar) learns this he wants revenge. Mahishasura has also taken a princess for a queen but, against her wishes, decides to do rigorous penance and acquire powers to use against the gods; as in *Bhukailasa*, the gods become jittery because they cannot refuse him the boon. Mahishasura, made powerful by the boon from Brahma goes on the rampage in heaven and wreaks havoc. Eventually, it is once again Narada who devices a method and the gods induce Parvati to take a form—as the goddess Durga—that helps neutralize the strength granted to the asura by Brahma's boon, and it is the goddess who kills Mahishasura in battle.

The two films have several features in common, but before I get into that there is an aspect of *Mahishasura Mardhini* that requires commentry. While Mahishasura is arrogant, molests celestial nymphs, and (like Ravana in *Bhukailasa*) does not follow the code of dharma, his queen nonetheless conducts herself as the devoted wives do in films like *Harishchandra*, *Bedara Kannappa*, and *Bhakta Vijaya*. Since the wife is devoted to a husband who challenges the gods, there is effectively a conflict of loyalties that needs resolving. The film hits upon having her being equally devoted to her husband and to Parvati and being perpetually in prayer. At the conclusion—and before her husband's death—her devotion is acknowledged by Parvati (as Durga) and she becomes a garland around the goddess' neck.

Coming to the similarities between the two mythological films just cited, the major one may be identified as the god and the king being treated roughly as equals with a democratic transaction between them rather than unconditional submission. In fact, the king as 'devotee' has a self-important swagger that is unmistakable. In both *Bhukailasa* and *Mahishasura Mardhini*, the king engages in rigorous penance and demands powers from the gods as though they were his right. In both films the king responds to the divine visitation (during his penance) as though the god was an expected visitor and this is different from the rapturous way the protagonist receives the gods in *Bedara Kannappa*. Narada also plays a different role in these films and another mythological—to be discussed later. While in films like *Harishchandra*, Narada is a mischief maker, in these films (and more briefly in T.V. Singh Thakur's *Kaivara Mahathme*, 1961) he plays the more worthy role of intermediary between heaven and earth. Since the gods do wrong in these films and their wrongs cannot be indicated to them by someone who is merely a human, Narada becomes the moral agent pointing out the ethical deficiencies in their conduct.[10]

The relationship between gods and kings appears transformed after 1956 and in order to interpret the new relationship it is necessary to revert back to what kings and gods represented in the earlier films. As I argued, a king or a prince was a way of allegorizing the princely state and it is reasonable to assume that the representational habit continues after 1956. In the same way the god may be taken to represent the object of loyalty/adulation placed above the state—that is, the nation. If this is admitted, the interrogation of the gods through Narada finds correspondence in the mutually respectful relationship between the state and the nation. The relationship between the king and the god gradually becoming one between equals is consistent with this. The motif of interrogation of the gods perhaps has a parallel in the court-room scene in Hindi cinema of the 1950s in which the judge is interrogated (*Dhool Ka Phool*, 1959) for a wrongdoing.

This explanation appears to account for the change in the shape of the mythological film but one difficulty remains, which is why the representation should alter only after 1956—when Mysore had come under democratic rule in 1947. An argument which may be advanced is that the reorganized state after 1956 was different in a fundamental way—it was not even notionally a former 'nation within a nation' but integrated with India. Having become part of the nation not on their own but due to the decision of the central state, the citizens of Greater Mysore were perhaps more aware of their claims upon the nation. Since Kannada cinema was still produced in the region that was once constituted by princely Mysore, it may be surmised that these two films in Kannada cinema believe that they represented Kannada and not Mysore, but still represented the Kannada nation by employing the vocabulary of princely Mysore. This representation of the reconstituted state as a 'king' or 'prince' persists in Kannada historical and mythological films much longer—virtually as long as the genres remain current—till into the 1980s.

While dealing with the mythological film of the late 1950s there is another motif that requires notice, a motif that I identified in the introduction while discussing kinship ties and family networks in princely Mysore. The motif is perhaps seen earliest in K.P. Bhave's *Chiranjeevi* (1936). In films of this category a child-less couple is divinely blessed with a child and when the child grows up he becomes distant from his family and has thoughts only for god. I remarked earlier that this motif could be a measure of the aspiration on society's part to move away from narrow attachments defined by kinship ties towards higher loyalties. The years up to 1960–1, as has been observed by critics, was the period in which optimism over the nation was made palpable in Hindi cinema.[11] It would be expected that such a period of nationalistic optimism would also be the most appropriate moment for narrow loyalties to be abandoned.

Two Kannada films of around this period—Y.R. Swamy's *Bhaktha Kanakadasa* (1960) and T.V. Singh Thakur's *Kaivara Mahathme* (1961)—display the motif just described. In both films the protagonist moves away from the identity determined by his birth and embraces god although it involves hardship and being ostracized.[12] *Chiranjeevi* itself appeared when there was a move away from 'narrow loyalties' towards nationalism. The year 1936 marks the cruicial moment when a movement gathered strength to unify the opposition to princely rule in Mysore—when the Mysore Congress moved away from being a local entity by establishing stronger ties with the INC. This also occurred just before the non-Brahmin movement—through the People's Federation—merged with the Congress.[13]

The 'Social' Genre and the 'Modern'

The 'modern' is a key notion in the Hindi cinema of the 1950s where it holds out both a promise and a threat. The promise is often made through the figure of the doctor, who embodies science and freedom from superstition, and while the threat finds expression in the nightclub and the gambler, the abandonment of tradition. The Kannada socials deal with the notion of the 'modern' but the epithet does not mean the same things to them that it does to the Hindi films. The socials arriving after 1956 are different from one like *Gunasagari* in as much as they decline to employ the motif of intervention by the divine. In fact they announce their intention by including key characters describable as 'agents of Nehruvian modernity'—a doctor in K.S. Murthy/R. Ramamurthy's *Rayara Sose* (1957) and a schoolteacher in B.R. Panthulu's *School Master* (1958). It is as though the presence of these agents keep the gods out of the films.

Rayara Sose is set in the family of a miserly moneylender and revolves around the old man sending his daughter-in-law back to fetch the dowry her father was required to pay him. The daughter-in-law's father is a rationalist with nationalist sympathies (pictures of Nehru and Gandhi hang on his walls) and he is prone to giving away whatever wealth he has to the needy. The moneylender's son (Kalyana Kumar) is goodhearted but will not oppose his father openly. There is no criticism of his 'weakness' here and it is as if opposing a father would not be correct; the code of dharma is still operating here, unlike in Hindi films which frequently include violent confrontations between fathers and sons as in *Awaara* (1951).

In order to persuade his daughter-in-law to return with the dowry, the moneylender proposes that his son to marry a second time—although the son loves his wife dearly. If the son expresses his unwillingness the moneylender is even willing to adopt the son of a woman-servant (the cook), and nominate the young man Ganapa (Narasimharaju) as his sole heir. The film takes a curious twist here because Ganapa gets it into his head that becoming the moneylender's 'adopted son' entitles him to his daughter-in-law as well. Given the position granted to 'servants' in popular cinema, in both Kannada and Hindi, the notion of a servant desiring the married heroine is anomalous—even as comedy—and the motif therefore merits interpretation.

The stratification of major characters in the narrative into rigid classes is not a characteristic of Hindi cinema of the 1950s and generally admitted are only two categories: 'rich' and 'poor', with commerce between the two not being prohibited. Kamal Amrohi's *Mahal* (1949) and Mehboob Khan's *Amar* (1954) are apparent examples here. In contrast, the early Kannada films examined in the introduction suggest a more rigid kind of social stratification because it is not only 'rich or 'poor' that is the criterion. I have already noted the reference to the Brahmin caste and there are other social categories owing nothing to financial criteria—like 'merchants', 'farmers', 'courtesans', 'ascetics', and 'servants', with a suggestion that no legitimate commerce is possible between them. In *Gunasagari*, the villain employs two criminals to liquidate the heroine (his sister-in-law). While the criminals have a change of heart, it is only important that they are represented by racial stereotypes—they are dark, pot-bellied, and bare-chested. The keeper of the cremation ground in *Harishchandra* also appears to belong to this category. The explanation offering itself is that Kannada cinema comes from a more rigidly hierarchical society because princely Mysore was a Hindu kingdom with a limited exposure to colonial rule. What is crucial to Hindu hierarchy, as opposed to other kinds of hierarchy, is that it is not imposed by the exercise of power and access to wealth alone, but is actually separate. The highest caste in Hindu society was neither the wealthiest nor exercised political power, but was associated with 'ritual purity'.[14] The acquisition of wealth and power did not, therefore, alter one's position in relation to 'purity'. Kannada cinema does not invoke 'purity', but the films examined hitherto regard hierarchy as inviolable. It is in this specific context of 'inviolable hierarchy' that the motif in *Rayara Sose* becomes an anomaly.

Ganapa's comic desire to have the married heroine as his wife at the moment when she is most vulnerable is unusual and our discomfort is accentuated by her husband not being a pillar of strength. For all their comic excesses, Ganapa's antics even seem threatening. If we look at what makes the heroine vulnerable— she comes from the same caste or hierarchical category as the hero since their marriage was 'arranged'—it apparently rests in her father not being wealthy enough to meet her dowry. The issue of 'money' makes the moneylender consider substituting the existing family ties with ties outside hierarchy—through adoption. To phrase it differently, since the father-in-law and the cook (Ganapa's mother) come from different hierarchical categories, the film perceives a threat from wealth prevailing over the traditional notion of hierarchy. This is complicated when the husband's doctor friend (Rajkumar) arranges it so that the wife is restored to her husband and the existing order is re-established—although the moneylender changes his ways.

The film leaves us in no doubt that the doctor is an agent of modernity[15] but the doctor being used to affirm the existing familial/patriarchal order is a departure when we compare it to Hindi films like *Dil Ek Mandir* (1963) in which the doctor is the agent bringing the family situation to crisis. In Hindi films of the late 1950s, the doctor is the person standing against traditional prejudices and becomes the agent of change, but *Rayara Sose* does the opposite when the doctor restores the 'status quo'. Since it is difficult to understand the employment of the 'modern' in the Kannada cinema of the period on the basis of *Rayara Sose* alone, I propose to examine two other socials from the same period which also involve 'agents of modernity' and conclude with an examination of the the 'modern'.

While the other films use cultivated urban Kannada, K.R. Seetharama Sastry's *Anna Thangi* (1958) is entirely in the rustic Kannada spoken by farmers in rural Mysore and Mandya districts. This film is a drama about enmity between relatives within the same extended family. The hero played by Rajkumar toils hard to send his sister to be educated in Bangalore while his uncle, who has denied him his rightful share in the property, sends his son to the city as well. The two cousins are, unknown to their guardians, in love. They signal their city attachments by breaking off into English—with words like 'nonsense' frequently uttered. Modernity in this film is also signalled by the telegrams from the city brought to the illiterate (apparently Vokkaliga) landowner by his literate (apparently Brahmin) accountant (Balakrishna). It is also signalled by the dark glasses worn by the two lovers when they descend from the train and their cultivated cavorting. Modernity is signified in the film but it is not as important an element in the story as it is in *Rayara Sose*. It neither makes a promise nor holds a threat and when a resolution is reached it is only the coming together of the reconciled family—with 'modernity' rendered irrelevant.

The film chooses 'love' over an 'arrangement' in marriage but 'forbidden love' is still restricted to the confines of a single family. Family networks and kinship ties are apparently in place and still influential. *Anna Thangi* is perhaps also the first Kannada film in which the police appear, although their role is nominal. There is, as in the Hindi cinema of the period, an association made between them and the Indian state and the police are evidently its emblem.[16] This film being partly conceived as comedy, there is a passing acknowledgment at the conclusion that the troubles caused by the characters to each other are frivolous and, though the Indian state chooses to intervene briefly, it is really preoccupied with more important matters.

B.R. Panthulu's *School Master* (1958) is a more ambitious film, evidently intended as a nationalist statement and needs deeper scrutiny. In this film, the noble schoolteacher Ranganna (B.R. Panthulu) returns as headmaster to the primary school in his own native village and proceeds to set it right. The other characters in the village are Gundappa, an incompetent teacher (Balakrishna), and Nagappa, the corrupt chairman of the village panchayat. Ranganna, as may be expected, not only wins the loyalty of his students (especially an orphan named Vasu) but also Nagappa's undying enmity.

In the second part of the film Ranganna's own children grow up and find different love interests. Ravi marries Nagappa's daughter Radha, Gopi does well, becomes an amuldar (civil servant) and marries a rich girl from Shimoga. Ranganna's sons are now better off than he is but they do not pay their parents enough attention and the two aged people find themselves separated and unwanted in their sons' homes.

In the last part of the film Ranganna is in financial trouble on account of the money he has spent on his children and his house is auctioned. The house is secretly purchased by his old student Vasu (Shivaji Ganesan), who is now a senior police officer. When Ranganna is wrongly accused by Nagappa of stealing Radha's jewellery and taken to the police station, he is terrified of the law and the stern police officer till the police officer reveals that he is his former student Vasu and returns Ranganna's house to him with a gesture of immense respect. The false nature of Nagappa's complaint has also come to light by this time. The film concludes with reunion of family with Vasu (in civilian clothes) also present.

School Master is important to Kannada cinema for the number of new motifs it introduces. Ranganna is a local person from the village but is still being transferred from 'outside', implying that whatever qualities he needs to reform the local system were acquired outside. The 'village' is a way of allegorizing the nation, as in Mehboob Khan's *Mother India* (1957), and I propose that 'village' and 'outside' in *School Master* correspond to Greater Mysore and India, respectively. If this is conceded, the schoolteacher Ranganna is an agent of Nehruvian modernity coming in to reform the local system. The modern nation as a moral agent is also in accordance with the spirit of the late 1950s. The chief aspect of the village in need of change is its corruption. Hindi cinema of the 1950s is replete with zamindars, moneylenders, smugglers, gamblers, gangsters, and aristocrats as villains, but there appear to be few corrupt officials or politicians—which is how Nagappa is portrayed in *School Master* because of corruption being endemic to Mysore. At the same time, modernity in Kannada cinema has none of the technological/scientific/rationalist implications that it has in Hindi films where the doctor rather than the school teacher is its preferred agent—as in *Baazi* (1951) and *Dil Ek Mandir*. Even in *Rayara Sose*, in which the doctor is the agent, he does not save lives as in the Hindi films.

The second aspect of *School Master* is that it is the perhaps the first Kannada film to propose 'romance' as a basis for marriage, rather than family ties. Considering that a boy from Malur (in

Kolar district) is shown to marry a girl from Shimoga (300 kilo-
metres away) suggests that the family networks described earlier
are not a determining a factor in contracting marriage alliances
and Bangalore is the site in which 'love' (alliances across networks)
happens. There is a suggestion that the girl from Shimoga is a
Veerashaiva while the boy from Malur is not, and the fact of the
girl being rich overrides caste/sect as a consideration in alliances.[17]
Since this marriage turns out badly—with Ranganna's wife having to perform the duties of a menial in her son's household—the
film regards (like *Rayara Sose*) the possibility of wealth prevailing
over other kinds of hierarchy as threatening. The motif of the rich
wife's wishes prevailing over the husband's is also associated with
the notion of hierarchy. As already explained, the relationship
between wife and husband was once an allegory of the one between
subject to ruler and it is therefore hierarchical. The wife's money
helping her override the husband's wishes apparently points to the
undermining of traditional hierarchy. This is a motif that keeps
reappearing in Kannada cinema subsequently.

School Master accepts the possibility of alliances across family networks, but at the same time the places named—Kolar and
Shimoga districts—are in former princely Mysore—the areas
outside it are still outside the possibility of marriage alliances. It
should also be noted here that in *Rayara Sose* there are two other
servants apart from Ganapa's mother. One of these servants speaks
Mangalore Kannada (from former Madras Presidency) and the
other speaks Belgaum Kannada (from former Bombay Presidency),
and these servants are segregated hierarchically from Ganapa and
his mother who speak Mysore Kannada. These aspects suggest
that the integration of the Kannada areas into a single 'nation' is
still incomplete in the late 1950s.

The third aspect of *School Master* that draws our attention is
the way in which the police are regarded. When Ranganna is taken
to the police station having been accused of stealing his daughter-
in-law's jewellery, he is terrified of the police. The officer Vasu,
who respects him deeply, is unmistakably harsh towards him—so
that the surprise of getting his own house back as a gift is made
more pleasant! It is pertinent here that in the Hindi cinema of
the 1950s the police are not viewed with such awe by law-abiding
people and the relationship between the citizen and the policeman is more matter-of-fact. There is a clear recognition that the

state is a creation of the citizen and can be interrogated. Inspector Vasu revealing his true identity to Ranganna can be interpreted as the Indian state being the citizen's creation—Vasu is after all 'Ranganna's creation'—but this commonplace sentiment is even startling to the schoolteacher. Since the policeman is an emblem of the Indian state in Kannada cinema (as also in Hindi cinema), it points to the Indian state being removed from the citizens of Greater Mysore. This aspect will, however, need further examination in the light of how it develops.

The three films discussed here all acknowledge the pull of Nehruvian modernity, a notion that dominated Hindi cinema in the same period but the Kannada films are different. As I said earlier, Nehruvian modernity, *by itself*, neither makes promises nor threatens Kannada cinema in the late 1950s. This is very different from Hindi cinema where the club dancer and the gambler were symptoms of alarm and the good doctor emblematic of modernity's promise. The reason that Kannada cinema does not react in such a manifest way is perhaps because modernity had already been ushered into Mysore much earlier. The period 1910–18 constituted the most active years in the economic history of princely Mysore. They were characterized by far-reaching industrialization programmes and efforts at achieving economic self-reliance, quite unique in India at the time. Unlike the Gandhian model with its emphasis on *swadesi*, Dewan Sir M. Visveswaraiya actually anticipated the Nehruvian model because for him development was a race in which the western nations had already a huge lead. Visveswaraiya, like Nehru, also favoured a 'mixed economy' with state investment to hasten industrial progress—although this was often opposed by the British. Although Visverswaraiya had to resign in 1918 due to the caste issues that had come to the front, his policies were not dropped. In fact, Sir Mirza Ismail, who remained dewan from 1926–41, was an admirer of Visveswaraiya and continued many of the same policies.[18] Mirza Ismail resigned in 1941, ostensibly due to the controversy over a proposal for a project to produce cars in Mysore in collaboration with an American manufacturer.

The 'modern' may not have the implications for Kannada cinema that it did for the Hindi film but it is the notion that is most manifest when the Nehruvian nation 'penetrates' Kannada cinema. If we were to make an inventory of the motifs in the three socials just discussed in this section which pertain to this 'penetration', they could be divided into 'promises' and 'threats' although of an entirely different kind from those seen in Hindi cinema. The 'promises' would include the eradication of corruption and the arrival of impersonal authority in the shape of the policeman. They would also include the weakening of the arranged marriage with the admission of people outside the marriage networks into families. The 'threats' would incude traditional hierarchy being overturned by money and official power. The 'threats' and 'promises' are nominally demarcated but there is still uncertainty about what penetration by the 'modern Nehruvian nation' might imply. While the doctor does not perform the 'rationalist' function entrusted to him in Hindi cinema—perhaps because science and rationality were not new to Mysore—his presence is reassuring and helps to reaffirm traditional hierarchy. At the same time, the figure of the policeman, while promising much, still creates a sense of discomfort. *Anna Thangi* is abashed at the need to involve the police in local conflict, while in *School Master*, the policeman elicits terror. Overall, it would seem from Kannada cinema that Mysore is welcoming the Indian nation only guardedly and the major fear is that its admission might weaken Mysore's hierarchical stability. The authority of the nation state—as emblemized by the police—is perhaps also too unknown a quantity not to be regarded without trepidation in the late 1950s.

The Two Nations

It is now acknowledged that historical films partly project the concerns of the present back into the past[19] and this is true of Indian cinema as well. Kannada cinema beginning in the late 1950s was also actively engaged in constructing a Kannada nation by appealing to the past—especially empires like the one in Vijayanagar and to heroic kings and queens. The three films examined in this context are N.C. Rajan's *Ranadheera Kanteerava* (1960), R. Nagendra Rao's *Vijayanagarada Veeraputra* (1961), and B.R. Panthulu's *Kittur Chanamma* (1961).

Ranadheera Kanteerava is a story of palace intrigue under the Wadeyars and the film begins with a young king who loves pleasure, being accosted by his mother the dowager queen and his uncle Kanteerava (Rajkumar). The young king sees the error of his ways and intends to reform but he is poisoned at the behest of his minister. His uncle Kanteerava is installed in his place as king by the political lobby in the palace. It is expected that Kanteerava will be pliable but he becomes powerful in his own right and triumphs.

The film is preoccupied with defining a Kannada identity, and apart from the opening song eulogizing Kannada, proceeds about it in two ways. On the one hand are Kanteerava's friendly dealings with various chieftains or emissaries who speak different kinds of Kannada. Kanteerava is also allowed to have two wives and the second is a 'romance' signifying the knitting of Kannada areas outside the traditional marriage networks—as also suggested in *School Master*. On the other hand are Kanteerava's deeds against the Tamils. The chief of these acts is his defeating a Tamil wrestler in Tiruchi. Characters who speak Tamil and Malayalam are placed by the film in the position of Kanteerava's adversaries. After Kanteerava's killing of the Tiruchi wrestler, the wrestler's brother who is intent upon revenge attempts to enter into a secret alliance with the crafty minister trying to undo Kanteerava.

Ranadheera Kanteerava sets about trying to define an inclusive Kannada identity but it is still former princely Mysore in its address. Evidence of its covert exclusivity is its lampooning of the Kannada spoken outside Mysore. It also refers to a glorious moment in the history of Mysore as a way of eulogizing the Kannada nation alongside the recognition that Mysore's Hindu rulers were usually decadent and idlers. Still, there is one feature about the historical film that needs acknowledgement. Since the kings were actual individuals with their own histories, they weaken the single representation of 'king-as-lord'—which was a way of allegorizing Mysore state as an ideal monarchy. There are therefore two kinds of kings posited by *Ranadheera Kanteerava*: the ineffectual, pleasure-loving kind, and the courageous, responsible kind. The distinction implies recognition that the loyalty of the subjects is not the only issue but also the fairness of the ruler, which could only have happened under democratic rule.

Vijayanagarada Veeraputra is a historical romance about an assassination plot against the King Krishnadeva Raya (Udaya Kumar) by a vassal named Guruvaraya (Nagendra Rao). Guruvaraya is an arrogant chieftain who is resented by his subjects and when his chariot runs over a child, the boy's father kidnaps Guruvaraya's son and brings him up as his own son Vikrama (Sudarshan).

Vikrama grows up into a Robin Hood figure (with bow, cap, and feather) and saves Krishnadeva Raya's life. Eventually, Vikrama takes his place as the chieftain in his real father's place.

Two aspects of *Vijayanagarada Veeraputra* are immediately pertinent. On the one hand is the idea of the king being answerable to his subjects (as in *Ranadheera Kanteerava*), and on the other is the notion of the subjects being ruled by two different sovereigns, one subservient to the other and the greater monarch deserving more loyalty. It may be recollected that in the introduction (while discussing *Mahakavi Kalidasa*), I had interpreted the two objects of loyalty as corresponding to the former princely state and the Indian nation. If in *Vijayanagarada Veeraputra* the two objects of loyalty correspond to the Greater Mysore and the Indian nation respectively, it is the Indian nation that deserves more loyalty.

If *Vijayanagarada Veeraputra* confirms the subordination of the Kannada nation to the Indian nation, *Kittur Channamma* is a straightforward product of Indian nationalism. *Kittur Channamma* deals with the colonial period and makes an attempt to enlist a national heroine from Belgaum district (Bombay Karnataka) on behalf of the Kannada nation. The film begins with a schoolteacher (B.R. Panthulu) invoking Rani Channamma of Kittur as a heroic precursor of Gandhi. The film remains fairly true to the actual story of Rani Channamma of Kittur and explains concepts like the 'Doctrine of Lapse'. Channamma (B. Saroja Devi) is the second wife of the Raja Mallasarja (Rajkumar) who is captured by Tipu Sultan but escapes—with Tipu duly appreciating his valour. As opposed to the Mallasarja's first marriage, his wedding to Channamma takes place after a 'romance'—once again suggesting a discourse about the knitting of territories not linked by marriage networks.

Much of actual story of Mallasarja and Channamma involves bickering with other Indian rulers and the film does not avoid this aspect when it upholds Indian nationalism. But what it does is to present the British as the primary enemies. In fact, Mallasarja comes to grief at the hands of the Peshwas but Channamma persists in seeing them as the lesser of the evils. Part of the conflict in the film comes from Channamma's step-son continuing to see the Peshwas as the primary enemies. As in *Ranadheera Kanteerava*, there is treachery by ministers in the pay of the British. Most of the events in the film pertain to the early nineteenth century, after the fall of Tipu in 1799 and the reinstatement of the Wadeyars in Mysore.

In praising the kingdom of Kittur, the film briefly pours scorn on the rulers of Mysore—as lackeys of the British. At the same time, Channamma speaks the Kannada spoken in Mysore while her two ministers/advisors (who are British agents) speak the language of Belgaum (Bombay Karnataka). The film is apparently identifying a suitable icon for the Kannada nation while at the same time, through its use of different Kannada dialects, showing Mysore as synonymous with Kannada—not sincerely conceding that the Kannada areas outside it are also legitimately 'Kannada'. There is a privileging of Mysore over the other Kannada-speaking areas, an aspect noticed in *Rayara Sose* in which the servants who speak Mysore Kannada are hierarchically distinguished from those who speak other kinds of Kannada.

While the creation of Greater Mysore was expected—by its advocates like Alur Venkata Rao from Dharwad—to result in an undifferentiated Kannada nation (and the growth of Kannadatva/ Kannadaness as an emotion), there were (and are) apparently several impediments. As indicated earlier, the clamour for a Kannada nation came from outside Mysore, from Kannada speaking sections who had suffered under the yoke of other languages. Since this feeling was born out of a sense of deprivation, it did not find resonance in former princely Mysore where Kannada enjoyed the status of a ruling language. While 'Kannadaness/Kannadatva' would have been a sentiment best expressed by someone from the deprived areas where language had brought people together, it was expressed by people from the privileged monarchical state of princely Mysore where language could not be as critical in the forging of an identity.[20] This was not helped by political power being wielded from Bangalore and the enlarged state being called 'Mysore' until 1973.

Melodrama or Realism

Whenever we deal with Indian cinema of the 1960s it is always best to keep in mind the fact of the military debacle in the Sino-Indian War which interrupted the optimistic nationalism of the early Nehru years in India and had a profound effect upon popular cinema. While in Hindi cinema it led to a new kind of escapism,[21] it is interesting to examine the response of Kannada cinema

through a film from 1963. The film is G.V. Iyer's *Bhoodana* (1963),
a film that had all three major male stars of the era—Rajkumar,
Kalyana Kumar, and Udaya Kumar. This film is different from
any Kannada film coming before in as much as it is closer in spirit
to realism, than to the domestic melodrama of the earlier years.
To elaborate, melodrama is not only a matter of exaggerated gestures (in which *Bhoodana* abounds), but contains identifiable
narrative elements such as moral polarization, strong emotional-
ism, extreme states of being, persecution of the good, and a final
reward for virtue.[22] But even more importantly, the centre of interest in the underlying drama resides in what has been called the
'moral occult'[23]—a metaphysical system encoded in the narrative
to reward virtue and punish wrongdoing. The metaphysical agent
rewarding virtue in early Kannada cinema was god—in mythological films like *Harishchandra* and *Bedara Kannappa*. If 'king'
was a way of representing Mysore, then 'god' became a way of
allegorizing the Indian nation after 1947. When 'god' does not figure, the Indian nation, or an affiliated idea, still helps in the moral
resolution. While *Kittur Channamma* is about a small monarch's
sacrifice for the idea of the nation, *Vijayanagarada Veeraputra*
proposes a smaller and a greater monarch with loyalty to the
greater monarch being total. This greater monarch is also the
conduit through which true justice flows and this means that the
loyalty is not unquestioning but has been thoughtfully accorded.

Apart from these films that support the view that the Indian
nation is the moral agent in the historical film, it must be recollected that the social also does not differ in its emphasis—before
1962. In *Rayara Sose* the moral agent is the doctor (an emblem
of Nehruvian modernity), and in *School Master* the two moral
agents are the schoolteacher (representing Nehruvian modernity)[24]
and the Police Inspector (emblem of the Indian state). *Bhoodana*
is different in as much as there is little evidence of either a
metaphysical—or a political—agent rewarding virtue and this
makes it deeply pessimistic. This also takes it closer to realism[25]
although it has songs and emotional scenes as in other Kannada
melodramas.

In *Bhoodana*, Dasanna (Rajkumar) is a poor peasant with a
daughter and two sons, Ramanna (Udaya Kumar) and Lakshmana
(Kalyana Kumar). He is hopeful of getting land when Acharya
Vinobha Bhave's Bhoodan movement gets under way. The cunning

landowner Lakshmipathy (G.V. Iyer) decides to gift away five acres
of land to the movement, which is duly made over to the peasant. Dasanna is overjoyed but the land turns out to be unfit for
cultivation. He therefore borrows from Lakshmipathy to develop
the land and in the process gets into debt and loses the little
wealth that he has. His sons go to work on a coffee plantation and
marry a Christian and a Muslim respectively, getting some land
as incentive. Dasanna is therefore left with neither any wealth
nor any sons and he loses his sanity. The film opts for a forced,
'happy' resolution when the Bhoodan administrators return and
Lakshmipathy is exposed. The landowner is contrite and gives
away his entire wealth to the movement. The film concludes with
the people cheering for the Bhoodan movement.

The Bhoodan movement was a failure for the reason cited by the
film—the landowners giving away only uncultivable land, and the
film is being truthful.[26] What is however singular is the subject
being dealt with in the idiom of popular cinema,[27] and yet taking
this shape. If the universe of melodrama has a just 'god' watching
over the virtuous, the universe of realism is 'godless'—virtue is
left unrewarded and wickedness goes unpunished. Considering
that 'god' was a way of representing the Indian nation in Kannada
melodramas, the 'godlessness' of *Bhoodana*[28]—and the absence
of any other signifier for the nation—is perhaps indicative of
the local consciousness putting the Indian nation aside after the
Chinese debacle when nationalism was subdued. It is perhaps also
the fact of the film being 'godless' that also allows Dasanna's son's
to change their faith—abandon god, as it were.

Faith and the Devotional Film

I have hitherto attempted to demonstrate how linguistic reorganization led to generic differentiation in Kannada cinema which had
till then, by and large, restricted itself to mythological subjects.[29]
By the early 1960s, Kannada films could be broadly classified as
mythological and 'folklore' films (for example, *Bhukailasa*),
'socials' or domestic melodramas (for example, *School Master*),
historical and adventure films (for example, *Kittur Channamma*
and *Vijayanagarada Veeraputra*). Films resisting such categorization include *Vasanthasena*, an adaptation of a literary classic, and
Bhoodana, which is the closest that Kannada cinema came to
realism until 1962. This is not to say that further differentiation

within these genres is not feasible. The domestic melodrama, for instance, includes an agrarian category exemplified by *Anna Thangi* as well as the urban one represented by *School Master*. The devotional film (*Kaivara Mahathme*) is also different from the Kannada films that tell stories derived from Hindu mythology like *Bhukailasa* and *Mahishasura Mardhini*.

As indicated earlier, 1962 appears to be a critical year for Indian popular cinema as a whole, because of the military debacle of 1961. Kannada cinema produces several important mythological films in the next few years, as exemplified by Sundarrao Nadkarni's *Sant Tukaram* (1963), Hunsur Krishnamurthy's *Sathya Harishchandra* (1965), and T.V. Singh Thakur's *Manthralaya Mahathme* (1966), with Rajkumar starring in all of them. While in films like *Rayara Sose* (and, perhaps, *Bhoodana*), Rajkumar could still share the limelight with other actors, he occupies centrestage in every film he is in from 1963 onwards.

While the mythological thrives in Kannada cinema like never before in the years after 1961, there is a movement away from its earlier Shaivite bias towards Vaishnavism, perhaps because of the need to integrate—and this is true of *Sant Tukaram* and *Manthralaya Mahathme*. More important, however, is that these later mythological films are different from the earlier mythological films in another (more) covert way. To clarify, they are more difficult to read as allegory and can perhaps be categorized as 'escapes' into devotion because of their disinclination to engage with the present in any discernible way.

The first two of the three films cited are faithful remakes of earlier films—the Kannada *Harishchandra* of 1943 (already discussed) and Damle and Fattelal's Marathi classic *Sant Tukaram* (1936)—but an examination of the differences between the films of the 1960s and the originals is revealing. *Raja Harishchandra*, at first glance, appears to replicate everything in the film by Nagendra Rao but its effect is strangely 'campy'[30] with extended comedy sequences absent in the original. Nakshatrika, sent by Vishwamitra to accompany the royal family is a pest in the original film because he has the explicit role of persuading the king to abandon the path of dharma. In the later *Raja Harishchandra*, Nakshatrika is played by the comedian Narasimharaju who, in films like *School Master*, generally plays the kind-hearted and honourable clown. Even when he is an associate of the villain (as in *Bedara Kannappa*), he places obstacles in the villain's path and is in sympathy with the hero. The same thing happens in *Raja Harishchandra* when Nakshatrika, instead of being an unwelcome pest, actually becomes the king's sympathizer, even admonishing Vishwamitra for causing so much harm to the king. We see the same moderation (as comedy) being applied to the Queen's travails in the Brahmin household—in which every effort is made to mitigate her suffering and her son's.

While the king in *Harishchandra* is played out as a man genuinely put through hardship, the king in *Raja Harishchandra* is charismatic, upstaging everyone even as a slave—everything in Rajkumar's role is redolent of 'performance'. That this is deliberate is also suggested by the way the keeper of the cremation ground is introduced—as a robust individual with a deliberately blackened face (rather than as racial type), introduced through a supremely entertaining folk song and dance sequence. To summarize the effect of *Raja Harishchandra*, it is a work of entertainment in which characters go through the motions associated with the story, but with little faith in its instructive or devotional value.

Sant Tukaram is not different—partly because the villain is played by the comedian Balakrishna. While in the original, the Brahmin villain Salomalo (Kusum Bhagwat) appeared genuinely threatening, Balakrishna is notable for playing ineffectual villains—unable to overcome even the misgivings of their own assistants. The actor G.V. Iyer (from *Bedara Kannappa*, where he plays the scheming Brahmin) might have been a more credible choice although Balakrishna is more amusing. Second, the film deliberately plays down the 'anti-Brahmin' aspect of the original and opens with Brahmins prostrating themselves before the saint. The Brahmin villain is also deprived of his caste traits and given a beard. As played in Damle and Fattelal's version, Tukaram is an ineffective householder and his shrewish wife Jija must compensate in order to keep the family going but, here, there is a self-conscious element in her shrewishness—as though it were mere play-acting and this is supported by her gestures of love not to be found in the Marathi film. Rajkumar as Tukaram (for all his 'otherworldliness') also upstages Jija (Leelavathi) and we are not convinced of his troubles. If this film (also like the later *Manthralaya Mahathme*) is simply going through the procedures of the devotional story—with little faith in its real intent—it can be argued that this finds correspondence in the 'godlessness' of *Bhoodana*, for which an explanation has been offered. In these films devotion appears a posture rather than a matter of faith.

History Subdued

I have already tried to demonstrate how historical films like *Vijayanagarada Veerraputra* deal with both the Kannada nation and the Indian nation through the device of two monarchs, one subordinate to the other. Since it is the lesser monarch whose worth is questioned it can be argued that, until 1961, the Indian nation is the object of greater loyalty. The other historical films cited are either straightforwardly nationalistic (*Kittur Channamma*) or (as in *Ranadheera Kanteerava*) are concerned with upholding the democratic obligations/accountability of the monarch to his subjects—instead of the loyalty of the subject to the monarch, which was the tendency observed when Mysore was under princely rule. Although *Ranadheera Kanteerava* treats the non-Kannada areas (that is, Tiruchi) nominally as 'foreign', the emphasis on the accountability of the monarch points to the Indian nation being privileged over the Kannada one. To elaborate, the new political ethic that makes the government accountable originates in the independent Indian nation. *Ranadheera Kanteerava* also acknowledges this by portraying the dowager queen as the 'sacred mother'—the way many Hindi films like *Mother India* portray the Indian nation—and it is the dowager queen who expresses distress at the way the young king is governing.

If all this suggests that it is the Indian nation that is the ultimate object of loyalty in the Kannada historical film, the question is what happens when the nation has a subdued presence in the psyche of the audience, that is, after 1961. Since it is difficult to imagine Kannada cinema without Rajkumar in the 1960s, we should perhaps look at the actor's filmography to identify the historical films made after 1961. The *Encyclopaedia of Indian Cinema* (1995) reveals that Rajkumar's first historical after 1961 was *Immadi Pulakeshi* in 1967.[31] Since this tends to confirm my hypothesis about the decline of the historical film in the aftermath of the Sino-Indian War, the next step is to scrutinize the discourse in two of the few historical films made in the period, B.S. Ranga's

Amarashilpi Jakannachari (1964) and Hunsur Krishnamurthy's
Veera Sankalpa (1964).

Amarashilpi Jakannachari is not a film about princes and their
doings (the staple of the Kannada historical film) but about the
legendary sculptor responsible for the Hoysala temple at Belur—
constructed in the twelfth century. Jakkanna (Kalyana Kumar)
watches the courtesan Manjari (B. Saroja Devi) dancing and he
is inspired to do a life-size sculpture of her. The dancer sees his
work and falls in love with him. Jakkanna comes from a long line
of sculptors and, although his father initially disapproves of it, he
marries Manjari, who gives up dancing. But Manjari's mother and
her patron—the local chieftain—want her back and they hatch a
plot to get her to dance. Jakkanna discovers this and he is crushed
by the discovery. When Manjari is told that Jakkanna will not
want a tainted woman back and also finds her husband gone, she
flees and tries to kill herself by jumping into a river. Manjari is
saved by some fisher folk who also discover that she is with child.
Manjari and her son Dankanna are well looked after by the fisher
folk until she decides that the boy must be a sculptor like his
father. At the climax of the film father and son encounter each
other at Belur, where the construction of the temple is reaching its
final stages. The boy points out a flaw in a statue to Jakanna without knowing that Jakanna is his father. When the boy is eventually
proved right, Jakkanna cuts off his right hand in the presence of
the Hoysala king. A miracle however occurs and Jakanna's hand
is restored after an interlude of devotion. The film concludes happily with father, mother, and son being reunited. As a subplot, the
film also introduces the religious reformer Ramanujacharya who
is historically credited with having converted the Jain Hoysala
king to Vaishnavism.

Amarashilpi Jakannachari was the first Kannada film in colour
and pays tribute to a cultural showpiece. What is nevertheless more
interesting from my perspective is that it also uses the motifs of
the two 'monarchs'—a minor chieftain involved in deceiving the
sculptor, and the Hoysala king, Vishnuvardhana, who commis-
sioned the great temple at Belur. The film uses familiar motifs
but the King Vishnuvardhana is strangely subdued even when he
appears. At the climax, for instance, the verbal duel between father
and son over the sculptures—and their subsequent reconciliation

happens with the king standing unobtrusively behind—as though he was an inconsequential onlooker, very different from the earlier films in which submissions are made to the monarch and his appreciation is climactic. The temple at Belur is not less revered than the one at Hampi and King Vishnuvardhana is almost as important to Kannada culture as Krishnadevaraya was but there is a huge difference between the way the two kings are portrayed in *Amarashilpi Jakannachari* and *Vijayanagarada Veeraputra*, respectively. This, it can be argued, is not related to the two kings and the respective importance of their achievements, but rather to the years in which the two films were made: the 'Great King' in *Amarashilpi Jakannachari* was portrayed when the nation was subdued.

Veera Sankalpa is a much stranger film which uses a celebratory tone to eulogize the Kannada nation but is actually dark and pessimistic. It deals with the Vijayanagar Empire after its heyday, beginning with the aged king Venkatapathy's death. This film has several motifs that are highly anomalistic—a conspiracy by which the king's chosen successor the courageous Srirangaraya is imprisoned and beheaded and the throne occupied by an effeminate and timid boy (played by the comedian Dwarakish) because of the doings of the wicked prime minister. The heroic General Lakshmana Nayaka (Hunsur Krishnamurthy) fights the enemies—from without as well as from within—and an honourable Muslim commander from Bijapur dies in the service of the Kannada nation. Apart from the Kannada nation (rather than only Mysore) reigning supreme as the professed object of loyalty, the comic motif of the timid person in a position of authority has a parallel in Chanakya's Telugu film *Ramudu Bheemudu* (1964), which I have interpreted[32] as a comical allegory of the leaders of a nation humbled in war. Another factor—that the general stands virtually alone against cowardice and treachery—echoes the sentiments of films like *Sangam* (1964) and *Haqeeqat* (1964) in which the defeat of 1961 is invoked, but the military exonerated.

Moral Instruction in the Social

Where the Kannada social appears to change most significantly after 1960 is in the way hierarchy is treated, as also the denotation of caste. While, in the earlier films, people were segregated into caste/occupational groups (servants, courtesans, Brahmins, farmers, etc.) with little commerce between them, there are fewer signs of it in the 1960s, with even the Brahmin villain absent after *Chandavaliya Thota* (1964). It is however apparent that hierarchy persists in a relatively subdued way and these are usually in the comic servant romances through separate subplots. *Rayara Sose,* as indicated earlier, threw hierarchy into crisis through a subplot involving a servant but in films like *Nandadeepa* (1963), the 'below-the-stairs' romance is independent with little impact upon the main story. This implies a hierarchical segregation of plot components and is in evidence till much later. But as a way of playing down hierarchy without interrogating it, Kannada film narratives of the 1960s try to deal exclusively with one class—for example, a Brahmin class straddling both the village and the city as in *Nandadeepa* (1963), or a rural landowning Vokkaliga class as in *Chandavaliya Thota* (1964). This is different from the representation in *Bedara Kannappa* (1954) which introduces Brahmins, tribals, and courtesans as discrete (and exclusive) social groups within a single story. From the evidence of Kannada cinema it appears that the 1960s represent a phase in which Mysore strives to integrate with the Indian nation.

Another factor to be taken note of with regard to the socials of the early 1960s is that there is only the Mysore kind of Kannada spoken although this may either be the Brahmin Kannada of *School Master* or the Vokkaliga Kannada of *Anna Thangi*. The Kannada spoken in Mangalore (former Madras Presidency) or Belgaum (Bombay Karnataka) is no longer heard. Kannada cinema is now speaking 'on behalf of Kannada' perhaps presuming that the spaces outside former princely Mysore are integrated with the Kannada nation. Since there is no difference in the dominant speech in Kannada cinema, this does not mean that audiences outside 'old' Mysore are now being addressed, but simply that the assimilation of the Kannada-speaking areas outside Mysore within the Kannada nation is not an issue that is current.

As indicated earlier, another key aspect demarcating the Kannada social of the 1950s from the Hindi domestic melodrama pertains to its treatment of the family. The family in Kannada cinema was built through 'arranged' marriages rather than through romance and this I attributed to the family network system prevailing in princely Mysore. In the late 1950s, in films like *School Master*, romance appears because of the need to knit the Kannada areas together—areas not covered by the family networks. But once the anxious period is over, Kannada films appear to revert back to 'arranged marriages'—although 'romance' is allowed between two people connected through their families (as in *Anna Thangi*). While the Hindi film of the 1950s is indifferent to the joint family,[33] the motif of the single family with more than one brother is a common feature in Kannada cinema—for example, *Gunasagari*, *School Master*, and *Bhoodana*. Although families with one son are also not uncommon (for example, *Rayara Sose* and *Anna Thangi*) there is still a covert discourse in many of these films valorizing the joint family.

While the Kannada mythological film upholds devotion and the historical film eulogizes the just ruler, the socials of the late 1950s and early 1960s appear to place their moral emphasis elsewhere. Greed appears the quality most abhorred in films like *Rayara Sose*, *School Master*, and *Anna Thangi*, in which it is the uncle's denying his sister's family their share in the property that causes the trouble. Greed still invokes the code of dharma, which (as we saw) dominates ethical discourse in early Kannada cinema because it suggests the prevalence of artha. But while the threat to the protagonists may arise out of greed or selfishness, this selfishness is wicked (as in *Rayara Sose*) because it threatens the family. In *School Master* as well, the selfishness of sons leads to the breakup of the family. In *Anna Thangi*, the initial disturbance caused by the uncle leads to the break-up of the extended family. In M.R. Vittal's *Nandadeepa* (1963), Ravi leaves the household to seek his fortune in Bangalore, where he marries his boss' daughter, leaving his father in debt and his family in poverty. Once there, he is sent to London for training but selfishly decides to settle down there with his wife.[34] His father-in-law takes a second wife through the exertions of a former corrupt official, a girl who is none other than the Ravi's younger sister Gowri. The need to keep this secret leads to tragedy but what is important here is that regardless of what the nature of the wickedness, this film like the others sees the disintegration of the family as the primary threat and the ideal state is the undivided Hindu family, which has a natural ally in the *dharmic* code. T.V. Singh Thakur's *Chandavaliya Thota* (1964) is entirely about the break-up of a joint family and needs to be examined.

Chandavaliya Thota is based on a major Kannada novel by T.R. Subba Rao (TaRaSu) of the Pragatishila (progressive) school and is about an agrarian community living in harmony. Their troubles start when they need a priest and invite a poor young Brahmin outsider to live with them. Although they gift the Brahmin enough land to live happily, he is greedy and proceeds to poison the community by spreading envy and malice. The film takes pains not to be 'anti-Brahmin' by having a wicked insider in the (perhaps, Vokkaliga) community and the priest being introduced by another Brahmin, honourable and well-meaning. There are other aspects of the film that owe to the period—the disintegration of the community being initiated by lawyers who help widen the schisms, the police (and the judiciary) reduced to mechanically following the letter of the law. There is a courtroom scene in the film in which the sentence is simply read out without our hearing the pleas. This is in tune with Hindi films like *Bandini* (1963) and *Guide* (1965) in which punishment is perfunctorily awarded for crimes without there being a dramatic courtroom scene where guilt is either established or admitted[35] as in the 1950s.

As Patricia Uberoi observes in writing about *Hum Aapke Hain Koun...!* (1994), for more than a century public opinion in India was obsessed with the spectre of the imminent break-up of the Hindu joint family through processes like urbanization, westernization, industrialization, and the emancipation of women.[36] While the joint family has perhaps not actually been the institution it is credited with being, sociologists concede that it is a nonetheless deeply held traditional *value* in India.[37] Since Kannada cinema in its earlier years was deeply attendant to the traditional notion of dharma, more so than Hindi cinema which was influenced by the colonial encounter, it seems reasonable to attribute Kannada cinema's eulogy of the joint family to the same sociological facts— but with the important rider that the emblem of the joint family in Kannada cinema also represents the social networks created with hierarchy as the basis. Perhaps more difficult to explain is why this preoccupation leaves Kannada cinema temporarily in the mid to late 1960s. One way of determining this could be through identifying the ethic that replaces family dharma.

The Return of the 'Modern'

Examining Hindi cinema of the late 1950s, we find that much of the ethical conflict in the cinema of the period comes from the clash between the modern and the pre-modern. In *Kaala Pani* (1958) this manifests itself as the intrepid newspaper reporter's pursuit of dispossessed feudal authority—in the shape of a former dewan. In *Naya Daur* (1957) the climax has a race between a bullock cart and a motor vehicle. Since the modern is closely associated with the Nehruvian nation, the conflict abruptly leaves Hindi cinema after the military debacle of 1961. Still, we may surmise that the effects of Sino-Indian War were mitigated after 1965, when India was more successful in the war with Pakistan. Although the war reached a stalemate, it was apparent that it was India who had the better of the exchange.[38] The Nehruvian modern—for the reasons already explained—is not such a strong issue in the Kannada cinema of the late 1950s and its strong appearance in the late 1960s, therefore, needs some attention.

The discourse in *Chandavaliya Thota* suggests a 'conservative' outlook in as much as law and justice are shown to work against the interests of the community and essentially divisive. The idealization of the pristine state of the community also suggests the same thing. One could contrast this film with one that came later—B.R. Panthulu's *Emme Thammanna* (1966). The two adversaries in this film are an altruistic lawyer named Narasimhaiah and a crooked municipal president named Sheshanna. The film has Rajkumar playing a double role—that of Thammanna, the cowherd, and Narasimhaiah's junior, Murali. There is a large portrait of Jawaharlal Nehru in Murali's home and there is evidently an association made between the law and the Indian nation/state. Considering that the corrupt municipal president is emblematic of what was wrong with 'old' Mysore, the film appears to be suggesting the cleansing of the Mysore ethos by the Indian nation. This discourse is comparable to the one in *School Master* and it appears as though Nehruvian modernity were having a second coming in *Emme Thammanna*, although this is eight years later[39] and it is a lawyer rather than a doctor who is its agent. Another feature to be reckoned with is that the cowherd and the lawyer are being played by Rajkumar with no explanation of them being separated at birth being provided. The cowherd becomes educated and the two Rajkumars marry the two heroines on the same day. This perhaps also suggests that the traditional notion of hierarchy has now weakened, even if only briefly.

Since *Emme Thammanna* begins with the story of the cow-herd (and privileges him in its title), another way of looking at its discourse is to regard it as addressing those in his position and persuading them about what they might gain through modernity. The same discourse is evidenced in R. Ramamurthy's *Rowdy Ranganna* (1968) in which the protagonist is a farmer who is threatened by the elements of tradition (municipal presidents and moneylenders), but finds an ally in modernity (doctors and lawyers). *Emme Thammanna* and *Rowdy Ranganna* are set in unnamed urban milieus but Bangalore city begins to make a forceful appearance in the cinema of this period with films taking the viewpoint of the Bangalorean.

Bangalore: A Rise and Fall

Among the films we have examined in this study the first film to suggest the presence of Bangalore as a space is *Nandadeepa* (1963), but the viewpoint is that of the heroine, a girl brought up in the village. Srikanth (Ashwath), whom she marries, apparently repre-sents private enterprise in the city. Since the large industry in Bangalore in the early 1960s was government owned, we may sur-mise that Srikanth finds correspondence in the first generation entrepreneurs owning the ancillaries springing up around the public sector enterprises.[40] But where *Nandadeepa* took the view-point of the rural person to whom Bangalore was still distant, Ravi's *Bhagyada Bagilu* (1968) identifies with the upwardly mobile resident of Bangalore. The poor protagonist of this film is befriended by a wealthy man who becomes his benefactor. The general sense in the film and in B.R. Pathulu's *Beedhi Basavanna* (1967) is of the (legitimate) opportunities available in Bangalore for material advancement but there is more than this in the city motifs of the period. Specifically, there are other key films in which the city is the moral site in which the modern resides.

Many of the films do not name Bangalore but only refer to a 'city' but there is a difference in the way Bangalore is perceived—vis-à-vis Mysore. M.R. Vittal's *Hannele Chiguridaga* (1968) is set in the home of a wealthy patriarch who heads a joint family.

The family is so large that the patriarch has difficulties even recollecting the names of his children. The daughter Malathi (Kalpana) is married but the son-in-law expires soon after the wedding. Malathi decides to study further and finds herself avoided because of her widowhood. Meanwhile, her sister-in-law's bother Prasad (Rajkumar) is also widowed and the film is about how the patriarch's resistance to the two widowed people marrying is overcome. What is interesting here is that the story is set in Mysore and not Bangalore, although the milieu is urban. It might perhaps not have been appropriate to set the story—about a family needing to think afresh on social mores and needing to become more 'modern'—in Bangalore.

Bangalore features in another 'reformist' film, B.A. Arasu-kumar's *Bangarada Hoovu* (1967). The story of this film is told from the viewpoint of Anand, a young 'development officer' who wants to marry his friend's sister Seetha (Kalpana) although his mother has set her heart on his marrying her niece. The crisis in the film occurs when Seetha is diagnosed as having leprosy but it ends with Anand marrying her after she is cured. Anand is from Bangalore and the film begins with a 'modern dance' by young women in tight clothes trying to attract Anand's attention in a park. The two aspects of the modern—represented by dancing and medicine—get due attention in this film, reminiscent in its thrust of the Hindi films of the late 1950s.

The caste representations in Kannada cinema change gradually after 1956 and alongside the move away from Shaivism is the absence of Veerashaiva traits in the characters. While, as I emphasized in the introduction, it may not be correct to see denoting of caste in the given names, there are still suggestions that should be recognized. Whenever a film has a farmer as a character, he speaks the kind of Kannada associated with the Vokkaligas of princely Mysore and the title 'Gowda' is applied, which suggests the same thing. When films move to the city and need to show progressive people, usually with wealth, the names tend to have Brahmin associations. Since the Brahmins were traditionally the best-educated in Mysore, Kannada films from 1966 onwards introduce the figure of the wealthy Brahmin family from Bangalore as in *Bangarada Hoovu*.[41] I propose that this is due to Brahmins not being associated with the land and, therefore, being natural candidates to bridge the cultural gap between the local milieu and the nation. Moreover, as M.N. Srinivas observes,[42] an important social process in Mysore was the urbanization of Brahmins. This would imply their portrayal as agents of progress, which is different from their portrayal in *Chandavaliya Thota*, in which the Brahmin is a rural presence.

Considering all the aspects of the 'modern' seen in Kannada cinema between 1965 and 1968, the notion would appear to be especially related to Bangalore where Brahmins apparently dominate. Bangalore had not achieved its prominence in the late 1960s and until the 1970s it was not even considered anything more than a modest-sized state capital, although it was the site of several major sized public sector industries.[43] It is difficult, therefore, to see Bangalore's growth as being responsible for its being viewed as the site of modernity in the late 1960s and the reasons evidently lie elsewhere. Since the clash between tradition and modernity is also represented in the films as the clash between entrenched corruption in Mysore and 'Indian modernity', we should perhaps look at the national arena for an answer.

That it is the 'nation' rather than Bangalore that is actually the moral agent is also suggested by a dissenting portrayal of Bangalore in A.C. Narasimhamurthy's/S.K. Bhagawan's *Sandhyaraga* (1966), in which the joint family breaks up after it moves to Bangalore, where the eldest son (an advocate) is tempted by corruption. At the same time, the younger son becomes a nationally renowned singer, performing in places like Madras, Benares, and Delhi. The motif of the train journey across India seen in this film is reminiscent of Hindi films of the 1950s like Bimal Roy's *Devdas* (1955) and Sohrab Modi's *Jailor* (1958). Another motif in the film is the portrayal of the newspaper as representing the values of the nation as in Raj Khosla's *Kaala Pani* (1958).[44]

Even more convincing evidence of Mysore state drawing closer to the Indian nation is provided by Chaduranga's 'historical' film *Sarvamangala* (1968), about the sacrifices made by peasants in Mysore district for India's freedom. At no point does *Sarvamangala* even acknowledge that there was a princely government between the citizens and the colonialists.[45] The film, perhaps for the first time for a Kannada film, also has a conspicuous Muslim character who is a sympathetic onlooker at key moments. This is perhaps intended to announce Mysore's secular credentials in the scheme of the Indian nation.

While some films bypass Bangalore in their fervour for the Indian nation, it is the association between the Indian nation and Bangalore that is more common. It can be argued that the reappearance of the nation and the 'modern' in Kannada cinema owes to Mysore regarding itself as increasingly important to India. The motif of Bangalore gaining importance is perhaps because of the city's position as state capital and not due to any developments within the city. Moreover, with huge central government investment in Bangalore, the city is consistently viewed in Kannada cinema as closer to India than to Mysore.

While the Congress was perceived to be weakening after Nehru's death, it continued to remain strong in Mysore state. It was this strength that made Nijalingappa one of the most powerful people in the Congress and a member of the shadowy group known as the Syndicate even during Nehru's lifetime, when he was declining physically.[46] The Congress party's internal crisis came to a head with the results of the 1967 elections. For the first time, it lost nearly 60 seats in the Lower House, managing to win only 297 seats. Until 1967, the Congress had also never won less than 60 per cent of all seats in Assembly elections. It also suffered a major setback as non-Congress ministries were established in Bihar, Kerala, Orissa, Madras, Punjab, and West Bengal. It was Mysore's importance that led to Nijalingappa's elevation to the post of president of AICC in 1968 when his protégé Veerendra Patil replaced him as chief minister.[47]

The sense of well-being displayed by Kannada cinema in the period perhaps reaches its apogee in Dorairaj-Bhagwan's 'spy thriller' *Jedara Bale* (1968). This film is about a Bangalore-based secret agent Prakash a.k.a CID 999 (Rajkumar) who is after a gang of counterfeiters. The film combines James Bond's appeal to women with the traditions of Mysore when CID 999 is approached by well-placed men who want him for a son-in-law. More importantly, the Indian Airlines Bangalore-Delhi flight is seen carrying personages in Mysore turbans—as if to signify Mysore's importance in the scheme of the nation.[48]

There are several factors in *Jedara Bale* that point to Mysore state's self-importance—the confidence that technology is in Bangalore as well as the sense that the fate of the nation is in local hands. The film also mimics many of the aspects of the Hindi films of the late 1960s—gaudy 'cabaret' dances and gambling.

To convince us that Bangalore is 'international', the film locates much of its action in the vicinity of Hotel Bangalore International, then an up-market hotel with floor shows advertised in the daily newspaper. The 'cabarets' in the film are watched by family men accompanied by women in saris, as if to assert that the 'modern' signified by these dances is not in contravention of Mysore tradition. But if 1968 was the year when Mysore's self-importance and well-being was at its highest in the decade, everything changes abruptly in 1969.

The Nation Suddenly Distant

As I proposed earlier, Mysore's 'proximity to the nation' in 1968 owed to S. Nijalingappa taking up the assignment of president of the AICC. Indira Gandhi was already prime minister but this was because she had been installed there by the Syndicate, of which Nijalingappa was a key member. The Congress won the general elections in 1967, although much less convincingly than in the past. Instead of being disconcerted by the Congress' weak showing in 1967, Mrs Gandhi saw it as an opportunity and seized it by radically altering the party's strategy. She circumvented the Syndicate by shifting her rhetoric to the left. Her gambit was to dissolve the 'vote banks' traditionally governed by the regional bosses and appeal directly to the electorate.[49] In 1969 she did the unthinkable and split the Congress over the choice of the presidential candidate, finding enough support to have V.V. Giri, rather than Sanjeeva Reddy, installed as president. While Mrs Gandhi won a landslide victory when the next election was held in 1971, it is enough to recognize here that Mrs Gandhi's victory in 1969 was a conclusive defeat for the faction in which Nijalingappa had been powerful. This could have made a difference to the way people in Mysore viewed Delhi. Mysore was perhaps not so close to the nation after all, with Nijalingappa no longer so powerful in the central Congress leadership. This is registered in Kannada cinema in the years 1969–71 through transformations in several familiar motifs.

Some tendencies of Kannada cinema from 1969 onwards are sharply contrary to what was in evidence in 1968 and in Siddalinaiah's *Mayor Muthanna* (1969), Bangalore is the site of criminal activity and injustice. This is not to say the village is idealized either because the film begins with an attempted rape in a rustic milieu. Rajkumar, in this film, plays a farmer wrongly accused of stealing temple possessions, because of his protecting a man from Bangalore who has actually done it. Apart from all this is the casual and indiscriminate way in which pictures of national leaders are hanging in people's houses—as though to downplay their significance. This is in sharp contrast to a film like *Bangaraaa Hoovu* that came out only two years earlier, where pictures of national leaders had positive connotations impossible to ignore. Other changes in Kannada cinema around 1970 will be examined in the next chapter.

The Meaning of Rajkumar in the 1960s

Most of the films discussed in this chapter have Rajkumar in the key male role and no understanding of Kannada cinema can ignore the actor's central position. If Rajkumar dominated Kannada cinema in the late 1950s, he attained even greater importance in the 1960s. The notion of the actor as 'parallel text' has been used to study the way stars like Amitabh Bachchan influence the text,[50] but Rajkumar by the end of the 1960s goes beyond Amitabh Bachchan and films often have the appearance of being constructed around him. It has been suggested that Rajkumar's acting career can be roughly divided into three phases.[51] The first phase is categorized as the 'high mimetic' mode, deriving from the 'company theatre' or the indigenous dramatic tradition and largely in the genres of the mythological and the historical (*Bedara Kannappa*, *Bhukailasa*, *Ranadheera Kanterava*). At the softer end of the 'high mimetic' mode are devotionals like *Sant Tukaram* and *Manthralaya Mahatme* in which the dominant emotion sought for is bhakti. The second phase has been called 'low mimetic' and is illustrated through films like *Naandi*, sometimes identified as the best work done by Rajkumar, while the third phase is apparently the uncomfortable 'lover-boy' one—films perhaps beginning with *Jedara Bale*. My own understanding of Rajkumar's roles in the period just examined is that in between the 'high mimesis' and 'low mimesis' phases, he has a series of rustic intimate roles where he uses his personal charm to considerable effect (*Anna Thangi*, *Chandavaliya Thota*). But there is also the beginning of the most important aspect of Rajkumar noted by cultural critics, which is the building of a 'super-ethical hero'—in contrast to the Tamil ideological hero in M.G. Ramachandran and the Telugu religious hero in N.T. Rama Rao.[52] Rajkumar is so important in the 1960s that we cannot go ahead with our inquiry unless we hypothesize on the meaning of his persona and how it was created.

Much work has already been done on the creation of the MGR persona[53] and it well-known that it had its origins in the Dravidian movement, which perhaps began officially with the founding of the Justice Party in 1917. The anti-religious stance of the Dravidian movement can be traced to its opposition to Brahmin domination, and DMK films like *Parasakhti* (1952) starring Sivaji Ganesan (and not MGR) being more anti-priest rather than anti-religion.[54] The Dravidian eulogy of Tamil can also be understood as a way of subjugating Sanskrit. The ideological hero therefore came out of a politically *polarized* milieu in which mass mobilization had taken place and adversaries identified. As regards N.T. Rama Rao, there has been little definitive work done on his significance as a 'religious hero' but he appeared in a milieu in which (because Hyderabad was under the Muslim rule of the Nizam) religious identity was determining. The common man's Telugu was perhaps also placed in opposition to the elitist Urdu,[55] which is why this manifested itself as language nationalism.

Rajkumar the 'ethical hero' came from another kind of milieu and his significance can be understood best by looking at Mysore. As indicated earlier, the milieu in which Kannada cinema originated had not had the benefit of mass mobilization and this tended to accentuate the effects of 'one party dominance'. The Congress came to power in India not as a political party but as a movement for Independence and reform. With Independence the Congress did not immediately become a political party and it continued to be a 'movement'. The difference was that, having acquired Independence from foreign rule, it now took upon itself the task of building a nation and it tried to achieve its ends through a consensus.[56]

In Mysore, 'one-party dominance' meant a virtual absence of political polarization. Although there had been a non-Brahmin movement in the state, it was not based on mass mobilization but was simply the manifestation of the non-Brahmin elite trying to secure for itself privileges (within an authoritarian system) that were enjoyed by the Brahmins. It is perhaps for this reason that there is little strength to the 'anti-Brahminism' in early Kannada cinema, which leaves it in the 1960s. When the Congress came to power in Mysore, the absence of any opposition also meant the absence of clear-cut political programmes. It has been recorded that in the pre-Independence period the only programme that the Congress leaders offered to the public was that the Congress raj would be a 'panacea to all public ills'.[57]

While writing about *School Master*, Kannada cultural critic D.R. Nagaraj compares the film to Raj Kapoor's work with some interesting results. Raj Kapoor, Nagaraj notes, was an enthusiastic modernist who endorsed the revolt of the young against stifling traditions while *School Master* explores the disintegration of societal values, which have their roots in tradition.[58] Nagaraj perhaps had *Awaara* (1951) in mind when he made this comparison and I would like to extend his observation.

In *Awaara*, the protagonist's opposition is not so much to 'tradition' as to his authoritarian father. The authoritarian father is a pre-Independence motif in Hindi cinema that can be associated with colonial rule. Apart from P.C. Barua's *Devdas* (1935) there are other films like *Kismat* (1943) and *Taqdeer* (1943) in which the motif of the authoritarian father appears though 'rebellion' is muted before 1947. Considering that the father in *Awaara* is a judge and the judge (like the police) is a way of representing state authority in Hindi cinema, there is covert political allegory in the son's rebellion against his father in *Awaara*[59] which needs to be taken into account.

Raj Kapoor was making films in a milieu that had seen an anti-colonial movement—which is very different from B.R. Panthulu's case in *School Master*. This film, it must be observed, does not place 'tradition' in opposition to 'modernity' (which was the way of Hindi cinema in the 1950s) but simply expands on the individual selfishness of the children. This means that it cannot be interpreted *politically* as resistance to social change—as a conservative Hindi film like *Naya Daur* (1957) can be. *School Master* is simply taking an 'ethical' stand on a matter of consensus, as the films with Rajkumar tend to do in the 1960s. If *School Master* attacks the ingratitude of children after using their parents for advancement, *Bangarada Hoovu* attacks superstition, specifically the notion that leprosy is the consequence of one's past sins.

I would like to argue here that the 'ethical hero' represented by Rajkumar comes out of a milieu in which there was little political polarization. Rajkumar in the later films of the 1960s is the voice of the 'good' and his adversaries are not identifiable as traders, landowners, the upper-castes, or servants of the state, etc. (which are all *political* categories), but simply as 'bad people' who do things that are not legally and ethically correct. 'Incorrect' is initially going against dharma but it also takes other shapes gradually—like promoting superstition as in *Bangarada Hoovu* or forging currency as in *Jedara Bale*. Unlike Raj Kapoor's films, which always have a political agenda, Rajkumar's have none, and this has a parallel in the pronouncements of the first Congress government in Greater Mysore. If the first Congress raj promised that it would be a 'panacea for all public ills', Rajkumar's films exhort against the same ills without identifying them politically.[60]

Rajkumar dominated the Kannada film perhaps even more than MGR and NTR dominated their respective cinemas, and there was much public speculation on why he did not enter politics. The explanations offered have generally been of a personal nature—his simplicity, his Gandhian beliefs, etc.,[61] but the most plausible solution to the problem lies elsewhere. For someone to stand for a political principle, he must identify the principles he is against and therefore also be clear about his political adversaries. What an icon represents only means something in relation to the forces or ideas it is against, and in Rajkumar's case it is difficult to identify them because (being a 'good man') he was 'for everyone'.[62]

The films with Rajkumar do not differ in their ethical emphasis from other Kannada films of the period but he is only an actor even until *Chandavaliya Thota* (1964) in which he is playing identifiable fictional characters. But perhaps beginning with the mythological films like *Sant Tukaram*, he plays fictional characters less and less in the 1960s and is fully installed as a figure for public veneration in the 1970s—not as an individual but as an emblem of local values. Rajkumar does play negative roles in many mythological films (from *Bhukailasa* [1958] to *Bhaktha Prahalada* [1984]). Villains in mythology are as much players in a divine drama as the heroes are and the films recognize that, but there are no negative roles outside the mythological film.

In the earlier socials of the period, Rajkumar contributes to the fiction—as in *Sandhyaraga* (1966)—but later increasingly becomes a 'voice of conscience'[63] with the message of the film articulated through him. An indication of how pronounced this is can be gathered from *Mayor Muthanna* in which he begins by playing a rustic (with the appropriate Kannada) but switches to an urbane Kannada when he is delivering his sermons against social evils. The building-up is perhaps to create a self-image for the Kannada speaking public within the Indian nation, with which their space had now become fully integrated. Needless to add, there is a significant quantity of hagiography about Rajkumar written in Kannada[64] because of the star's evident importance to the region.

2. The Distance from Delhi
1970–9

Loyalty Undivided

Hitherto, I have partly been taken up by the way Kannada cinema
negotiates the space between Mysore state and the Indian nation.
Mysore state, which appears to be getting closer to the Indian
nation in the late 1960s because of the importance of the state
Congress to the centre, is abruptly distanced in 1969—arguably
because of the defeat of the all-powerful Syndicate, in which S.
Nijalingappa was a key member—by Indira Gandhi. Nijalingappa
was a kingmaker within the Congress from the Lal Bahadur
Shastri period onwards and his political fall in 1969 is registered
by Kannada cinema partly through the way it changes its response
towards the 'modern'. As already indicated, the Nehruvian modern is not treated with the same reverence by Kannada cinema as
it is by the Hindi cinema of the 1950s because the 'modern' had
already been ushered into Mysore much earlier by able administrators like Sir M. Visveswaraiya and Sir Mirza Ismail. A strategy
employed by Kannada cinema while dealing with the twin objects
of loyalty—Mysore and the Indian nation—is to feature two kings
in its historical adventure films, one smaller and one greater, with
loyalty to the greater king being paramount. Kannada cinema
provides evidence of its studied distance from the Indian nation in

B.R. Panthulu's *Sri Krishnadevaraya* (1970) by dealing with only one monarch. This film is a 'biopic' of the most celebrated king of the Vijayanagar Empire—with the king expectedly played by Rajkumar.

Sri Krishnadevaraya is made in an especially elaborate Kannada with an opening song in the older version of the language which is no longer spoken. The legend at the commencement of the film extols the king and reverentially announces the project undertaken. The film is quite faithful to the actual events of the king's life, which means that it does not provide the emotional satisfaction that melodramas strive for. Towards the end of the film, the crown prince is poisoned by unknown persons and the villains are not brought to justice. The king is also unable to prevent his loyal minister Thimmarasu (B.R. Panthulu) from being blinded. The king also has two queens (played by Bharathi and Jayanthi) with one of them being a former courtesan. The two remain devoted to each other despite efforts to drive them apart. The major liberty taken with history is that the king is the embodiment of Kannada virtues—including his generosity to his defeated Muslim enemies and his honouring of their god. While the earlier historical film invoking the same king (*Vijayanagarada Veeraputra*) brought in the motif of the two royal personages—also paralleling Kannada mythological films that provide twin objects of loyalty—*Sri Krishnadevaraya* has only one: the king represents Kannada, and adulation is directed only towards him.[1] An allegory of the Indian nation is notably absent in *Sri Krishnadevaraya*. Treating Muslims from Bijapur as people eventually loyal to the king is also a way of making Kannada the ultimate object of loyalty, instead of either Mysore or India.

Another motif that becomes conspicuous around 1970 is that of the sacred mother figure. In Hindi cinema, the mother is sacred when she allegorizes the land or the nation as in the 1950s. One of the first Kannada films in which the sacred mother makes her appearance is *Bhale Jodi* (1970) an entertainer also starring Rajkumar, and in a double role. The film begins with a theatre performance in which the protagonist is playing a Vijayanagar hero. There is a eulogy in the opening dialogue of the Kannada land as mother. This is followed by the rest of the film in which the protagonist's actual mother is treated with the same reverence, a reverece not witnessed in the earlier cinema in which the mother features—for example, *School Master*. Another feature of *Bhale Jodi* is the film going on to become a 'masala film'—a mass entertainer about look-alikes in the mould of *Ram Aur Shyam* (1967), with the sententiousness suggested by the opening segments subsequently abandoned.

When one looks at the Kannada cinema coming in the years before 1969, it is apparent that it is the Indian nation which drives the moral discourse with Mysore playing only a subordinate part. This is as true of socials like *School Master* (in which the moral agents represent Nehruvian modernity) as of mythological films like *Mahishasura Mardhini* (in which the wife's devotion to the goddess takes precedence over her loyalty to her erring husband) and historical films like *Vijayanagarada Veeraputra* (in which it is the greater monarch to whom loyalty is primary). I would like to argue that *Bhale Jodi* does not implicate the Indian nation in its moral discourse and tries to substitute it with the 'Kannada nation'. The mismatch between the two aspects of the film—the sententious side from the earlier Kannada films and the 'masala' aspect reminiscent of Hindi films after the Sino-Indian War[2]—perhaps owes to its lack of faith in the Kannada nation as the ultimate object of devotion. The sacred mother in *Bhale Jodi* is perhaps an effort to provide a new moral signpost (instead of the absent Indian nation) but she does not justify her prominence though any decisive act, which is different from the way she features in comparable Hindi films where she inevitably makes sacrifices. The sacred mother figure is specifically associated with Rajkumar and her meaning will be explored again later.

The 'Brahmin' and the 'Modern'

A striking motif that proliferates in Kannada cinema in the years following 1969 pertains to a wealthy and generous individual who willingly gives away his wealth to people who are greedy for it. This motif is exhibited most forcefully by Dorairaj/Bhagwan's *Kasturi Nivasa* (1971) but continues in modified forms in B.S. Ranga's *Mr Rajkumar* (1971), Pekete Shivaram's *Kulagowrava* (1971), Puttanna Kanagal's *Sakshatkara* (1971), and Siddalingaiah's *Bangarada Manushya* (1972). Rajkumar plays the lead role in all these films.

In *Kasturi Nivasa*, Ravi comes from a wealthy family and resides in a palatial home with a history, which is named 'Kasturi

Nivasa'. Ravi is also the proprietor of a factory that makes matches with a dove as brand emblem. He is generous to a fault and is prepared to help anyone in distress. He has brought up a foundling named Neela who also works for him. Ravi is a widower, having lost his wife at childbirth, and his only daughter has drowned. Into Ravi's factory comes Chandru, also a widower but with a little daughter. Ravi trusts Chandru implicitly but Chandru gradually makes use of Ravi to embark on his own and set up his own match factory ('Eagle Brand'). Apart from becoming Ravi's competitor Chandru also marries Neela, just when Ravi himself has made up his mind to ask her to be his wife. Assisted by Ravi's gifts, Chandru becomes wealthy while Ravi himself is forced into penury. Also, while Ravi is proudly austere in his outlook, Chandru lives a life given to drinking and nightclubs. Eventually, a remorseful Chandru acquires 'Kasturi Nivasa' in an auction and tries to return it to Ravi, but proud Ravi will not accept such generosity. The film concludes with Neela visiting Ravi and wanting his pet pigeon for her child but Ravi, who has nothing to offer the visitor, has just sold the bird to buy food. He therefore collapses and is last seen lying dead on the ground with his right hand in the posture of someone who is giving.

Kasturi Nivasa has several aspects that are important to my inquiry. The first is perhaps the sense it conveys of being about 'Kasturi Nivasa' rather than about an individual, with the house becoming a contested site. Hindi films like *Mahal* (1949) and *Sheesh Mahal* (1950) allegorized the space of the nation as an enormous mansion with claimants from different classes.[3] Although the ownership of 'Kasturi Nivasa' passes from Ravi to Chandru in *Kasturi Nivasa*, it is not a contested site in the same sense—with warring players coming from different classes. The film is, rather, a paean to Mysore and the spirit of generosity associated with it. This generosity/tolerance is now wistfully regarded as characteristic of the Mysorean/Kannadiga[4] but Ravi's portrayal in the film needs to be examined in the specific context of its times.

Ravi in *Kasturi Nivasa* does not dress in traditional clothes but is always in a suit—complete with a bowtie—even when he moves into a dingy hovel. He and his ancestors have been owners of a match factory. A match factory, based on forest-based raw materials recalls the industries favoured by Visveswaraiya in his effort to make Mysore modern. My interpretation of Ravi is that he

represents the 'modern' but the Mysorean modern—ushered in by
Mysore's dewans—rather than the Nehruvian one. The generous
and refined modernity of Mysore needs no context—or cause—
and this is consistent with Ravi being shown as without parents.
Giving him a father or a mother might have reduced him in stature from an idea to a person. Kasturi Nivasa is perhaps Mysore
because it is a space with a tradition that Ravi is upholding.

The film also allegorizes two different kinds of modernity—the
one represented by Ravi's 'Dove Brand', and the more rapacious kind
represented by Chandru's 'Eagle Brand'. The two modernities, it
can be argued, find correspondence in the one initiated in Mysore
and the one introduced by the Indian nation much later. While
this distinction between the two kinds of modernity was deliberately avoided by Kannada cinema as long as Mysore was felt to
be close to the Indian nation,[5] the developments of 1969 may have
resulted in 'Indian modernity' falling out of favour. Moreover, by
the beginning of the 1970s, industrial suburbs had also sprung up
in Bangalore—in Rajajinagar and later around central industries
like HMT, ITI, and BEL,[6] and there was a conspicuous creation of
new wealth *through central intervention*. Chandru, with his new
wealth and vulgar willingness to display it perhaps represents
this new wealth. Ravi *not* accepting the gift of his house from
Chandru and Neela also has a parallel in Ranganna in *School
Master* accepting a similar gift from the police officer, his former
student. *Kasturi Nivasa* is perhaps deliberately invoking the earlier film and saying how humiliating accepting such a gift would
be to an emblem of Mysorean dignity.

Another connection can be made between *Kasturi Nivasa*
and the Kannada films of the late 1950s. These films, it may be
recalled, expressed alarm at traditional hierarchy being overridden
by the one imposed by wealth. Ravi, in *Kasturi Nivasa*, because
of his proud willingness to give away all he has, represents the
traditional scorn for the new kind of hierarchy created by wealth.[7]
Since Ravi repeatedly stresses his lineage, his pride can be associated with his inherited position in the hierarchy, which wealth
cannot take away. Ravi's caste is not specified in the film but he
has a loyal retainer Ramayya (Ashwath) who speaks the Kannada
of the farming community (Vokkaligas). The loyalty of this
retainer to Ravi may be equated with respect for traditional hierarchy and, since Ravi is placed at its summit, he can be identified

as 'Brahmin'. To spell it out—in case this is misunderstood—Ravi may not be *a Brahmin* but he occupies the position of the 'Brahmin' in traditional hierarchy. If this interpretation of Ravi in *Kasturi Nivasa* is allowed, the gracious 'Brahmin' appears to represent the Mysorean self-image. In this film—and in others from the same mould—Rajkumar consistently portrays the Kannada speaking Mysorean whose self-image is that of the Brahmin in traditional hierarchy; of someone at the pinnacle but who is too proud to take steps to realign if the traditional notion of hierarchy is overturned. The twin but associated notions of the 'modern' and the 'Brahmin' find a different kind of expression in the first Kannada art film—*Samskara* (1970).

Samskara

Kannada films frequently draw from literature in the 1960s but they draw from literary sources which can be adapted into the idiom of melodrama—the works of writers like A.N. Krishna Rao (ANaKru), T.R. Subba Rao, and Triveni. *Samskara*, a novel by U.R. Ananthamurthy written in 1965 is different because it is about an internal journey. *Samskara* is about a Brahmin scholar driven into moral crisis and therefore forced to question the tenets he has lived by. The novel was written by Ananthamurthy when he was in England and it was apparently inspired by Ingmar Bergman's *The Seventh Seal* (1956). Pattabhirama Reddy's film *Samskara* (1970)—which was scripted by Girish Karnad—was, initially, nearly banned[8] for hurting Madhwa Brahmin sentiments but widely seen by the public later on.

Samskara tells the story of a Vaishnavaite scholar named Praneshacharya (Girish Karnad) who lives in a small village in Shimoga district (in former princely Mysore) with his ailing wife. The crisis is created when Naranappa (P. Lankesh) is found dead. Naranappa was a Brahmin and a meeting of the Brahmins of the village is summoned. At the meeting, it comes out that Naranappa was a rebel and an iconoclast, having deliberately lived the aberrant life of a beef-eating and alcohol-consuming individual. He had also taken a low-caste mistress in Chandri (Snehlatha Reddy) and poured scorn on the Brahmins of the village. The meeting makes it clear that the Brahmins of Durvasapura are a greedy and despicable lot, with only Praneshacharya to compensate for their prevailing low moral standards. The question now being posed before the gathering is whether, having renounced his religious precepts in every way, Naranappa is eligible to be cremated, and, if he is, who is to perform the rites. The meeting reaches its high point when the good-hearted Chandri offers her gold jewellery to the Brahmins to overcome (through the appropriate rituals) the technical difficulties that may stand in the way of Naranappa's cremation. Vultures are flying in the sky and this is inauspicious. Plague is in the air but the villagers are still unaware of it—despite the rats dying in the street-corners.

When Praneshacharya is unable to come up with a satisfactory solution he hastens to a small temple in the forest and meditates before a stone idol of the god Maruti to seek guidance, but meets with a continued lack of success. Outside the temple, however, he runs into Chandri and, within a few moments, is in her arms and in the throes of passion. When Praneshacharya returns he finds his wife dying and he blames his own lack of self-control for what has transpired. His wife dies and he is so overcome by guilt and remorse that, when the other Brahmins visit him, he declares his inability to be of moral assistance to them.

Praneshacharya is now so overcome by pangs of guilt that he sets off on his own upon a journey of attrition without being certain of his destination. On the way he meets a lively young man named Putta who belongs to the lower Maleru caste. Putta is walking to a fair and needs company because he is loquacious by temperament. He is not put off when Praneshacharya makes a concerted attempt to evade him and follows behind the scholar asking riddles. Towards the end of his wandering Praneshacharya begins to feel a kinship with Putta and tells him of his turmoil— and the reasons for it—but Putta becomes condemnatory. A bullock cart going to Durvasapura comes by and Praneshacharya climbs in but Putta, who once wished to accompany him, suddenly demurs and departs on his own. The film concludes with Praneshacharya reaching his village—depleted by plague—and looking out over it.

It has been necessary to relate the story of *Samskara* at some length because it is not a continuation of Kannada cinematic tradition thus far and cannot be understood through a reference to another film—which is the way I have generally dealt with the cinema discussed above. *Samskara*, it can be argued, has the same position in Kannada cinema that *Pather Panchali* (1955) has in

Indian cinema, although this will need some elaboration. Ray's film is generally regarded as a realist film set in 1920s with no apparent discourse about the nation, but the question that engages me now is whether it could have been made before 1947.

Vibhutibhushan Banerji's *Pather Panchali* (1929) is a very different kind of work from Satyajit Ray's film version of it. The book consists of a string of isolated episodes about a small family of Bengali Brahmins. All the stories about Harihar's forefathers end in death and decay. People who die are forgotten, as is Apu's sister Durga, who is remembered only by Apu, that too a year later. In the destructive stream of time, actions do not develop continuously as a nexus of causes and effects. Narrative time is structured to draw the attention of the reader to certain memorable events—but not to any continuing relationship between them.[9] Ray changes Vibhutibhushan's story with the intent of sharpening its narrative and, consequently, amplifying its emotional impact.[10] Unlike in the novel, every event in the film is directed towards Apu's development as an individual and towards his eventual maturity. Many of the most memorable sequences in the film have to do with Apu's encounter with modernity—the telegraph wires, the train—and Ray's 'realism' conveys the acute sense of indigenous objects arriving for the first time, as it were, before the technology of cinema.[11] The film exhibits a certain pride at indigenous reality being captured by technology, a pride that could not have been felt by a colonized culture. Since Apu's is the 'new' consciousness through which reality is experienced, it is analogous to the position of the young Indian nation apprehending its own reality, through the use of a modern apparatus.

Samskara was made in 1970 around the same time that 'New Indian Cinema' arrived on the scene thanks to central government policy,[12] but it was made with finance made available locally. While Indian art cinema outside Bengal may roughly be said to have been initiated by government policy/FFC finance, *Samskara* is singular because it was made with local finance and also arrived too early to be attributed to a national initiative.[13] Second, although Kannada film already had a history of serious literary fiction, commencing even before 1947, it was not a novel by K.V. Puttappa or Shivaram Karanth[14] that was made into the first Kannada art film, but a (then) recent work by Ananthamurthy.

An enormous amount has been written about the novel *Samskara* but my interest is more in the film. Superficially, the film appears fairly faithful to the novel, but while a novel depends on a select, highly literate readership, even a faithful film version addresses a larger public. To be widely seen (as *Samskara* was) a film must connect more broadly than its literary source and, while sacrificing many nuances of the literary work, also address the immediate more closely. If the film *Samskara* is less concerned with religious issues than with being broadly humanist,[15] it also connects with the other Kannada cinema of the period—though perhaps not conspicuously.

Ananthamurthy's novel has been described as an 'allegory rich in realistic detail' by its translator, A.K. Ramanujan.[16] He observes that the allegory results from an abstract human theme reincarnated in a recognizably realistic milieu. In Praneshachaya, he suggests, is an allegory of the Brahminical life wrestling with the psychological complexity of the realist novel. The film *Samskara* is also allegorical but, I would like to argue, a different kind of allegory, an 'allegory of the modern'. The term 'modernist' has different connotations but *Samskara* is broadly 'modernist' in the sense that it involves a break with the traditional past.[17] I have already explored the association between the 'Mysore modern' and the 'Brahmin' in Kannada cinema of 1970 through an examination of *Kasturi Nivasa* and, I would like to argue, *Samskara* makes a similar association, though in a different way.

Samskara was originally taken to be 'anti-Brahmin' by a conservative segment of the Brahmin community because it attacked institutionalized Brahminism but a deeper examination of the film reveals how superficial such a reading is. It is true that the film has a number of despicable Brahmin characters and the positive counterpoints are 'low-caste' individuals like Chandri and Putta. But the film also has a more complex discourse when it makes Praneshacharya and Naranappa the only people who question the tenets into which they are born and both of them are born Brahmins. There are two kinds of Brahmins in the film, the low kind (the priests in the village) who use the favourable circumstances of caste to benefit personally, and the kind which reflects upon its station in the hierarchy, and it is their reflection/rebellion that makes Praneshacharya and Naranappa 'modern'.

Chandri's devotion to the two men perhaps betokens the same respect for traditional hierarchy and the 'modern' exhibited by Ravi's retainer Ramayya in *Kasturi Nivasa*.

The twin notions of the 'Brahmin' and the 'modern' apparently dominated Kannada cinema around 1970–2 and the art film that came after *Samskara*, Girish Karnad/B.V. Karanth's *Vamsha Vriksha* (1971) based on a novel by S.L. Bhyrappa, exhibits many of the same concerns although it may be regarded as more conservative. Satyajit Ray, when asked about the Kannada art cinema of the time, apparently remarked that the cinema was too preoccupied with Brahminism and ritual. My own understanding is that Apu and Praneshachaya are actually comparable because both are associated with the 'modern'. The difference between the two is that while Apu's consciousness parallels that of the young nation awakening to modernity, Praneshacharya represents Mysore staking a claim upon the same modernity by demonstrating its ability to question tradition to the point of breaking with it.

Puttanna Kanagal and the Woman's Melodrama

I have been dealing with popular cinema hitherto but *Samskara* is in a different idiom—that of the art cinema. If one were to characterize the primary difference between Indian popular cinema and Indian art cinema one might say that while the former is derived from mythology and the oral tradition, the latter owes enormously to the modern Indian novel. This means that while characters in popular cinema are types, those in the art cinema tend to be individuals. Types are vehicles for allegory because they do not have to be emptied of psychology. Conversely, it is difficult to read art cinema as allegory and critics have therefore been confused by art films that exhibit the same motifs as the popular films of the same period.[18] Apu and Praneshacharya are more individuals than types, but my interpretation has depended on both of them being typical in some sense. Apu's consciousness is in many ways simply that of a child while Praneshacharya (as generic type) corresponds to the religious believer confronted by an existential dilemma and proliferates in the films of Bergman and Dreyer.[19]

A Kannada filmmaker who rose to prominence in the 1970s as an auteur (although within popular cinema) with an identifiable sensibility and a consistency in his choice of subjects was Puttanna

Kanagal. He was an auteur primarily in the sense that in a cinema dominated by stars the films he directed were sought out because of their themes. I did not discuss his first Kannada film *Bellimoda* (1967) in the context of the 1960s because it was too exceptional and found few motifs in common with other cinema of the period. In this film (based on a novel by Triveni) the only daughter of the wealthy owner of a plantation Indira (Kalpana) is engaged to marry a young man Mohan (Kalyana Kumar). Her father funds Mohan's study in the US with the understanding that he will return and marry her. Before he completes his studies, however, the heroine's parents have a son and her mother dies soon after. When the male protagonist returns, he begins to behave strangely and wishes to break off his engagement to Indira. She guesses correctly that the situation has arisen because she will no longer inherit her father's wealth, because of her younger brother. She consents to the breaking off of the engagement but Mohan has a serious accident thereafter. Indira now tends to him so selflessly that Mohan understands the errors of his ways and begins to genuinely love her. When he recovers fully, however, she tells him that she will not marry him.

The film may be interpreted as roughly 'feminist' but it is difficult to find a film from the era of women's emancipation in Hindi cinema—namely, the 1930s and early 1940s[20]—that is comparable. Puttanna Kanagal went on to make a series of films with women as focal characters, and his choice of themes is distinctly unconventional—prostitution, incest, adultery, madness, an older woman's relationship with a much younger man,[21] with feminine desire being a key motif. What Indira feels for Mohan is not only 'love' but also 'desire' because of the physical aspects that are given emphasis—like a song in which she responds wildly to a kiss.

While Puttanna's working with the same kind of themes more than a decade later means that it is difficult to interpret each of his films in the context of a historical moment, this does not imply that his films are too 'personal' to be interpreted through a reference to the milieu because films in popular cinema inevitably have public connotations. Puttanna's films are from Mysore and therefore appear to favour the same themes pertaining to Brahmin families, although the caste is not spelt out. In *Bellimoda*, for instance, we only know that the heroine's father is a wealthy estate owner. When people are described as the landed gentry (sometimes denoted by 'sowkar') it stands for the Vokkaliga group because the Kannada spoken also suggests it. But when a rich person is a 'plantation owner', it could mean any caste. But unlike 'landowner', the plantation owner signifies 'refinement' and education as well as wealth which may, in turn, imply 'Brahmin'. The term 'sowkar' means 'wealthy person' and drawing attention to wealth can perhaps be termed 'unrefined' in the context of the Kannada film. In *Bellimoda* there are also Brahmin name associations, and assuming that arranged matches are between those of the same caste we can say that the film is entirely about people of the Brahmin caste. This, of course, excludes the comedy sections which apparently involve people lower in the caste hierarchy. Needless to add, the comedy sequences run parallel to the main story and influence it in no way, implying that commerce between different hierarchical stations (or castes) is still disallowed as in the earliest Kannada films.

An important aspect of Puttanna Kanagal—his preoccupation with feminine desire—comes into prominence in three key films of the early 1970s—*Gejje Pooje* (1970), *Sharapanjara* (1971). *Gejje Pooje* (which is based on a novel by M.K. Indira) is about a girl born into a devadasi household. Chandra (Kalpana) is Aparna's daughter and Aparna (Leelavathi) is an orphan brought up by devdasis. In order to see her daughter educated, she agrees to take a 'sowkar' lover and moves to a Brahmin section of Mysore town. Chandra grows up there and does extremely well in her examinations while the Brahmin boy Somu who loves her, fails. Chandra looks upon the Somu's father as a spiritual father because it is his liberal outlook that sees her accepted despite being a courtesan's daughter. Chandra has never known her real father but he reveals himself one day as a respectable Brahmin who was forced by circumstances to abandon his wife, who then went on to become a devadasi. He is now too weak to assume responsibility for Chandra and her mother but, instead, asks Chandra's help in getting his daughter by his official wife married to her former sweetheart Somu. Chandra consents and when the two are married agrees to go ahead with the 'Gejje Pooje' (the worship of the anklets) that will initiate her into the life of a devadasi. Before she does this, however, she proceeds to Somu's house to take his father's and her own father's (now Somu's father-in-law) blessings. But ironically Chandra has also consumed poison (a crushed diamond gifted by her father) and she dies, as does her mother, out of grief.

In *Gejje Pooje*, Puttanna employs some of the motifs used in *Bellimoda*. When Puttanna portrays a strong woman (Indira, Chandra) he contrasts her with the man she loves but who abandons her casually (Mohan, Somu). *Gejje Pooje* makes a token gesture towards the plight of devadasis but its story is really about a Brahmin (or part-Brahmin) girl forced to become one and is, therefore, interpretable as an upper-caste lament over the state to which it has been reduced. While this throws suspicion on the film's 'social concern', *Gejje Pooje* should perhaps be read allegorically with 'Brahmin' representing the same things as in films like *Kasturi Nivasa* rather than as standing for an actual caste identity.

The notion of feminine desire is also a key one here as in the next film *Sharapanjara*, which is based on a novel by Triveni. In that film a woman develops a hysterical condition after the birth of her child and, although subsequently cured, finds herself shunned by her husband and family, separated from her child, and virtually cast out. The theme of feminine desire—explored in Hindi cinema of the late 1950s, with films like *Dhool Ka Phool* (1959)—has been studied and associated with the modernization programme. While these women's melodramas, in Hindi films, were male centred with Rajendra Kumar in the lead role, many of them raised the question of women's desire and broached questions connected with the emancipation of women from the oppression of orthodoxy.[22] Although it is normally men who feel desire in most Hindi films and women who are its passive objects, these films have a much more active role for the woman. Feminine desire is usually illicit in the Hindi cinema of the late 1950s and the woman gets a second chance when she finds a husband without the sexual appeal of the lover.

While the illicit nature of desire in films like *Dhool Ka Phool* and *Gumraah* (1963) can be linked to modernity acting as a threat to tradition and the family, Puttanna's three films are different in as much as it is within a socially sanctioned relationship that the woman feels desire.[23] This bonhomie between sanctioned relationships and feminine desire parallels the one between caste and modernity, which I had remarked upon in the context of *Kasturi*

Nivasa. It suggests that modernity had already been assimilated such that it could co-exist with traditional hierarchy and orthodox family, with neither of them being in conflict with it. Puttanna continued with the theme of feminine desire in much later films but that is perhaps because he was an auteur, whose personal preoccupatio... were historically engendered in the 1960s.

Nagara Haavu and Conflicting Authority

While these three women's melodramas only suggest Puttanna's ties to traditional Mysore, his biggest hit *Nagara Haavu* (1972, based on a novel by T.R. Subba Rao [TaRaSu]) is much more explicit. This film—set in Chitradurga town around the fort—is about a wayward Brahmin youth named Ramachari (Vishnu-vardhan) who will listen to no one except his former teacher Chamaiah (Ashwath), also a Brahmin. Ramachari's classmate Varada promises to give his sister Alamelu (Arathi) to him in marriage but breaks his promise although Alamelu loves Ramachari. Chamaiah intervenes and makes Ramachari give up Alamelu. A Christian girl named Margaret has meanwhile fallen in love with Ramachari and he, after Alamelu goes away, becomes involved with her. Ramachari now finds employment with three reprobate 'sowkars' who go on trips to Bangalore to indulge themselves. During one of these visits Ramachari discovers that the girl procured for them is Alamelu. After he draws Alamelu away she reveals to him that her husband turned out to be a despicable sort who made money in this way. She suggests to Ramachari that they run away but Ramachari has now given his heart to Margaret. In the last part of the film, Ramachari's relationship with Margaret is resisted by both families and the teacher Chamaiah once again tries to intervene. The confrontation takes place on one of the fort's battlements and in the heat of the moment Ramachari pushes Chamaiah, who falls to his death. Ramachari and Margaret decide to follow and they too kill themselves by jumping off the Chitradurga hillside.

Ramachari in *Nagara Haavu* is rebellious and can be mistaken for the 'angry young man' but he is more impetuous than heroic. If one were to characterize Ramachari's rebellion one could say that it is institutional authority that he resents. There are two representations of authority in the film and while Chamaiah is the moral authority he reveres, the principal is his natural enemy because he is vested with actual power. Ramachari therefore ties the principal up to a pillar in the middle of the night after ransacking his garden.

Puttanna provides an indication of how the two figures of authority should be interpreted because while Chamaiah is associated—through portraits that hang on his walls—with Visveswaraiya and Kannada cultural figures, the principal has a portrait of Nehru hanging on the wall behind his chair. There is therefore an indication here of different attitudes towards Mysore and the Indian nation, with the attitude towards the latter being more ambivalent. Overall, the general sense conveyed by Ramachari is of a person in whom the moral values associated with Mysore remain but only in traces and almost at the unconscious level. His undirected rebelliousness owes itself to his being subjected to different kinds of authority and his inability to distinguish the right kind of authority from the wrong kind.

Another factor to be taken note of is the negative portrayal of Bangalore in the film. All Puttanna's films discussed so far are set outside Bangalore—in Mysore, Chikmagalur, and Chitradurga. Although Bangalore is the home of the Kannada film industry, Kannada cinema has had ambivalent feelings towards it.[24] Being the site of huge central government investment—industries, educational, and research institutions—as well as being a cantonment town, perhaps, makes it less of Mysore and more a creation of the Nehruvian nation/state. The reprobate 'sowkars' in the film do not recognize Alamelu when she comes to them in Bangalore. The 'consumers' and the 'commodity' come from the same small town, but Bangalore (as marketplace) mediates in the transaction.

Politics and Hierarchy

The years beginning with 1972 represent a new era for Mysore because of happenings at the national level influencing the local arena. Kannada cinema responds to this sharply, as will be evident from the next few sections in this chapter. In the years between 1969 and 1972 Indira Gandhi went from strength to strength outside Mysore, especially after the successful war with Pakistan in 1971. The government led by Veerendra Patil, the Congress (O) as it was called after the split of 1969, finally fell in March 1971 and Mysore was placed under President's rule. When Mysore went to the polls a year later, Mrs Gandhi's Congress (R) secured an over-whelming mandate and D. Devaraj Urs became Mysore's chief minister. As already elaborated upon, caste was always an important factor in Mysore and this continued after the linguistic reorganization of 1956 with the Veerashaivas/Lingayats and Vokkaligas—because of their numerical superiority and their economic status—dominating politics. The two groups had come together before 1947 against the Brahmins who had dominated the bureaucracy in the princely state. Urs belonged to the same caste group as the erstwhile Maharaja representing less than 1 per cent of the population. The community numbered only around 25,000 at the time and was concentrated almost exclusively in the district of Mysore. Devaraj Urs had not distinguished himself particularly in the early part of his career. But when the Congress split in 1969, while most of the Congress leaders in the state sided with Nijalingappa, he chose to be with Mrs Gandhi.[25] In 1972, when elections were held, Urs did not contest but remained Congress (R) party president with a control over the distribution of tickets. When Mrs Gandhi began her own campaign to woo the weaker sections, Urs with his own 'minority' caste status was the perfect choice to represent her. When the Congress (R) had won a solid victory in the state assembly elections Mrs Gandhi engineered the selection of Urs as chief minister with the expressed intention of making her party more broadly based, erode the power of the dominant caste groups, and serve those groups which had never shared power. In the process, Mrs Gandhi apparently expected to leverage her own position in the state.[26] The ascendancy of D. Devaraj Urs represented a new era in the state of Mysore. It registers in Kannada cinema (predictably) once again as a weakening of hierarchy which, in the preceding few years, is more rigidly drawn as we see in films ranging from *Bellimoda* to *Kasturi Nivasa*.

If *Nagara Haavu* has one aspect that is most unusual for a Kannada film, it is the way in which so many caste and religious groups are actually named. Ramachari is a Brahmin, Varada and Alamelu (Arathi) are Iyengar Brahmins, the three 'sowkars' are clearly Vokkaliga, Margaret is a Christian, Jaleel (Ambarish) is a Muslim, and Margaret has an 'uncle' who is called 'Naidu', which is also a caste name. A closer look at the film reveals something

else, which is that unlike in much of the earlier cinema, the different groups all 'transact' with each other in some sense. This
last assertion perhaps needs some more elaboration.

As explained in connection with *Bellimoda*, the film has
extended comedy sequences involving people who are not involved
in the main narrative. There is no commerce between the protagonists and the comedians in the sense that although they are in the
same space their stories are independent of each other. This is in
contrast to Hindi cinema which provides for separate comic relief
but there are transactions between the protagonists and the comic
characters. In *Sholay*, for instance, the comic relief is provided
by the jailor (Asrani), but Jai and Veeru escape from prison by
'transacting' with the jailor—that is, by threatening his life with
a fake pistol. Puttanna's *Gejje Pooje* provides another instance
of the lack of commerce between different caste groups because
while Chandra (being partly Brahmin) transacts with the Brahmin
family, we never see her mother engaged in similar exchanges,
being confined entirely to devadasi society. *Sharapanjara* is set
in an apparently Brahmin household and if there is the seeming
anomaly of the cook casting aspersions on the heroine's sanity
and causing her separation her from her own child, the cook is
made distinctly Brahmin.

Nagara Haavu, on the other hand, is unusual for the way in
which transactions are allowed between different social groups.
I pointed to the presence of a Muslim character in an earlier
Kannada film *Sarvamangala* (1968), but while that Muslim was
a passive onlooker and not allowed to participate in any transaction, Jaleel in *Nagara Haavu* is actually beaten up by Ramachari.
Similarly, there are transactions between Ramachari and the
Christian girl Margaret, Ramachari, and the 'sowkars'. One way
of reading the Brahmin girl Alamelu being forced into prostitution by her husband is that it points to commerce between the
different hierarchical groups becoming unrestricted.

When I notice the weakening of hierarchy (as a defining notion)
in Kannada cinema due to ascendancy of Mrs Gandhi's chosen
politician(s), the implication is not that cinema becomes more
egalitarian—because *Nagara Haavu* appears to regard the new
equations with alarm. Virtually every one of the relationships
just commented upon is portrayed as ominous. The love between
Alamelu and Ramachari may be gentle but the one between

Margaret and Ramachari is characterized by unmasked desire and there is a suggestion that Ramachari is uncomfortable with it. Puttanna Kanagal being an 'auteur' means that he can admit his prejudices without hesitation, but there are other films in which the weakening of hierarchy manifests itself more blandly as in Y.R. Swamy's *Nanda Gokula* (1972). Before we take up this film starring Rajkumar, however, we need to recapitulate how caste is represented in Kannada cinema.

Castes in the Kannada cinema of the period are rarely denoted, only connoted. If the protagonist is a Brahmin, his sacred thread is never in evidence but there are other indicators like names and spoken dialects that are effective markers. Wherever castes are denoted by professions, we can gauge caste from the trade practised. Vokkaligas are usually denoted as farmers and Brahmins are professionals where education may be assumed—like teacher, doctor, accountant, lawyer, etc. One group that is not connoted is the Veerashaiva or Lingayat sect, although the cinema of the 1950s and before did do so—as in *Gunasagari* (1953). The reason why it is inconvenient to use the Lingayat sect to connote hierarchical position is perhaps because the sect arose out of a rebellion against caste and, therefore, accommodates the different former caste groups within itself. The protagonists in *Gunasagari* are from the trader or Vaishya caste, although they are also apparently Lingayats.

Nanda Gokula is about a poor Brahmin family. The father Seetharamaiah (a Brahmin name) works as an accountant in the flour mill owned by Veerabhadraiah (a Lingayat name) and has two sons, Ravi (Rajkumar) and Sridhar. There are different conflicts within the narrative. The first comes out of the mother's brother being married to a rich woman named Dhanalakshmi, who does not respect her husband because she is wealthy. The second is Sridhar studying medicine because of the sacrifices made by Ravi but being ungrateful. Sridhar gets his FRCS (Fellow[ship] of the Royal College of Surgeons) from London but marries Dhanalakshmi's daughter and rejects his own family. The third comes out of Veerabhadraiah's brother-in-law plotting against Seetharamaiah and having him removed when he falls ill. Seetharamaiah (Ashwath) eventually dies when Sridhar refuses to attend to him but the narrative is resolved when the good Veerabhadraiah seeks Ravi's hand in marriage for his daughter,

Jaya. Veerabhadraiah's son also marries Ravi's sister; Sridhar and his wife regret their past conduct, and everyone is happy. The film uses the familiar motif of money interfering with traditional hierarchy (wife and husband here) but more interesting is the Lingayat-Vaishya businessman[27] seeking his Brahmin employee's son for his own daughter's husband. The weakness of endogamy in the period is also suggested by *Bhoothayyana Maga Ayyu* (1974) and Vijay's *Gandhada Gudi* (1973), both favouring romantic attachments—rather than marriages within the extended family. Also significant in *Nanda Gokula* is Bangalore being seen in positive light once again.

A factor to be taken note of in the Kannada cinema of the period is the unstable relationship between hierarchy and occupation. Siddalingaiah's *Bangarada Manushya* (1972), the biggest Kannada grosser for several decades, follows the same model of which *Kasturi Nivasa* is the supreme example. The motif of the selfless Brahmin continues in *Bangarada Manushya*, but the protagonist (Rajkumar) takes up farming to support his widowed sister's family. The film nonetheless takes the precaution of making the protagonist a 'progressive farmer' and, in order to demonstrate that hierarchy is still intact, introduces a neighbouring farmer—traditional and apparently Vokkaliga—with a separate comic subplot to his family. A film that came two years later, Dorai/Bhagwan's *Eradu Kanasu* (1974), goes a step further in its ambiguity over occupations when the same extended family includes city dwelling Brahmins and farmers, without the farmers being labelled 'progressive'.

Towards Delhi

To recollect some of the earlier observations, many of the changing motifs in Kannada cinema after the linguistic reorganization of the states in 1956 can be associated with the way the Indian nation is perceived in relation to Mysore. The characteristics that mark out Kannada cinema hitherto have pertained to the emphasis on hierarchy, and hierarchy is weakened whenever Mysore has felt itself closer to the nation as in the years leading to 1969, and after 1972 when D. Devaraj Urs was seen as the chosen agent of the centre. Another feature is the way Bangalore becomes a rough index of Mysore's distance from Delhi. The city is viewed positively whenever Mysore has felt itself close to the nation but negatively when it has felt itself distant. The content of Kannada mythological and the historical films has also, generally, been interpreted in terms of this distance and these genres, though weakened, continue into the 1970s. *Bangarada Manushya* (1972) includes a twist involving a family in Belgaum with is secretly cared for by the selfless protagonist. This relationship is misinterpreted by his greedy nephew until it is revealed (too late) that the protagonist's relationship with a woman in Belgaum is a noble one—and without its basis in conjugality. While the protagonist is associated with Mysore modernity (the film has footage showing Visveswaraiya), there is a picture of Nehru hanging on the wall in the Belgaum household. It would, of course, have been incongruous to associate Visveswaraiya with Belgaum because he is a Mysore hero and Belgaum was part of the Bombay Presidency. Still, there is suggested bonhomie here between Mysore and the nation, which is denied by most films in 1970–1.

Kannada cinema of the 1970s registers both the political concerns of the times as well as an increasingly arrogant central authority—although in a covert way. Since Devaraj Urs was neither a Lingayat nor a Vokkaliga his only hope of political survival was to alter the logic of Mysore politics. He did this not only by extending patronage to members of marginalized groups in regional politics but also by placating key Lingayat and Vokkaliga leaders. More importantly, he undertook several populist measures such as freeing debtors from obligations to pawnbrokers (mainly non-Kannadiga) and providing houses for the poor.[28] Although many of these measures had the appearance of being radical, they were devised not to upset the classes that were actually powerful.[29] His most important contribution was perhaps the amended Land Reforms Act which was passed in 1973 and came into effect in 1974. Under the act the only persons eligible to hold land were those engaged in personal cultivation. This act was not directed at landlessness but towards tenancy[30] which meant that many poorer landowners who had leased out their lands to those with the wherewithal to cultivate it lost the little they had. Another very visible move made by Urs was the Urban Land Ceiling Act by which many old Mysoreans who lived in large ancestral houses in the cities but who were otherwise not rich were dispossessed. The 1970s were an important socio-economic period for Mysore (renamed Karnataka in 1974) but three aspects perhaps have a greater bearing on Kannada cinema. The first is that the amendment to the Land Reforms Act had its greatest impact outside former princely Mysore—largely in the coastal districts of Uttara Kannada and Dakshina Kannada.[31] The second is that Urs' having to extend his patronage to functionaries at the lower levels to strengthen his own hands as a minority leader resulted in a huge increase in corruption.[32] While Urs did much on his own initiative, he did it in the name of Mrs Gandhi and the central leadership. He paid the price for it eventually when he split with the Congress and could not take credit for whatever he had done[33]—his Congress (U) being virtually wiped out in 1980.

The amended Land Reforms Act of 1973 was perhaps the legislative measure that Devaraj Urs will be best known for. *Eradu Kanasu*, which I mentioned earlier, includes an element that can perhaps be best explained through a reference to it. The hero Ramachandra Rao (Rajkumar), who is a professor in a Bangalore college, is officially engaged to marry his own cousin (Manjula) until her once acquiescent father comes in the way without any reason being given. Ramachandra Rao therefore marries another woman (Kalpana) and the film is about how he grows to love her. The hero's parents notice his coldness towards his wife and try to bring about a rapprochement by leaving the couple alone in their city house for a while. The excuse tendered is that they have to attend to their lands and harvest the grain but there is a suggestion that being 'absentee landlords' could threaten their holdings. The uncle's sudden decision not to allow his daughter to marry his nephew is also never explained. But by convention, 'estrangement' within a landowning family—as in *Chandavaliya Thota* and *Anna Thangi*—is associated with the division of land. Conversely, marriages between landowning families suggest enlarged landholdings. The lack of a reason for the proposed alliance being cancelled in *Eradu Kanasu* leads me to seek out an extra-textual explanation. In *Eradu Kanasu*, the motif of the cancelled engagement, I propose, implies the impossibility of enlarging landholdings because of the land ceilings now stipulated. The absence of an explanation for the broken engagement is strange but perhaps it was expected to touch the right chord with audiences—because of the enormous effect the Act had at the time.

The courtroom and the police (as in Hindi cinema)[34] are emblems of the Indian state, which is why they are less in evidence in Kannada than in Hindi cinema. Whenever there are hints of litigation, as in *Chandavaliya Thota* and *Bangarada Manushya*, we see lawyers but rarely judges and the courtroom. The police officer is, by and large, also an elusive presence in the earlier Kannada cinema. I have already explained his presence in the context of the 1950s, in films like *School Master* and *Anna Thangi*. *Jedara Bale* (featuring CID 999) can be understood as a celebration of state authority when Mysore believed it had a hand in ruling India—because of the ascendancy of Nijalingappa at the national level. With Nijalingappa's political marginalization in 1969—which registered as a defeat for Mysore—CID 999 apparently went into hibernation. *Jedara Bale* had two sequels, *Goadalli CID 999* and *Operation Jackpot*, made in 1968 and 1969, respectively. Another sequel, *Operation Diamond Racket*, was announced in 1969 but the project was postponed indefinitely, with the film coming out eventually only in 1978.

An important film with a key place for the courtroom scene is Siddalingaiah's *Bhoothayyana Maga Ayyu* (1974), based on a novel by Gorur Ramaswamy Iyengar. *Bhoothayyana Maga Ayyu* is a rural melodrama about the doings of a villainous gun-totting Brahmin moneylender named Bhoothayya (M.P. Shankar). The saintly figure in the village is the Vokkaliga farmer, Devaiah. Bhoothayya has a son named Ayyu (Lokesh) while Devaiah has one named Gulla (Vishnuvardhan). Although Devaiah is prosperous and not in debt, Bhoothayya gets his signature on some pretext and the result is that Devaiah ultimately hangs himself after losing a prolonged court case. The enmity continues between Gulla and Ayyu until their wives decide matters have gone far enough. Ayyu transforms into a good person and saves Gulla's wife from drowning. The film concludes with Ayyu's goodness becoming known and peace being established. The film also introduces other backward castes and Dalits, all of whom hate Bhoothayya and make common cause with Gulla. A prominent character in the film is played by a Siddhi actor—a tribe in Uttara Kannada whose ancestors were African slaves in Portuguese Goa. All these are new motifs for Kannada cinema and apparently owe to Devaraj Urs' economic measures, the new political alignments, and the public acknowledgement that the marginalized classes need to be represented.

Bhoothayya's Brahmin caste is deliberately invoked in *Bhoothayyana Maga Ayyu*, but the man has none of the 'Brahmin traits' eulogized in Kannada cinema of the 1970s. M.P. Shankar, who plays him, plays the keeper of the cremation grounds in the 1960s version of *Sathya Harishchandra* and also the gymnasium-owner who gets Ramachari employment with the 'sowkars' in *Nagara Haavu*. He has the physique of a wrestler and it is difficult to understand why Bhoothayya is portrayed thus. Even stranger is the revolver he carries with him in a holster worn over his dhoti. All this is perplexing but my own understanding is that Bhoothayya is not from Kannada cinema but is a hybrid engendered by Mysore's proximity to the nation.

India was a relatively radicalized space around 1974 because of Mrs Gandhi's populist rhetoric. There was a new kind of radical middle-class cinema coming from directors like Shyam Benegal and, even if his *Nishant* (1975) was made a year later, there had already been, in the mainstream Hindi film, portrayals of feudal brutality and melodramatic examinations of rural oppression. The murderous Brahmin moneylender, I propose, is a hybrid composed of 'feudal oppressor' from a north Indian milieu (as portrayed in the Hindi film) and Brahmin from local hierarchy. While Hindi films portray the Kshatriya caste (or Thakurs) as feudal oppressors, *Bhoothayyana Maga Ayyu* relies on the more docile local priestly caste—but imparts Kshatriya attributes to it to make it fit the pan-Indian stereotype of 'caste oppressor'.[35] There is also an attempt here to accommodate local caste relationships within a pan-Indian framework, perhaps owing to some kind of political theorizing current at the time due to left-wing academics who had been enlisted by Mrs Gandhi. Devaraj Urs also attempted to make himself a pan-Indian political theorist of sorts and tried to equate local caste with class, invoking 'class war', and citing E.M.S. Namboodaripad on the issue.[36]

As observed earlier there is little evidence of the courtroom scene in the cinema prior to *Bhoothayyana Maga Ayyu*. While Mysore's 'proximity to the nation' may account for the presence of a motif common to Hindi cinema in this Kannada film, it does not explain why lawyers and the courtroom are shown in negative light here. In this film and in earlier films like *Chandavaliya*

Thota and *Bangarada Manushya*, the implication of litigation is not that justice will be obtained but that a local solution is more efficacious and less expensive. The hypothesis that the judiciary represents the Indian state is borne out by these films representing official justice as always distant. In *Bhoothayyana Maga Ayyu* official justice also involves difficult trips to Bangalore, which I have tried to show is associated with the nation. But *Bhoothayyana Maga Ayyu* is different from other films in as much as litigation is not merely contemplated (as suggested by the presence of lawyers in films like *Chandavalliya Thota* which has no courtroom scene); rather, there is actual action in the courtroom as in Hindi films like *Aradhana* (1969). This, I propose, suggests a situation in which the Indian state has a more intrusive presence locally.

'Twins'

Interpreting films without Rajkumar takes a different course from those in which he stars because they are conceived differently. The roles played by Rajkumar in the 1970s always include a characteristic bit of moral rhetoric and not usually to be found when other actors play the lead. In *Bhoothayyana Maga Ayyu*, for instance, the protagonist Gulla is himself too flawed and impetuous to stand for any moral principle. The viewpoint upheld by Rajkumar's roles can be roughly identified with the moral principles that Mysore might have liked to be known by and identified as essentially 'Brahmin', this term perhaps made flesh and blood by Visveswaraiya.

Most characters played by Rajkumar in the 1970s tend to be upright, courageous, and possess a barely concealed contempt for material success—especially when represented by wealth. The protagonist played by Rajkumar upholds the chastity of women and inevitably regards his own mother as worthy of worship. There is a fundamental difference between the 'oedipal mother' from Hindi cinema as seen in films like *Awaara* (1951), *Mother India* (1957), and *Deewar* (1975), and the sacred mother in these Kannada films. The difference is that in the Hindi films the mother is required to earn her children's devotion through her acts. In all three Hindi films, she brings up her son(s) alone when she is deserted by her husband and her suffering is given emphasis. In the Kannada films of the 1970s she is an object of devotion even when she does nothing significant. In one or two films the mother is equated with language but even when this equation ceases, the protagonist's devotion to his mother continues. Since the motif of the mother is less often found in the films without Rajkumar, I propose that this ploy has a double purpose. The first is to erect Rajkumar as the personification of every value that Mysore once stood for and the second is to give him a stable object of devotion. Indirectly, therefore, the mother allegorizes Mysore. The fact that the mother plays no active role is arguably because she represents a defunct political entity. An alternate argument is that the mother is the Kannada language but, even long after linguistic reorganization, the motifs in Kannada cinema appear to invoke only former princely Mysore and not the enlarged state—which includes huge areas outside the former princely state. Greater Mysore was renamed Karnataka in 1974 and, by all accounts, this was met with jubilation in northern Karnataka while there was a sense of loss in Mysore.[37] Hitherto, I have used the term 'Mysore' for the territory addressed by Kannada cinema since the original state and the enlarged one had the same name. But since the territory addressed by it from the late 1970s onwards—whether it is Karnataka or Mysore—remains uncertain, the simplest course is to refer to the territory addressed by Kannada cinema as the 'region'.

There are series of films starring Rajkumar made after 1974 in which the actor plays two or three roles, and in which one role represents the quintessential regional hero complete with the ubiquitous mother figure. The first of the films is Pekete Shivaram's *Daari Thappida Maga* (1975). In this film about twins, Prakash is kidnapped by a gang of thieves and brought up as a master criminal. The other twin, Prasad, grows up to become a professor in a Bangalore college. Prakash is amoral, murderous, and promiscuous, while the absent-minded Prasad respects the chastity of women. An interesting factor is that Prakash's nefarious activities are conducted outside the region and the two come into contact only when Prakash comes to Bangalore for a robbery. Prakash's first operation is in Bombay in the vicinity of the Taj Hotel and involves smuggling of idols and the second is in a palace in north India and involves the stealing of the queen's jewels. The parts of the film involving Prakash are overrun by policemen and CBI officials, while Bangalore is relatively free of them until Prakash virtually brings them along. Eventually, Prasad and

Prakash come face to face and their relationship is understood. There is a disquieting development when Prakash begins to cast covetous glances at Prasad's sister-in-law and, given the context of Kannada cinema, it is as though a once docile animal brought up in the wild were exhibiting the behavioural traits acquired there and become treacherous. Prakash is eventually killed off but the motif of the feral twin brother is strong and makes us strangely uneasy. *Dari Thappida Maga* was released in the year of the Emergency and though it may have been made before the Emergency was announced, it was still conceived when the Indian state was fighting with agitations mounted by Mrs Gandhi's political opponents on several fronts—notably in Bihar and Gujarat. Karnataka was not beleaguered territory in the same way and this, I propose, is suggested in the film not only by the local space being free of policemen—until Prakash arrives in Bangalore—but also by Prasad's stability, especially in relation to Prakash's. Prasad's absent-mindedness also appears suited to a character from an untroubled milieu.[38]

The motif of the look-alike finds mythical expression in Hunsur Krishnamurthy's *Babruvahana* (1977), although they are father and son instead of two brothers. The story deals with a segment of the Mahabharata set after Dharmaraya has been enthroned as king in Hastinapura but before the Kurukshetra war. The first half of the film deals with his younger brother Arjuna (Rajkumar) going off on a pilgrimage but being married to two different women—made possible by loss of memory created by the Sri Krishna. Arjuna is therefore unaware that his son by Chitrangadha—Babruvahana (Rajkumar)—has been brought up by her and another wife Uluchi and grown into manhood. The second part of the film deals with the arrogant Arjuna and Babruvahana in battle when Babruvahana tethers the sacrificial horse sent out by Dharmaraya to mark his dominance as king. The film does not have Kunti on the scene. It is therefore only Babruvahana who has a sacred mother—or rather, two of them. We may, consequently, understand Babruvahana—rather than Arjuna—as the regional hero. The battle between father and son takes place eventually with the two mothers aligned on either side—the real mother with Arjuna and Uluchi with Babruvahana—and Babruvahana not only conducts himself more correctly but he also wins. The film concludes with the dead Arjuna brought back to life through Sri Krishna's intervention and everyone bowing before his presence. In the end everyone respects and honours god, to whom everything has a purpose.

In this mythological film, as in others of the 1950s and 1960s, there is the motif of the king and the god. The king here is apparently Babruvahana, although Arjuna and Dharmaraya also wear crowns. Overall, however, one gets the sense of Babruvahana and his two mothers being together, while the Pandavas under the guidance of Sri Krishna represent a unity of sorts. Seen thus, the film can be read as a story about a king—who upholds the values that the region is known by—holding his own against a divinity whose agent is drunk with power. While the actual battle between Babruvahana and Arjuna is difficult to interpret allegorically, the region's loyalty to the nation despite its agent being drunk with power is recognizable when we relate it to 1977, the year when Mrs Gandhi's abuse of power saw her defeated.

The third film, K. Somashekar's *Shankar Guru* (1978), is a more innocuous effort about twin brothers separated at birth. Rajkumar also plays their father, who deserted their mother because he was accused of murder (unjustly) and therefore fled. As may be anticipated, the earnest son lives in Mysore with his mother while his more frivolous—although good—twin lives in Kashmir. Much of the film is set in Kashmir because the villains and the father of the twins, Rajashekar, and other Kannada-speaking Mysoreans featuring in the narrative own estates there. Smuggling of idols continues to be a key motif in the film but more important is perhaps the fact that the resolution happens in Kashmir with no one making a move to return 'home'. While the smuggling of idols is a key motif in the Hindi films of the 1970s[39] and suggests the region's support of national preoccupations, the abandoning of the local space by the protagonists indicates a degree of 'ambition' in Kannada cinema to become 'national' instead of regional. This ambition is also suggested by Dorai/Bhagwan's *Operation Diamond Racket* (1978). Here, CID 999 has no dealings with the region, and even his 'romance' is with an outsider—without the family which might have helped locate her. In the film *Goadalli CID 999* (1968), the protagonist gave his occupation as 'estate-owner from Chikmagalur' to conceal his identity but this untruth still indicated that his personal moorings were in the region. This is not the sense to be got from *Operation Diamond Racket* in which, to all appearances, CID 999—or Mr Prakash—has no regional identity at all.

Devaraj Urs continued to remain strong in 1978, although Mrs Gandhi had been unseated and he assisted her to get back into Parliament in that year through a by-election in Chikmagalur. The two films were perhaps released before she won—which was only in November—but the changed equation between a triumphant chief minister and his humbled leader could not have been lost on the region. Moreover, where Mrs Gandhi had been assertive as the prime minister, the government that replaced the Congress was hardly forceful and may have appeared lax. Kannada cinema's not being confined to its own territory in 1978 may owe to a strong region not meeting external 'resistance' from a strong central authority. National identity is strong when the nation is opposed from without (as in war) and weak when there is no such opposition. The characteristics common to *Shankar Guru* and *Operation Diamond Racket* may be related, thereby pointing to the weakening of regional sentiment because of a soft Indian state.

The pan-Indian Art Film in Kannada

Three art films made in the 1970s after Indira Gandhi's Congress came to power in Karnataka under Devaraj Urs are of interest if only to understand how later Kannada art cinema differs from *Samskara* in its implications. Pattabhirama Reddy's film, as already explained, has a special significance for Kannada cinema because it represents Mysore staking a claim upon Indian modernity. Although different in theme from *Pather Panchali* it is as important to the region as Satyajit Ray's film is to the nation. Three subsequent films made by cultural stalwarts Girish Karnad, B.V. Karanth, and Girish Kasaravalli are more pan-Indian than regional, and I propose to examine this aspect of Girish Karnad's *Kaadu* (1973), B.V. Karanth's *Chomana Dudi* (1975), and Girish Kasaravalli's *Ghatashraddha* (1977).

Girish Karnad's *Kaadu* is based on a novel by Sri Krishna Alanahalli and is set in two villages dominated by Vokkaligas. The focal character is a little boy named Kitty who has come to visit his uncle Chandre Gowda and is witness to the happenings. Chandre Gowda (Amrish Puri) is the head man of Koppalu and he lives with his wife Kamali. Kamali's greatest woe is that Chandre

Gowda has a mistress in the neighbouring village Hosuru and visits her every night. Tensions between Koppalu and Hosuru mount when Chandre Gowda punishes a local person who works for a Hosuru strong man named Shivaganga. The head man of Hosuru tries to make peace but violence erupts at a local fair. Chandre Gowda makes a show of bravado but Kamali is raped and brutalized by Shivaganga and she dies. The villagers of Koppalu under Chandre Gowda raid Hosuru and slaughter Shivaganga and his men. The film concludes with the police arriving and the 'miscreants' being arrested.

Kaadu is neatly made and is not without lyricism but one can be confused about its meaning and purpose today. The film places no emphasis on power equations and caste politics/relationships. It does not examine gender issues either, and if it tries to see the world through Kitty's eyes, we remain uncertain about what he sees or learns. The film is episodic and Kitty sees the various things that might go into a 'growing up' story—a couple fornicating in the bushes, a woman's anxiety at her husband's infidelity, group rivalry, and violent death. Ray's Apu may be the model for Kitty but where the 'modern' was the key element in Apu's education, Kitty's eyes open only to 'adult reality'. This gives us a clue as to the covert discourse in the film because everything in *Kaadu* is pointed towards an 'authentic' rendering of a way of life. Even the music by B.V. Karanth is not theme music but uses instruments that might have been actually used in the milieu depicted. But if 'authenticity' is the film's purpose, who or what is its authentic vision being held up to?

The Film Finance Corporation (FFC) had been set up in 1960 on the recommendation of the S.K. Patil Film Enquiry Commission Report of 1951. In 1971, the Information and Broadcasting (I&B) Ministry laid down, as part of the FFC's obligations, the directive that it would develop film in India into an effective instrument for the promotion of national culture, education, and healthy entertainment by financing (through loans) modest but off-beat films. Overall, the effect of FFC policy and Mrs Gandhi's interventions in the field of cinema was to encourage off-beat films, which could succeed financially only if they conformed to the following aesthetic criteria: (a) human interest in the story, (b) Indianness in theme and approach, and (c) the films being about characters/people with whom the audiences might identify.[40]

While *Samskara*, it may be argued, deals with too esoteric a dilemma for audiences to 'identify' with Praneshacharya, *Kaadu* presents us with no such difficulty. Kitty's innocent viewpoint being the focal one is perhaps even a way to facilitate audience identification with the characters. Moreover, the absence of social detail pertaining to the way local power is exercised in the village, the local caste equations, relationships within the family, etc., makes the film an emblem of 'Indianness'. I therefore suggest that *Kaadu* is a film that conforms to the notion of a pan-Indian realist cinema current in the 1970s in a way that *Samskara* is not. The story being resolved only through the arrival of the police suggests that the conflicts portrayed—slight though they are[41]—have no local solution. The police being an emblem for the Indian state is perhaps significant here and can be interpreted as *Kaadu* showing more faith in the nation state than in the ability of the 'local' to administer itself.

B.V. Karanth's *Chomana Dudi* (1975) is based on a more important novel by K. Shivaram Karanth. Published in 1933, the novel came out when India was fired by the spirit of social reform and was part of the Pragathisheela movement in Kannada literature but distinguishes itself from the other works of the movement through its emphasis on naturalism instead of naïve idealism.[42] *Chomana Dudi* tells the story of Choma, a low caste Holeya or untouchable from a village in present day Karnataka during British rule. Choma belongs to a sub-caste so lowly placed that it has to live on leftovers or animal carcasses and cannot till land, which Choma desperately wants to own. Choma loses his children one by one, one to an illness while another is allowed to be drowned by the Brahmin onlookers. The remaining son becomes a Christian—as a way to own land—but the last straw is his only daughter Belli not resisting the advances of the Christian overseer.

The differences between the novel and B.V. Karanth's film adaptation have been written about and analysed.[43] The main difference noted is that the film privileges the notion of 'superstition' much more—through Choma's (Vasudeva Rao) fear of his deity Panjurli—than in the novel, in which Panjurli is only one thread in the complex fabric of Choma's existence. Another difference is that when Choma is shown doting on his oxen, there is no acknowledgement in the film that it is also common for his people to eat cattle. A sequence in the book showing him feasting joyously with his friends on a dead ox is omitted in the film, as if with disapproval. There are other differences[44] but those just cited suggest that the film is being offered to a modern India in which the eradication of superstition is a primary concern[45] and which, perhaps, has a centralized notion of cinematic propriety. Choma being denied a local community also finds correspondence in Hindi films like Govind Nihalani's *Aakrosh* (1980), which deal with tribals and other marginalized groups but are not able to imagine a local community to which they might belong.[46]

The third film Girish Kasaravalli's *Ghatashraddha* (1977), which is based on a story by U.R. Ananthamurthy and deals with ritual as *Samskara* does, but is very different from the 1970 film. This film, like *Kaadu*, has a child as a focal character. The boy is witness to a cruel turn of events in a Brahmin village. A Brahmin widow who has become pregnant because of an affair is ostracized by the community through a ceremony which acknowledges her as dead even when she lives—her head is shaved and she is cast out by her family. The film has extended sequences showing the cruelty of adolescent boys, learning to be priests, to each other and is a powerful indictment of ritual and superstition. But it is also true that Yamunakka's plight cannot be extended to include gender issues of today. *Ghatashraddha* deals with a past state of affairs as though it were current. If a comparison were to be made with a western film, Jacques Rivette's *La Religieuse* (1967), which is based on a work by Denis Diderot may be appropriate. But that film, while dealing with the life of a woman in the eighteenth century who is forced to become a nun, is concerned with relating a story and not with criticizing a 'social evil'. *Ghatashraddha*, on the other hand, is too claustrophobic for us to see anything except its purpose, which is to attack superstition and ritual—as though such a purpose would only be appropriate to a modern nation. Also, while *Samskara* raised key religious issues that could cause sincere dilemmas to a believer like its protagonist, *Ghatashraddha* subsumes everything under the terms 'superstition' and 'ritual' with little attention to the religious logic pertinent to its setting. *Chomana Dudi* and *Ghatashraddha* also attack the doings of the Church and Christians in order not to be read as anti-Hindu but as anti-superstition.[47] It is perhaps pertinent to my argument that *Ghatashraddha* was remade as *Diksha* in Hindi by Arun Kaul in 1991.

The Kannada New Wave, as the art films of the period were called, had a large number of films by cultural personalities and filmmakers like P. Lankesh (*Pallavi*, 1976), Prema Karanth (*Phaniyamma,* 1982), M.S. Sathyu (*Kanneshwar Rama*, 1977), T.S. Ranga (*Geejagana Goodu*, 1979), T.S. Nagabharana (*Grahana*, 1979), and Chandrashekhar Kambar (*Kaadu Kudre*, 1978). The films they made were not all alike and the arguments I have just offered may not apply to many of them. While there was the influential factor of a generous state government subsidy which may have created filmmakers more readily than may have been otherwise possible, the fact that much of this cinema had no local roots has been commented upon by cultural critics.[48] The Kannada New Wave continued well into the 1980s but also lost its relevance. Although many of these art films are important to cinema, they are not helpful if our interest is in understanding the local ethos. W.H. Auden's remark about what a poet hopes for his work may be especially pertinent here: these later Kannada art films are perhaps like some valley cheese, local but prized elsewhere. I will therefore not be examining much Kannada art cinema in the rest of the book.

The Fading Community

A phenomenon that I have not explored hitherto is why so many Kannada films of the 1960s and 1970s are based on works of litera-ture,[49] which is not so in the 1950s and earlier. While popular films found the dramatic novels by writers *from Mysore* like Triveni, AaNaKru, M.K. Indira, TaRaSu, and Gorur Ramaswamy Iyengar most suitable, art films depended on the works of writers like Shivaram Karanth, U.R. Ananthamurthy, and S.L. Bhyrappa, which are more reflective and sometimes from *outside Mysore*. In writing about the spread of nationalism, Benedict Anderson[50] describes the nation as an 'imagined community' because nation-hood as experienced is associated with imagining and with creation. To elaborate, the possibility of the nation depends upon the development of the book, the novel, and the newspaper. It also presupposes a reading public capable of using them within a terri-tory and able to imagine themselves as a single community. There are other imagined communities in India apart from the nation and I have tried to argue that former princely Mysore remains inscribed as a territory in Kannada cinema long after it had ceased to exist as a political entity. Drawing loosely from Benedict Anderson, I also propose that although 'Mysore' became defunct as a political entity in 1956, it existed in the place in which it might have existed—in the collective memory of the people of the region, and given shape and manifested in the region's literature. If Mysore had not become defunct as a political entity (that is, it had been 'living' like the nation), adapting literature might have been redundant. 'Mysore' was not only a space but also an ethos that faded as the last generation of Mysoreans passed on. Already, in the late 1970s, we find popular cinema less dependent upon literature. Art cinema continued to adapt literature, but more as a way of invoking its cultural authority than to tap into the manifestation of an ethos.[51] Most of these art films were not widely seen locally. Given the hypothesis about the relationship between Mysore and Kannada cinema up to the end of the 1970s, it will be interesting to see what Kannada cinema becomes in the 1980s and the properties of the 'region' it helps to imagine. At the end of the 1970s it still imagines its territory as Mysore, but this apparently cannot continue indefinitely, with the fading of 'Mysore' as a cherished memory.

3. Vestiges of Mysore
1980–9

Changing Patterns

My observations about Kannada cinema in the 1970s may have conveyed the impression that there is a rigid consistency in the development of the motifs exhibited by it, but this is not entirely true. There are many aspects of the earliest cinema that continue well into the 1970s although some of the films appear to abandon them. As an instance, the endogamy of the 1940s and 1950s cinema continues into the 1970s, although 'love' and 'romance' often find a place. My own approach is to treat departures from the norm as anomalies and try to explain them. I explained the 'love across castes' in *School Master* (1958) in this way as I did the 'arranged marriage' between people from different caste groups in *Nanda Gokula* (1972). This chapter is important because the 1980s represent a period in which some genres in Kannada cinema—the mythological film, the historical film—died out and new genres like the youth film appeared. At the same time, these new genres are not 'stable' like the mythological film, the historical drama, and the family melodrama, and fade away almost immediately.

The term 'genre' is perhaps not an exact term for categories in Kannada cinema but I use the term loosely. Genres are dependant on conventions created by the myths engendered by historical moments. To cite Roland Barthes again, myth is a kind of language and a set of conventions by which the exigencies of a specific historical moment are given eternal justification.[1] Hollywood genre films refer back to mythologies of their own and, phrased very simply, the conventions of the western can be associated with the origins of the American nation state because it shows the 'westerner' as the civilizing influence in a savage land.[2] Post-war Germany produced the genre of the *Heimatfilme*. 'Heimat' is the feminine German word for 'homeland' as contrasted with 'Fatherland', which is a masculine term with martial connotations. The Heimatfilme was a response to the war and Germany's defeat but war was characteristically the subject it neglected to invoke—except in the manner of a natural calamity.[3] 'Third World' cinemas have historical genres of their own and Indonesian cinema has two different genres dealing respectively with the colonial period under the Dutch (the *Kompeni* genre) and the struggle against the Japanese (the *Perjuangan* genre).[4] Egyptian cinema has the genre of the war film, which deals largely with the Arab-Israeli struggle of 1948, the historical spectacle genre, which includes *Cleopatra* (1943) and *Saladin* (1941), and another genre that deals with contemporary politics.[5]

In Kannada cinema, as in Hindi cinema, there do not appear to be genres in the same sense because all films appear to draw sustenance from the same values which owe to 'pre-history'. To illustrate, I interpreted the set of films constructed around the generous 'aristocrat', beginning with *Kasturi Nivasa*, by invoking the modernization of princely Mysore. But the discourse promoted in the film owes to the notion of hierarchy derived from the caste system—which is ancient. This is different, for instance, from a western like John Ford's *The Searchers* (1956) in which the discourse pertains to the white family bringing civilization to the savage West, a specific response to a historically identifiable moment. As I have tried to explain elsewhere,[6] traditional aesthetics, poetics, and dramaturgy in India apparently sought out truths which were 'transcendental' and 'immutable' and did not depend on the exigencies of the moment. The 'pre-capitalist' content of Kannada and Hindi cinema,[7] noticed by other critics, is due to the 'immutable' truths having been conceived in a 'pre-capitalist' era. *Kasturi Nivasa* does not even invoke 'caste' but the 'eternal values' on which the notion of caste hierarchy is itself based.

If there are no genres in the strictly accepted sense, what are categories like the mythological film (*Babruvahana*), the domestic melodrama (*Nanda Gokula*), and the spy film (*Jedara Bale*) in Kannada cinema? I would like to argue that the different categories are all family dramas but in different settings.[8] Although CID 999 remains single[9] at the commencement of each film his relationship with women always culminates in an implicit marriage. The protagonist's concern for feminine chastity and her family make this apparent. Even in a film like *Operation Diamond Racket*, the woman's dead brother is his friend and one cannot imagine CID 999 (alias Prakash) taking advantage of the sister of a friend. It can also be argued that 'technology' in these spy films plays the same part that divine intervention plays in the mythological film—in as much as it is 'magical' and/or reassuring. Divine intervention is not intended to induce belief—as it is in, say, *The Ten Commandments* (1956)—but merely a ploy accepted without demur, as one might accept an automobile also functioning as a submarine in a James Bond film.

On the other hand, there are also films that do not fit into the dominant patterns of the moment and have different discourses. If the films I have discussed from the late 1970s play down the notion of endogamy central to the earlier cinema, there is a low-budget 'horror film' (or a family film with 'horror' elements) made in 1979 in which endogamy is even central. Vijay's *Na Ninna Bidalare* (1979) is generally inspired by *The Exorcist* although it is about a newly married man—rather than a child—who is possessed, and by a dead college-mate who had tried to seduce him. The interesting thing in this film is that the protagonists are cousins who marry after a long courtship but the intruding ghost tries to destroy their marriage by claiming (falsely) that seduction by the man had led her to suicide. While the suggestion is that the husband (Ananth Nag) and wife (Lakshmi) are Brahmins, the background of the dead seductress remains unspecified. The ghost is eventually got rid of by application to Raghavendra Swamy of Manthralaya, once the patron saint of the Madhwa Brahmin community but now with a substantially wider following. One can see in this film a threat to endogamous relationships from the cosmopolitan city—since the man was a student in Bangalore and his wife is from a village. But princely Mysore *was constituted by endogamous relationships* and there is, hence, a larger regret[10] here that goes beyond the threat to endogamy—not found in films like *Shankar Guru*. The producers of *Na Ninna Bidalare* had their office in Saligrama village in Mysore district. My observation here is that the makers of the film were likely to have been closer to the ethos of former Mysore than filmmakers from Bangalore. There is a significant gap between those who recollect Mysore and those who do not which is discernible. Although most films of the late 1980s, abandon the traditional signifiers associated with Mysore, there is still evidence in the Kannada films of the late 1980s that it once existed.

Acknowledging a Demise

Until late into the 1970s, Mysore can be identified as the region in at least some Kannada films—like *Na Ninna Bidalare*—but such identification becomes more difficult thereafter. Despite my approach of not dwelling on the preoccupations of individual film-makers but on the motifs engendered by historical circumstances, it is sometimes useful to compare similar films by the same direc-tor with the sole purpose of spotting and explaining differences. I did not discuss A.V. Seshagiri Rao's *Sose Thanda Sowbhagya* (1977) while dealing with the 1970s, but it becomes pertinent if we compare it to his *Pattanakke Banda Patniyaru* (1980). The earlier film is about a rustic family with two brothers; the older brother is educated while the younger one (Vishnuvardhan) is not. The conflict arises when the older brother marries a girl from Bangalore and she brings about a rift by making her husband selfish. This motif is familiar but the younger brother marries the educated younger sister of the first girl—who is not only unlike her sister but noble and clever, and she restores the balance in the family through her doings. The melodramatic crisis occurs when the family assets are divided between the two brothers with the par-ents themselves separated in the same way, one going to each son. The two sisters—one good and one bad—coming from the same family in Bangalore suggests that the film is deliberate in its mes-sage of neutrality towards the city, even if the family crisis is more important to the film. The indivisibility of the joint family in

Sose Thanda Sowbhagya being sacred supports my earlier contention that—like endogamy—it is emblematic of Mysore.

Pattanakke Banda Patniyaru plays with many of the same
motifs as *Sose Thanda Sowbhagya*, but its joint family is not
sacred. In this film an educated young man and his uneducated
younger brother marry an uneducated village girl and an educated
girl from the city, respectively. Both brothers love the land—like
the good brother in the earlier film—but the women embark for
Bangalore—because of its glamour—and have to be chastened
there. It is important that while the brothers and their wives
live together, the joint family is not valorized and its break-up
not invoked. In fact, the brothers live with an uncle rather than
their father—who is dead. The uncle is played by the comedian
Balakrishna while the father in *Sose Thanda Sowbhagya* was
played by the actor Ashwath (who epitomizes Mysorean dignity
in the Kannada cinema of the 1970s). This ruse is perhaps a way
of retaining the joint family as a motif but de-emphasizing its
significance.

Another film, Vijay's *Auto Raja* (1980), acknowledges the demise
of imagined Mysore by dealing with it in the past tense—through
a flashback. The heroine Bhavani (Gayathri), who believes herself
the daughter of the villain, discovers later that the villain cheated
her mother (Leelavathi) after killing her father (Ashwath) in a fake
accident. Her father was an estate owner and this finds correspondence in the imaging of Mysore gentility in films like *Bellimoda*
and *Bhale Jodi*. Also significant is the film moving to Bangalore
in the present. While *Pattanakke Banda Patniyaru* tried to substitute the land for Mysore as an object of loyalty, *Auto Raja* tries to
build a community around the urban working class as represented
by autorickshaw drivers. The heroine, although rich, finds true
love only in Raja (Shankar Nag) and the class differences between
them is left unproblematized. Bangalore, as already explained,
has an ambivalent presence in the earlier Kannada cinema but
with the fading away of Mysore, it now appears rid of its negative
connotations.

While these films suggest that Mysore is not a territory that
might mean much to audiences around 1980, the film that actually represents Mysore's demise is perhaps Puttanna Kanagal's
best work *Ranganayaki* (1981). This film is about a travelling

theatre company run by the patriarch Shamanna. The heroine Ranganayaki (Arathi) and a young actor Ramanna (Ambarish) were brought up by Shamanna. The son of a local businessman Nagaraj wishes to marry her and she consents, but she finds herself losing her freedom as a wife and yearns to go back to the theatre, which her husband will not allow. When she does go back to act during his absence, he finds out and deserts her, taking their son with him. Ranganayaki now goes back to the stage but the screen beckons her and she decides to leave—with Shamanna's blessings. The patriarch nonetheless collapses during a performance; her move to the film world and the demise of the theatre company happen concurrently. In the last part of the film Ranganayaki is phenomenally successful on the screen (as Mala) but runs into a young man Shekhar, who is infatuated with her. The film plays with the notion of incest—because Shekhar is actually her son by Nagaraj—but more important from my perspective is the sense of a community that suffuses the film up to the moment of Shamanna's death. This first part of the film is filmed in the small towns of Mysore, while the later part is shot in Bangalore. While Nagaraj's father was a prosperous Vaishya businessman from a small town, Nagaraj himself has moved to Bombay in the last part of the film and it is from Bombay that Shekhar arrives. Puttanna's films take an ambivalent view of Bangalore and *Ranganayaki* is not different. While the city represented the worst kind of 'commerce' in *Nagara Haavu*, here it is impersonality and its exclusion from the community that is most striking. *Ranganayaki*, being more complex, resists the kind of interpretation that I have given *Sose Thanda Sowbhagya* but the presence of the patriarch touches a chord because he, Ranganayaki, and Ramanna constitute a 'joint family' in the narrative, in some ideal sense.[11]

Inhabiting the Central State

To recollect briefly what has already been said, the years in which D. Devaraj Urs remained chief minister in Karnataka have large consequences for Kannada cinema. Between 1972 and 1980 he asserted himself more and more with the central leadership of the Congress and split with Mrs Gandhi in 1978 to form his own party. But since he had done everything only in Mrs Gandhi's name, he saw his party being wiped out in 1980 in the Lok Sabha elections, when Mrs Gandhi's Congress won 27 of the 28 seats in

Karnataka state. R. Gundu Rao, who had been a Devaraj Urs follower but who chose to remain with Mrs Gandhi became chief
minister thereafter until the Congress lost the assembly elections
in 1983.

The police officer, as I explained earlier, is an emblem of the
Indian state in Kannada (as in Hindi) cinema. Since Mysore always
felt itself somewhat removed from the nation, the police does not
figure prominently in Kannada cinema until 1980–1. Karnataka
sending twenty-seven MPs to parliament in 1980 apparently
had an effect and there are three films made in 1981–2 in which
the protagonist is a police inspector—S.V. Rajendra Singh Babu's
Antha (1981), G. Dattaraj's *Keralida Simha* (1981), and Joe Simon's
Sahasa Simha (1982)—and this is the equivalent of representatives
of the region inhabiting the central state. While this should have
gladdened Kannada cinema, all three films are noticeably dark.
This may be attributed to two important factors, namely, the
demise of Mysore, which the films register as the death of a father
or mother, and the central state being in a considerably weakened
condition from the last years of Janata Party rule onwards, that is,
1979–80.

According to political scientists, the 1980s were a period in
which 'divisive forces' had gained impetus within the Indian polity because of regional demands. If the last years of Janata Party
rule saw the squabbling between constituents (with regional loyalties) weakening the traditionally strong centre, Indira Gandhi also
ruled tentatively in her second reign. One of Mrs Gandhi's machi-
nations when out of power had been her initial encouragement of
a young Sikh religious preacher named Jarnail Singh Bindranwale
as part of an effort to weaken the faction-ridden Akali Dal, which
had participated in the Janata coalition. But when she returned
to power in 1980, she presumed he was dispensable and chose to
ignore him after he had campaigned for the Congress. Bindranwale
had however captured the imagination of many a Sikh youth by
now and he encouraged them to question the authority of the
Indian state and speak the language of secession. The centre was
also beset by conflicting regional demands since the states that
had done well like Punjab sought greater autonomy while others
like Assam, which believed they had been neglected, demanded
a larger share in central revenue.[12] Further, one result of 'vote
bank' politics—when group identities were actively promoted for

short-term electoral gain—was that the regional groups began to gradually assert themselves against the weakened central state.[13]

The experience of a Kannada film protagonist being a police officer is a new one for Kannada cinema and *Antha* betrays signs of uneasiness. The story is designed to look like a 'fable' and is set in another country. *Antha* however drops this pretence almost immediately and tells a story largely set in Bangalore. The story is about a young police inspector (Ambarish) who has a resemblance to an imprisoned criminal and this resemblance is used by his superiors to enable him to penetrate the underworld. While earlier Kannada cinema used local names, *Antha* has north Indian names for most people—as if it would only be proper to have north Indian names for Kannada people dealing directly with the nation. The male protagonist is Sushil Kumar and his underworld look-alike is named Kanwarlal. An underworld don is Dawood and the hero's policeman friend is Kulwant. The film attained notoriety for its violence (it was given an 'A' certificate) and the most infamous episode involves Sushil Kumar's pregnant wife (played by Lakshmi) being kicked to death. There is apparently a deep sense of the family threatened in the film and the death of the protagonist's mother suggests the termination of the joint family. At the conclusion, the protagonist discovers that the gang has the support of some top officials and politicians and he kills them one by one. This aspect of the film and another motif—in which the protagonist draws strength from a picture of the goddess Kali killing a demon—anticipates Hindi films of the 1980s, notably N. Chandra's *Ankush* (1985) and *Pratighaat* (1987).

The two other films are comparable to *Antha*. *Keralida Simha* (1981), has Rajkumar in the lead role and it is apparent that the star has abandoned his Mysore image of the 1970s. The film is about two policemen who are brothers and live with their mother. Shankar (Rajkumar) is accused falsely in an interrogation death and is hunted down by his brother. Shankar's mother is murdered by the gang he is fighting against and another interesting motif is Shankar being engaged to be married to a lawyer (played by Saritha) but she taking the side of the wrongdoers because (it later turns out) her mother is held hostage by them. The elasticity of legality—represented by the lawyer who can be enlisted for any purpose—is also a motif repeated later in the 1980s (for example,

Singeetham Srinivasa's *Halu Jenu*, 1982). *Sahasa Simha* (1982) is another film in the same mould with a fearless policeman Pratap (Vishnuvardhan) as its focus. Like *Antha*, it uses north Indian names like Shankarlal, Madanlal, and Rattanlal for its villains, while the protagonist's late father was a police officer named Gopal Rao (a Mysore Brahmin name) who was killed by these villains and who is avenged. *Sahasa Simha* has another interesting motif that will be examined later in the chapter.

Rajkumar and the Last Mythological Films

The 1980s marked the end of Rajkumar's career as a star and his career cannot be understood without his mythological films. I will briefly examine a mythological film made in 1983, Vijay's *Bhaktha Prahlada*, and make a few comments about Rajkumar as the star of the Kannada mythological film. *Bhaktha Prahlada* tells the familiar story of the arrogant demon king Hiranyakashipu, who challenges Lord Vishnu but whose son is the god's ardent devotee. As most readers will be aware, Hiranyakashipu is killed when his son declares that god is everywhere and the king seeks to know if he is in a pillar in the palace. When his son asserts that he is, the king smites the pillar with his mace but a frightful beast Narasimha, half-lion and half-man, emerges to kill him. This is the story as most people know it, but *Bhaktha Prahlada* begins when two celestial gatekeepers (wearing crowns) in Lord Vishnu's palace are cursed by some devotees for not granting them entrance. Vishnu tries to lessen the impact of the curse and offers the gatekeepers the option of either being reborn on earth for seven lives as Vishnu's devotees, or three as his enemies. The gatekeepers, not wanting to stay away from him for so long, choose the latter course. They are therefore born as two brothers, Hiranyaksha (played by screen villain Thoogudeepa Srinivas) and Hiranyakashipu (Rajkumar). The two are drunk with power and decide to take on the gods in battle, but Hiranyaksha is killed by Lord Vishnu who takes the form of a boar. Hiranyakashipu therefore undertakes penance to Brahma to attain invulnerability and then launches war on the gods, with the king of the gods, Indra (Gangadhar), conducting himself disgracefully and in a cowardly way. Hiranyakashipu arrests seven of the gods—including Agni, Varuna, Vayu, and even Yama, the god of death, and allots them menial jobs in his palace. Narada (Ananth Nag), the familiar celestial figure, is the intermediary who, while playing the part of the king's acolyte, plots and plans his eventual defeat.

We are aware of the motif of king and god in Kannada cinema and, as I have been explaining, the king represented the region because Mysore state was once ruled over by one. After 1947, with the king no longer ruling, this method of representation persisted but god came to allegorize the Indian nation, which was above the region and loyalty was finally directed towards it. If we were to assume that the king still represents the region (after the fading away of Mysore) in *Bhaktha Prahlada*, it would produce some interesting results. Unlike Mahishasura (in *Mahishasura Mardhini*) who seeks to conquer heaven, Hiranyakashipu's primary enemy is Lord Vishnu because the god killed his younger brother. But the film also creates a division among the gods with the others demonstrating their weakness. Considering that the king's arrogance is the result of Vishnu's boon to a celestial gatekeeper (who is presented as a 'king') it is apparent that the discourse in the film focuses on the fulfilment of a king's desire to come closer to god, although this god resides in a heaven that is weaker than it ever was in the Kannada mythological film.

Bhaktha Prahlada was one of the last mythological films in Kannada cinema, although Rajkumar did star in two more—remakes of *Mahakavi Kalidasa* (as *Kavirathna Kalidasa*, 1983) and *Bedara Kannappa* (as *Shiva Mechida Kannappa*, 1988). There are two aspects to be considered here, and while one is that the representation of the region as a 'king' had to cease because of the region losing all the qualities associated with princely Mysore, the other is that only Rajkumar could be associated with the role of the prince or king. The second is because Rajkumar's persona, being created as the embodiment of Mysore values, was the only one suited to playing the king. It should be noted here that in no Kannada mythological film does Rajkumar play god—the entity allegorizing the Indian nation—and it is inevitably Mysore's place that he takes in the allegory. This, of course, excludes *Babruvahana*, in which he takes both places through the double role.

The Motif of the 'Prevented Union'

A handful of films of the early 1980s also include the (sometimes bizarre) motif of the prevented union. In Shankar Nag's *Geetha* (1981), the heroine is a spirited girl who falls in love with a pop singer (Shankar Nag) who returns her love but their union is prevented when she is discovered to be terminally ill. Singeetham Srinivasa Rao's *Halu Jenu* (1982) stars Rajkumar as a white-collar worker who is perpetually using devious ploys to raise money because his wife is dying of cancer. One of these is to claim to be a bachelor and offer to marry a girl from a rich family. In order to convince them of his eligibility he claims to be the son of 'Singapore Seetharamaiah'. Identifying families through their ancestral place is a common feature of marriage networks—both in real life and in the Kannada film. There is apparently a parody of this motif when Seetharamaiah's ancestral place is named Singapore! The dying wife (Madhavi) wishes that he marry the rich girl but the motif of deceit suggests the impossibility of marriage—although the girl is good, beautiful, and loves the hero.

At the conclusion of the most unusual film of the lot—*Sahasa Simha* (1982)—a police officer has just killed the north Indian villain but the villain's daughter still loves him. The girl intends to marry him but he reveals at the last moment that his countenance is actually a mask and he displays his real face for what it is—burned and disfigured by acid. It is also revealed that it was her father who disfigured him thus when he was a child.

The Hindi films about terminal illness that appeared in the 1970s (notably Hrishikesh Mukherjee's *Anand* and *Mili*) are not like *Geetha* and *Haalu Jenu* in as much as they were about people bearing misfortune with fortitude and not about a prevented union. I have already described the political climate in India, beginning in 1980, with the state beleaguered but the troubles faced by the Indian state were predominantly in north India. In these Kannada films, the traditional notion of endogamy is abandoned (even parodied in *Halu Jenu*) and the prevented matches are all 'romances' outside the community and the marriage networks. Since this is anomalous—in a cinema in which endogamy is the accepted method of matchmaking—it demands interpretation.

Marriage networks, as I proposed earlier, represent the region in Kannada cinema and there is a suggestion in the films of a desired union outside the marriage network that is prevented because of a sickness or physical condition abruptly intervening. If we interpret the motif as allegory with one element as the region, it suggests that the prevented union is between the region and something outside it—specifically, the nation. And the nation is no longer vigorous but gravely ailing or disfigured, the messages propose. That Hindi cinema of the 1980s does not exhibit the motif tends to substantiate the reading because, the notion of region being foreign to it, it would have no means to deal with a 'union' of the kind suggested by Kannada cinema.[14]

A recapitulation of some 'motifs of distress' in Kannada cinema and the associated historical moments that perhaps engendered them may be in order before we go further. This may help us to broadly understand how cinema actually registers historical moments. The first motif (before linguistic reorganization) is the curse of poverty (*Bedara Kannappa*) and I associated this with the apprehension in former princely Mysore of the consequences when its own prosperous territory was merged with the undeveloped Kannada speaking regions. A second motif is joint family relationships thrown into crisis by 'romance' (*School Master*) due to the endogamous marriage networks thrown open to penetration from the outside—on account of the linguistic reorganization. India's defeat in the Sino-Indian War produced the darkest ever historical film made in Kannada (*Veera Sankalpa*) in which a trusted general is unable to prevent his noble ruler from being deposed and executed by a treacherous usurper, and an effeminate clown placed on the throne of Vijayanagar. The motif of the modern Brahmin being reduced to penury because of his willingness to give away to those who are more rapacious (*Kasturi Nivasa*) was associated with Mysore becoming distant from the Indian nation after Nijalingappa's fall in 1969, but recalling its past and upholding its own kind of modernity over the one associated with the nation. The 'prevented union' (*Sahasa Simha, Halu Jenu*), as I have just proposed, owes to the region having overwhelmingly endorsed a government at the national level, which could only rule hesitantly over a beleaguered territory.

The motifs of distress just enumerated have one aspect in common which is that they all testify to a political anxiety of some sort—whether an unhappy expectation or a destroyed hope. Political anxieties are apparently felt when there is a widespread sense that a development—although likely to be detrimental—is unavoidable and the motif of distress is perhaps like a visible symptom that surfaces when something is repressed. It is perhaps only as the symptom of a political anxiety that one can understand a film like *Sahasa Simha* because what it shows can hardly be attractive—if its purpose is 'mass entertainment'. The other interpretive possibility—that the anxiety is not political but psychological—can be neglected because of the bunching together of these motifs at particular historical moments.

All motifs do not arise out of political anxieties because there are positive motifs as well. Those motifs which can be described as 'optimistic' do not owe so much to heartening developments as to the expectations aroused by them. The Headmaster cleansing the establishment (*School Master*) mirrored the expectation that the Nehruvian influence would rid the region of its primary evil—corruption. The perception of Kannada cinema that the region was important in the scheme of the nation in the years leading up to 1969 saw traditional aspects like hierarchy weakening in cinema and the Nehruvian modern being celebrated (*Bangarada Hoovu, Jedara Bale*). The strength of the Devaraj Urs government when his mentor Mrs Gandhi had fallen at the national level was reflected as people from the region being important enough to own huge property in far flung corners like Kashmir (*Shankar Guru*) and in the revival of the CID 999 series in *Operation Diamond Racket*.

When newsworthy developments do not arouse public expectations, they do not find expression in cinema. The successful war with Pakistan after which Bangladesh was created did not find reflection in either Hindi or Kannada cinema, although the expectations of war had produced a patriotic film in *Prem Pujari* (1970). Bengali cinema perhaps registered the possibility of Bangladesh more distinctly before 1971 than its actual creation. Mass movements and agitations may cause public unrest but unless they arouse expectations of some sort they are not registered by cinema. This is significant because the Kannada film industry participated in a mass movement called the Gokak Agitation around the Kannada language in 1982, but Kannada cinema does not recognize it. Kannada nationalism is highest at other times when it has another purpose, for example, preparing for an enlarged Kannada nation after linguistic reorganization (*Ranadheera Kanteerava*), and the Kannada language becoming the sole object of loyalty when people from the region felt defeated and let down by the nation after Nijalingappa's fall (*Sri Krishnadevaraya*).

Karnataka Politics in the 1980s

Devaraj Urs' split with Indira Gandhi spelled an end to his political career in 1980. Urs had been chosen because Mrs Gandhi wanted to break the stranglehold of the dominant castes in Karnataka politics and Urs, accordingly, nominated members of the numerically small backward castes and tribes and members of the minorities to contest the election. He had the task of keeping his defection-prone MLAs in check and he evolved the strategy of making them chairmen of newly created public sector corporations. He extended his patronage to them and the result, overall, was a huge increase in the level of corruption in public life. Urs had not only implemented his progressive legislations and measures—which included directing planning away from its urban-centredness to improving the lot of those in the rural areas in Mrs Gandhi's name—but also strengthened the hands of the Taluk Development Boards to undertake works. But in 1980, those he had built up decided that Mrs Gandhi would be the better horse to back and that led to the defeat of his party in the Lok Sabha polls, with Mrs Gandhi's Congress (I) sweeping them in 1980. While Urs interpreted this as a defeat and resigned as chief minister, it was left to Gundu Rao, leader of the Congress (I) to engineer defections and form the government in Karnataka.[15]

Gundu Rao, being a Brahmin, perhaps rode on the circumstances that had weakened the dominant castes in Karnataka, but his years as chief minister were a disaster for the Congress. He had made his way up partly by being a Sanjay Gandhi acolyte when Urs fell out with Mrs Gandhi—because of Sanjay's interference in state affairs. Gundu Rao's three years were marked by gimmickry of various sorts and it was in his period that agitations were mounted against the government—like the farmers' agitation which he handled badly and to which he had to ultimately make several concessions. Another whimsical move by Gundu Rao was his declaration at a gathering of Sanskrit pundits that he would restore first language status to Sanskrit in the school curriculum. Earlier, Urs had demoted Sanskrit to the status of third language and, given the availability of teachers of Sanskrit, there was no way in which Gundu Rao's declaration might have been fulfilled. But his statement was widely interpreted as anti-Kannada by Kannada groups. To placate them, the chief minister formed a committee under V.K. Gokak to look into the question of introducing Kannada as a first language in schools and the Gokak Committee Report came out in January 1981. Since the government did not accept the recommendations entirely it led to a statewide agitation, and when the film industry under Rajkumar joined the movement, it became a mass uprising.[16] When the government belatedly accorded the status of sole first language to Kannada, the linguistic minorities—Tamils and Muslims, mainly—agitated against the move. At the time of the 1983 elections, Gundu Rao confidently predicted that the Congress would improve upon its seats and the Janata Party did not see itself snatching power from the Congress but that did eventually happen.[17]

The years in which the Janata Party ruled Karnataka under Ramakrishna Hegde and S.R. Bommai (1983–9) were good years, especially after the Gundu Rao period, and were marked conspicuously by the provision of drinking water to the villages—due to the efforts of Abdul Nazir Sab, a cabinet minister—as well as important measures in decentralization, but Kannada cinema does not respond to these happenings discernibly. It is apparent that the 1980s were not politically uneventful in Karnataka but there was no dominant political discourse in the public space—as, for instance, there was in the Devaraj Urs era—and this means that cinema does not register the events. Moreover, the Rajiv Gandhi era in the 1980s—although also eventful—generated no dominant discourse in the public space either. This can be grasped by contrasting it with the Nehru era, in which the discourse centred around modernization and socialism, and the Indira Gandhi era, when the discourse revolved around the admission of the poor into the social mainstream, western imperialism, and authoritarianism (at the time of the Emergency), and all these register as motifs in cinema. This absence of a dominant discourse both at the state and the central level gradually leads to a paucity of signifiers in Kannada cinema of the late 1980s. In other words, the stories proliferating in this cinema do not mean much and cinema tries to compensate by concentrating on spectacle and other 'attractions' at the expense of the story.

Vestiges of the Region

Before Kannada cinema abandons endogamy and the joint family as motifs is an interim period in which they are present as vestiges without moral significance. Kashinath's *Anubhava* (1984) is a shameless piece of titillation in which young man (Kashinath) working in Bangalore marries his adolescent niece, who has just attained puberty. The film introduces a wanton woman from the village (Umashri) who follows him to the city but begins to exploit him until she ultimately embarks for Bombay with a criminal neighbour. There is a suggestion that the neighbour is engaged in the flesh trade but *Anubhava* declines to shed tears over the woman's fate. What it does instead is to arrange a 'happy ending' with the male protagonist reunited with his bride. Since the other woman is not 'bad' the indifference of the film to her fate is disturbing. Important from my viewpoint, now, is only that the film is able to satirize endogamy instead of portraying it as sacred, and also treat Bangalore as a neutral space without negative connotations.

S.V. Rajendra Singh Babu's *Bandhana* (1984), which also plays with the notion of terminal illness, is about the unrequited love of a doctor Harish (Vishnuvardhan) for his colleague Nandini (Suhasini). Nandini marries a childhood friend named Balu who turns out quite despicable but Harish, meanwhile, develops an incurable heart condition. Balu, himself not above raping their maid, is jealous over Nandini's proximity to Harish. The film concludes with Harish dead and his spirit entering the body of Nandini's stillborn child and its coming to life. Nandini also signs the divorce papers sent to her by Balu at the conclusion. This film is initially confusing because Harish has a fond mother but just when we begin to interpret her presence we discover that Balu and Nandini have devoted mothers as well. This, I suggest, is another way of de-emphasizing the motif seen in the earlier films.

I have characterized these two films of the 1980s as belonging to an interim period in which the conventions of Mysore cinema persist but without their original significance. While this is a reasonable conclusion, it is also difficult to be certain about when the 'interim period' concludes because the notion of endogamy is invoked till much later in Kannada cinema, without it being valorized.

A Young Cinema

One of the developments of the Kannada cinema of the late 1980s is the rise of the youth film, as exemplified by V. Ravichandran's

Premaloka (1986), Singeetham Srinivasa Rao's *Anand* (1986), and M.S. Rajashekar's *Nanjundi Kalyana* (1989). *Premaloka* is an unusual film because its story is related much more in song than is common to Indian popular cinema. Inspired loosely by *Grease 2* (1982), the film tells the story of Ravi (Ravichandran), the scion of a rich family and Shashi, whose father (Srinath) is a police officer. After the initial period of coy hostility, Ravi and Shashi fall in love and wish to marry but Ravi's father wants his son to wed the chief minister's daughter, who has seen Ravi. He, nonetheless, believes in true love and lectures to his parents, about Shashi's and their marriage is finally solemnized in public in the presence of a large number of students. The film features several Kannada film stars like Vishnuvardhan, Ambarish, Srinath, Lokesh, Leelavathi, and Prabhakar, with none of them having roles that impinge upon the narrative. Ambarish, for instance, plays a waiter in a restaurant who brings the couple two cups of coffee and Vishnuvardhan is a teacher who sings a song in the classroom. The presence of the chief minister and a police officer means nothing and the film is empty of signifiers that might once have been interpreted. While youth films are normally about generational differences, the differences here are entirely around love. The film is set in the student world and therefore abounds in songs, dances, and fights, but none of them have much bearing on the narrative.

Anand is also a youth film although it is apparently more intricate than *Premaloka*. In this film Anand (Shivarajkumar) is a student who lives with his mother (Jayanthi), who is a nurse. Anand is perpetually in conflict with a rich boy named Srikanth whose father is a businessman named Raja Chandrashekar. Anand falls in love with Mala (Sudharani) whose father is a rich businessman named Kumar. While Mala wants to marry Anand, Srikanth wants to marry her and Raja Chandrashekar approaches Kumar in the matter. Kumar is a reasonable man and his opposition to the marriage is therefore not made an issue. What happens instead is that Anand's mother reveals that Raja Chandrashekar is actually his father. The rest of the film is about Anand going about getting his true father to acknowledge him. He is able to do this because Raja Chandrashekar is contesting an election and he is kidnapped by his rivals. How Srikanth and Anand might become reconciled to each other is not explored. *Anand* bears a superficial resemblance to the Hindi film *Trishul* (1978) but without the angry young man motif.

Nanjundi Kalyana begins, unusually for a film of the times, in a village. Raghu (Raghavendra Rajkumar) lives with his father and mother, who are landed and rich. His father is worried and he reveals that his sister and brother-in-law quarrelled with him and went to Bangalore. Raghu, he hopes, will marry their daughter because that was once the agreement. Raghu now goes to Bangalore and shows to us that he is a modern young man with friends there. Two of his friends love two sisters but they cannot marry until the girls' oldest sister Devi marries—and she is a tomboy who has frightened off many suitors. Raghu also discovers that the family is his aunt's and he decides that he will be Devi's husband. The rest of the film is about Raghu pretending to be 'Nanjundi', his father's younger brother who was drowned but has now returned miraculously. Raghu 'persuades' Devi to marry him by doing things to her—from defeating the wrestlers set up by her to having her locked up in a psychiatric institution. Devi marries 'Nanjundi' but plans her revenge—which turns out to be futile. Devi is finally 'broken' and family peace is established. *Nanjundi Kalyana* bears some resemblance to the Hindi film *Betaab* (1983), with the added element of endogamy.

The telling of the stories of the three films may have helped to demonstrate how empty they are of signifiers. All three stories are about 'love' to which there are no credible obstacles—although *Premaloka* has the chief minister's daughter, *Anand* has an interlude involving a call girl employed to bring discredit to the hero and *Nanjundi Kalyana* has the nominal resistance offered by the tomboy. As has been shown elsewhere,[18] 'love' in popular cinema is not subject matter but merely a strategy to bring the narrative to closure. For love or marriage to mean anything, the element opposing it is significant and this is as true of Kannada as of Hindi cinema—except that where Hindi cinema uses romantic love, Kannada cinema uses endogamy. In *Na Ninna Bidalare*, the opposition to the marriage between two cousins comes from the ghost of a classmate—who is from cosmopolitan Bangalore and outside the endogamous network. In *Pattanakke Banda Pathniyaru*, the attractions of Bangalore drive the marriages into crisis. In *Sahasa Simha* it comes out of the male protagonist's face having been disfigured by acid. In each of the three films it is the credible element opposing love that I have tried to interpret. The three youth films are different in as much as what is placed in opposition to 'love' is not credible enough to hamper its development and, in being about 'love', the films are really about nothing. The other motifs brought in deliberately—politics in *Premaloka* and *Anand*, rural life and the village in *Nanjundi Kalyana*—are extraneous and have little significance. The same remark can be made about the prominent use of the city locales in the three films. The city is perhaps simply a glamorous space with no specific connotations because while the action in two of the films takes place largely in Bangalore, *Premaloka* is shot in Madras, as though it really does not make a difference what city the story is set in.

The youth film, as I remarked earlier, is usually about generational conflict and this is as true of *American Graffiti* (1973) as about *Dilwale Dulhania Le Jayenge* (1995). This means that there tend to be youth films when there is a political turnabout in the public consciousness. *Dilwale Dulhania Le Jayenge* can be interpreted as a response to the end of Nehruvian socialism—or the economic liberalization instituted by the P.V. Narasimha Rao government—just as *American Graffiti* responded to Vietnam. 'Youthfulness' either takes the shape of disowning responsibility or deliberately forgetting/overlooking the past. The pointed exuberance of *Dilwale Dulhania Le Jayenge* comes in part from a second generation NRI trying to overlook 'tradition'. The 'rebellions' in three Kannada films are all over-assertions of 'love' but this needs further scrutiny. One film, *Premaloka*—is nominally about the triumph of romance over endogamy—if an arranged marriage between the chief minister's daughter and a businessman's son constitutes 'endogamy'. Another—*Nanjundi Kalyana*—is about endogamy asserting itself after the cosmopolitan city throws joint family ties into crisis, and the third—*Anand*—is about a inter-class romance becoming endogamy when a poor boy is acknowledged as a rich man's son. Endogamy continues to be a key motif in the films but it is not an issue—in as much as one can be either for it or against it and it does not matter. The youth motif in the three films can, therefore, be said to be constructed around forgetting what endogamy once meant. In other words, the youth motif in the films involves the forgetting of what Mysore one meant to the constituency of Kannada cinema.

Depletion of the Story

Earlier, I remarked that the absence of a dominant discourse in the political space had led to films concentrating on spectacle at the expense of the story. One of the pleasures in narrative cinema is 'narrativity', described as the process by which the spectator constructs a coherent 'story' out of the visual and aural data provided to him or her. Narrativity is hardly the only pleasure offered by cinema, but it demands more active engagement than spectacle. It has been suggested[19] that the proper way for narrative artists to provide experiences richer than submissive stupefaction is, rather than deny audiences the satisfaction of the story, to generate stories that require the most rigorous kinds of narrativity. If Kannada popular cinema has had any consistent virtue it has been its 'profligacy'—the intricate nature of film narrative brought about primarily by the proliferation of subplots—which has been an observed characteristic not only of Kannada and Hindi popular cinema but of South Asian cinema in general.[20] One has only to look at the twists and turns in a film like *Sahasa Simha* or *Bhaktha Prahlada* to recognize how depleted the youth films are in terms of the story. What they try to do to compensate is to crowd the films with songs, dances, and fights—or low humour as in *Nanjundi Kalyana*—to draw attention away from this depletion.

If a parallel has to be drawn with the Hindi film, the simplicity of the Hindi cinema of the 1990s—beginning with *Hum Aapke Hain Koun ...!* (1994)—can be traced to the Indian state not being an element in film narratives after the economic liberalization of 1991–2, when it announced its withdrawal from the public space.[21] The intricacy of a film like *Damini* (1992) comes out of the implication of the state (through the motif of the law) in the story, an element evidently absent in *HAHK*, which compensates for its simplicity (the absence of signifiers) by crowding itself with spectacle—of consumption and the rituals associated with conjugality. The Kannada youth films like *Premaloka* are even poorer in signifiers than *HAHK*. While the nation (allegorized as the ideal family) was implicated in *HAHK*, the region—the key element in the earlier cinema—is absent in the youth films. To substantiate this proposition is another Kannada film, Ravi's *Malaya Marutha*

(1986), which tries to compensate for the depletion of the story with 'classical' music and dance.

Caste in 1980s Cinema—Kannada and Hindi

A useful way of understanding the creation of meaning by Kannada cinema may be through a comparison with Hindi cinema. The earliest Kannada films of the 1980s bear a strong resemblance to Hindi cinema of the same period. The weakening of the law in *Antha* is a motif found in a large number of Hindi films like *Tezaab* (1988), *Pratighaat* (1987), and *Agneepath* (1989). The motif of vigilante justice, found in V. Somashekar's *Gajendra* (1984), is also prominent in many Hindi films like *Tezaab* and *Shahenshah* (1988). *Antha* was even remade in Hindi as *Meri Awaaz Suno* (1981) with Jeetendra. Strangely enough, while Hindi cinema continues with the motif of the weakened law even in the early 1990s with films like *Phool Aur Kaante* (1992) and *Damini*, Kannada cinema appears to move away, although some films like *Sangliana* (1988) nominally employ it.

Another key difference between the two is the attention to group/caste identity in Hindi cinema finding no correspondence in the Kannada film in the 1980s. Gang identity is a crucial motif in *Ankush* (1985), *Arjun* (1985), *Tezaab* and *Ghayal* (1990), and caste identity is a key factor in *Prem Rog* (1982), *Ghulami* (1985), *Batwara* (1989), and *Qayamat Se Qayamat Tak* (1988). While *Anand* does use the motif of conflict between youth gangs, the fact of Anand and Srikanth being brothers and their conflict virtually vanishing shows that the motif is not important—unlike the Hindi films in which members of gangs even kill one another. These motifs in Hindi cinema—the weakness of the law and the emphasis on narrower loyalties/identities prevailing—continue in the same manner for more than a decade while Kannada cinema changes swiftly between 1981 and the later 1980s.

The stability of the motifs in Hindi cinema over a period of more than a decade may be attributed to the absence of a dominant political discourse in the public space corresponding to India. While radical populism had dominated Mrs Gandhi's rhetoric in the 1970s, her second innings was marked by tentativeness and her replacement by Rajiv Gandhi in 1984 changes very little in Hindi cinema. Kannada cinema was perhaps differently placed because it ended the 1970s with the memory of Mysore not yet fully erased—as a film like *Na Ninna Bidalare* suggests. Kannada cinema begins the 1980s with the region and the nation still as distinct entities but the region appears to have faded away by the time we come to the youth films without the nation replacing it as an object of loyalty—despite the Indian nationalist rhetoric in films from *Sahasa Simha* to Joe Simon's *Hongkongnalli Agent Amar* (1989). Kannada cinema therefore continues on its journey away from Mysore in the 1980s and this perhaps accounts for the changing motifs.

Caste identity in the two cinemas is however a comparison that needs to be made, because while hierarchy was a key issue in Kannada cinema from the earliest period, Hindi cinema, by and large, only acknowledged the rich and the poor. The 1980s are however a different proposition because while Kannada cinema appears to abandon its traditional attention to hierarchy, Hindi cinema suddenly becomes 'caste conscious' as never before.[22] There is, nonetheless, a difference between what caste means in Hindi cinema and the notion of hierarchy in Kannada cinema. In the Hindi cinema of the 1980s caste does not mean hierarchy but represents identity: a reason for different *jatis*—like Jat or Thakur[23]—to band together, and summons a situation in which narrow loyalties take precedence over the nation. It is for this reason that there are narrow loyalties to other than jati specified in the cinema of the 1980s: that is, to gangs (*Arjun, Ghayal*), region (*Ek Duuje Ke Liye, Ankush*), and class (*Naseeb, Coolie*).

An examination of Kannada cinema suggests that while its notion of hierarchy is derived from caste, the jatis themselves are rarely invoked. We are made to infer caste from the given names and occupations: if education implies 'Brahmin', farming and landed wealth implies 'Vokkaliga', and merchant implies 'Vaishya'. As a corollary, schoolteachers, doctors, officials, and industrialists (*Kasturi Nivasa*) could be Brahmins, while owners of flour mills (*Nanda Gokula*) could be Vaishyas, and wholesale grain ('*mandi*') merchants could be Vokkaligas (*Nagara Haavu*). Other hierarchical categories could be managers of estates (caste unspecified as in *Bellimoda*), courtesans (*Bedara Kannappa, Gejje Pooje*), and dalits (a rare category present in *Bhoothayyana Maga Ayyu*). 'Servants' are also a category and if 'cook' is Brahmin (*Sharapanjara*), it does not mean that a cook occupies the same hierarchical position as his Brahmin employer. Caste here does not denote jati identity but hierarchical station—which is why marriages in certain films are contracted between people of different jatis. Hierarchy, also, does not mean only caste because it is also inscribed within the family. The wife, for instance, is lower down in the hierarchy than the husband. But hierarchy does not mean the submission of one group (or individual) to another and it would be more correct to say that all groups submit to hierarchy, which is perhaps definable as the social structure which keeps the groups apart and performing their own given roles. In *Samskara*, for instance, Chandri and Putta acknowledge Praneshacharya's hierarchical position but this is not presented as a relationship involving the submission of one individual to another. Putta also rejects Praneshacharya when he finds that the latter has not conducted himself according to his station. The notion of hierarchy that Kannada cinema drops in the 1980s is therefore different from the notion of jati that Hindi cinema often pays attention to during the decade.

Hierarchy after Mysore

There is a weakening of the notion of hierarchy in the Kannada cinema of the 1980s and the phenomenon needs to be explored. Hierarchy is synonymous with Mysore and since Mysore fades away from public memory in the 1980s, so does hierarchy, is the broad justification offered. Since hierarchical position is often indicated by vocation or occupation, it may be useful to examine how it figures in the 1980s through an examination of a few anomalous representations of occupation. Until late in the 1970s, there is no sign of the working woman in Kannada cinema perhaps because of the difficulty in reconciling the hierarchical position of 'wife' with an occupation. The motif begins to appear hesitantly in the 1970s perhaps due to the influence of Hindi middle cinema.[24]

One of the first Kannada films to deal with the working wife is Geethapriya's *Hombisilu* (1978). Nataraj (Vishnuvardhan) and Roopa (Arathi) are qualified doctors and their professional relationship is reconciled with their marital one by Roopa being Nataraj's assistant. The conflict arises when another woman doctor, Vasanthi, is also engaged as Nataraj's assistant and resolved when Roopa demonstrates her capability as doctor and a more credible assistant than Vasanthi, who finally admits it. The effort in the film is to retain the notion of hierarchy in accordance with a convention developed in former princely Mysore but still deal with the working woman.

Bandhana (1984) is also about two doctors, a man and a woman, with the woman unable to marry the man although she feels for him because she is betrothed. The first part of the film teases us into believing that the match between the two will happen but the woman's marriage takes the film into new territory. She behaves impeccably with her husband but he conducts himself in the basest fashion and shows himself to be unworthy of her respect and love. My argument here is that the film is deliberately moving into territory not circumscribed by the values connoting Mysore, chiefly by creating events that the Kannada film never dealt with. The chief of these is the arrival of the maid named Gowri who is raped by the husband. At the same time the film shackles the women to the erstwhile conventions and they do not even consider threatening the husband with prosecution. It is this partial repealing of film convention that makes *Bandhana* sexist in a way that the earlier films—which honour the convention—are usually not and this is also true of *Nanjundi Kalyana, Anand,* and *Anubhava.* In *Nanjundi Kalyana,* Devi is treated cruelly by the male protagonist—under the guise of pranks—and she submits. In effect, he is freed from the erstwhile conventions of the Kannada cinema while she is not. *Anand,* as I said earlier, includes a sub-plot in which a call girl is employed by the villain to besmirch the male protagonist's character. If one understands 'call girl' to be an extension of the 'courtesan' motif in the earlier cinema, the call girl is not treated with the consideration extended to the courtesan (*Gejje Pooje*).[25] *Anand* has a sequence in which a client burns the girl's face and neck with a cigarette butt—with the act being a mere detail and not justified by the story. The temptress in *Anubhava* also suffers a horrific fate—being sold into the flesh trade—not justified by the story and the 'happy ending' of both films do not include the other woman in the resolution. Overall, one could say that while film conventions of erstwhile Kannada cinema—with its affiliations in princely Mysore—are generally abandoned, the women in the films are shackled and made to submit to the same conventions. It is as if the film conventions dictate the woman's actual place in society. This makes the films distastefully sexist and the trend continues till much later.

One way of understanding the increasingly unhappy position of women in Kannada cinema beginning in the 1980s is perhaps through the distinction between 'Mysore modernity' and 'post-colonial modernity'. A characteristic distinguishing the two is that Mysore modernity was a much more limited concept in as much as had to do entirely with industrialization and state investment in creating productive capacity. Post-colonial modernity in India, on the other hand, included women's emancipation as a component because of the reformist movements of the nineteenth and early twentieth century,[26] and Hindi cinema bears this imprint. This means that when Kannada cinema moves out of the safety of hoary convention—which specified rigid roles for *all* individuals in social relationships—it emerges as a deeply conservative cinema prone to gender-related political incorrectness.[27] Also, where the empowerment of the marginalized groups leads to films being prudent when dealing with caste-based issues, the lack of a strong women's movement in the region sees them becoming sordidly patriarchal. Puttanna Kanagal's woman-centred films appear to be the only exception because, where the woman's emancipation films of the 1930s and 1940s like *Duniya Na Mane* propose a political reexamining of the woman's position, films like *Bellimoda* make room for it within the existing paradigm of patriarchy. This treatment of women in later Kannada cinema will come for discussion again in the next chapter.

Unstable Communities

I have examined the Kannada films of the 1980s from various perspectives but one more important aspect for the remaining part of this book is the issue of the community that Kannada cinema imagines—after the demise of Mysore. The earliest of the films—*Antha, Sahasa Simha*—apparently try to imagine India as their community by having north Indian names for many key characters but this does not become a trend. Nationalist feeling was low in the 1980s in Hindi cinema and Kannada cinema may have come to see the move as unviable. *Bhaktha Prahlada* allegorizes Indian nationalist discourse when it tells the story of the king's son being responsible for his father's death by becoming, primarily, a devotee of god. Subsequent films try to identify other groups/objects of loyalty as a basis for building a community—the urban working class (*Auto Raja*), the land (*Pattanakke Banda*

Pathniyaru), youth groups and/or the student community (*Premaloka, Anand, Nanjundi Kalyana*), and the classical tradition (*Malaya Marutha*). The fact that there are so many disparate efforts at building a community suggests that those constructed are unstable and tentative. Language, significantly, does not feature as the sacred object because it is not implicated in the narrative—as it was in *Sri Krishnadevaraya* (1970), for instance, when the film imagined a Kannada community that included Muslims from Bijapur. This observation does not mean that the sanctity of the Kannada language is not nominally invoked because many films include a line or two of rhetoric eulogizing it (alongside the nation, usually) without the notion being crucial to the story. After examining Kannada language cinema in the 1980s we come up with an unexpectedly bleak conclusion, which is that after the demise of imagined Mysore, Kannada cinema is unable to envision a community to replace it, and this is partly responsible for the decline that we sense when we compare the cinema of the 1980s with the earlier cinema.

4. Provisional Communities
1990–9

Signifiers

The last chapter explored briefly the depletion of the story in 1980s cinema and here I continue with the exploration. From the late 1980s onwards, Kannada cinema becomes depleted because of a lack of signifiers—the cinema does not 'mean' in the way it had done hitherto. The region is absent as an imagined community in these Kannada films and this perhaps accounts for them being unable to 'mean'. Most of these films are either 'love stories' or 'suspense yarns'. Since 'love' is not subject matter but a strategy to effect a closure,[1] love stories which have no more in their narrative than the rhetoric of 'undying love' are simply engaged in winding down. For them to sustain a 'local meaning' (of the kind that I have been excavating), there need to be other signifiers that appear along with 'love', for example, the protagonist's disfigured face in *Sahasa Simha*. Some 'love stories' of the early 1990s, which are difficult to interpret because of a paucity of signifiers, include P.H. Krishnamurthy's *Panchamaveda* (1990), S. Narayan's *Chaitrada Premanjali* (1992), Sunil Kumar Desai's *Beladingala Bale* (1995), and Nagathihalli Chandrashekar's *America! America!* (1995). The emptiness of these films can be gauged from *Beladingala Bale,* which is about a chess wizard trying to seek out a mystery woman whose voice he has heard on the telephone by following the clues given to him by her until he reaches her and finds her dead. The film contains no subplots or other kinds of detail but all of it is taken up by the 'clues' pertaining to the girl's name, her place of residence, etc. Many of these films abound in spectacle (usually landscapes or cityscapes), sexual titillation, and/or jokes which attempt to compensate. The 'suspense' films of the period revolve around crime and action—Sunil Kumar Desai's *Utkarsha* (1990) and *Nishkarsha* (1994), Nagathihalli Chandrashekar's *Baa Nalle Madhuchadrakke* (1993), Upendra's *Shh!* (1993)—but these are also marked by an absence of signifiers and a surfeit of 'attractions', as in the 'love stories'. *Utkarsha*, for instance, is about a serial killer who paints women in the nude and then stabs them to death. Where earlier Kannada cinema would have provided us with family backgrounds and other interpretable detail, *Utkarsha* provides none but allows us to see different women models in various stages of undress. One advantage of this absence of signifiers to the filmmaker is that the films can be remade in other languages or made by directors who have no knowledge of the region. Some of these films—for example, Dinesh Baboo's *Amruthavarshini* (1997)—were apparently remade in other languages and this would not have been possible with a Rajkumar film of the 1970s. Being poorer in interpretable content, most films of the 1990s cannot be read as allegories of the region—as *Bhaktha Prahalada* and *Ranganayaki* can be. It is the subtexts in the films that bear interpretation rather than the principal motifs, not so much the import of the stories as what is on the periphery. I expect to be able to make this point clearer as we proceed.

With the imagined region not invoked after the mid 1980s, Kannada cinema tries to call upon nationalist sentiments in S.V. Rajendra Singh Babu's *Muthina Hara* (1990), a war film straddling three wars, but its patriotism is spurious. *Muthina Hara* is unusual because it is about a Kodava (or Coorgi) army soldier (Vishnuvardhan) who fights in World War II for the British, when he marries a nurse (Suhasini), also a Kodava. Although Coorg or Kodagu is in Karnataka, Kodavas do not regard themselves as Kannada speakers; its two decorated generals Thimmaiah and Cariappa are not regarded as Kannada heroes and this makes *Muthina Hara* unusual. The film is a woeful experience because the protagonists lose their only child in an exchange with Pakistan in the 1950s, the man's mother dies of sorrow when she learns this and the soldier loses his own life in 1961 against the Chinese. Nothing goes right for the family and one begins to wonder about the purpose of such a film in 1990 until the protagonist is dying on the battlefield. At this point, he reaches into his pocket and asks a soldier—also from Karnataka and who dies subsequently—to assist him in drinking a few drops of sacred water from the Cauvery river which he has been carrying. Evidently, the film is providing a resumé of the various sacrifices made by people from Karnataka state on behalf of the nation. It is also reminding us that the Cauvery river rises in Coorg in Karnataka, just when (in 1990) a three man tribunal had been formed in Delhi for the sharing of Cauvery water with Tamil Nadu;[2] Indian nationalism is apparently not the film's true purpose and there is another agenda. There were anti-Tamil riots and deaths in Bangalore a year later with Cauvery water as the issue and the film is dealing with this sensitive topic. As regards the film's nationalist appearance, in contrast to a Hindi war film like J.P. Dutta's *Border* (1998), it is unable to imagine a community of soldiers because of its exclusive attention to the travails of a single family. This suggests that while Kannada cinema attempts to make the Indian nation an object for veneration around 1990 instead of the region, the attempt is hesitant.

The weakened state, principally in the motif of the threatened law and vigilante justice, continues into the 1990s in Hindi films like *Damini* (1992) and *Phool Aur Kaante* (1992). Some Kannada cinema of the early 1990s also continues with the motif of the threatened law but there is a key difference between these films and one like *Antha*, which came in 1981. P. Nanjundappa's hit film *Sangliana* (1988) has for its title the name of an actual IPS officer in Bangalore who made a reputation for himself as a maverick and later became a Bharatiya Janata Party (BJP) member of the Lok Sabha. The interesting fact here is that the officer H.T. Sangliana was not a Kannada speaking local but from Mizoram. The film does not allude to this and also does not explain the officer's unusual name—considering that he is played by Shankar Nag—and there is no hint that he is not local. Nanjundappa made a sequel in 1990, *SP Sangliana 2*, in which the officer is the superintendent of police, has an adopted son from the earlier film, the orphaned child of a murdered forest official, and marries the daughter of an intrepid journalist, after a romance. If we compare the later film with *Antha*, this is not as ferocious, with the officer and his family not threatened because he is always ahead of his foes.

Interpreting the figure of the policeman as representing the Indian state as hitherto, the general sense from the two films is not of the central state severely beleaguered but of local politics obstructing it in discharging its obligations. In *SP Sangliana 2*, the villain is a businessman who controls local politicians—three cowardly reprobates. The businessman is played by 'Mukhyamantri' Chandru who attained prominence playing chief ministers on the stage. It would seem that the region's politics obstructs the efforts of the Indian state, which is signified in many films of the decade. In another film which came much later—Dinesh Baboo's *Nishabda* (1998)—the villains are brothers who are ostensibly criminals but they dress in white as politicians do and the police are also in their service. In Dwarakish's *Shruthi* (1990), the police are involved in harassing migrants to the city and the farmers on the periphery whose wares are destroyed by them. Overall, the portrayal of the police is ambivalent in the 1990s although the portrayals are not all alike.

Parody and Propriety

An aspect of Kannada cinema that has distressed people who have followed it closely is the vulgarity that appears to overwhelm it in the early 1990s. While this is especially true of the coarse way in which women are portrayed, a scrutiny of this cinema suggests that there is, in the 1990s, a deliberate negation of the moral codes that Kannada cinema had once adhered to. Before we try to speculate on the reasons for the new impropriety in Kannada cinema, we should perhaps examine a few films to understand the shape it takes.

H.S. Phani Ramachandra's *Ganeshana Maduve* (1990) is set in a Bangalore *vattara* (the equivalent of a Mumbai *chawl*, a group of apartments in which lower income people live in close proximity). Ganesha (Ananth Nag) is a clerk in an insurance company and quarrels with his landlord and his daughter Ananthalakshmi (Vinaya Prasad). Ganesha is in love with a singer named Shruti whom he has heard only on the radio and his fan mail induces her to love him as well. Ganesha does not know that Shruti is actually Ananthalakshmi and that her father and his own are friends. When a match is arranged between the two, neither is inclined to agree. Devious methods are then employed to first get the alliance cancelled and then, when each of them understands who the other is, to have it rearranged. This film is a lively comedy but includes several tasteless segments of a kind not found in the earlier cinema. When there were tasteless jokes in the earlier films, the protagonists were still required to be dignified. The jokes here are not in any subplot but enacted by the protagonists. In *Ganeshana Maduve*, Ganesha writes a letter to his own parents purportedly from the girl's lover alleging that he has been 'sharing her bed'. Another 'joke' involves convincing Ananthalakshmi's parents that the man chosen in his place—the girl's cousin and a film director—is a bad match because he has contracted AIDS.

Upendra's *Tarle Nan Maga* (1992), a film that came two years later, is a film that defeats expectations. In this film—also set in Bangalore—Santhosh (Jaggesh), the son of a miserly shopkeeper, loves Lakshmi, the daughter of a teacher of music, but his parents want him to marry his voluptuous cousin Sundari, whose father is a landowner. Santhosh has a set of reprobates as friends, to whom he confides that Sundari is easy with her favours. There is a 'flashback' pertaining to their childhood (with the adult actors dressed as children) and the 'child' Sundari explaining to the 'child' Santhosh the 'wonderful stories' in sex magazines. Santhosh now arranges a series of deceptions to marry Lakshmi—including having her claim that she is pregnant by him. His friends impersonate the police (SI Saliana, who is SP Sangliana's stricter brother) and force the marriage. Much of the film has the tone of low parody because the things once held dear by Kannada cinema are ridiculed. Santhosh is duly married to Lakshmi but allowed to share her room her only because he convinces his parents that he wants to 'kick her' into granting him a divorce—so he can marry Sundari. The parents soon understand that this is a trick and try to kill Lakshmi, though unsuccessfully. Eventually Sundari becomes pregnant after an interlude in the dark with his degenerate friends and the film ends with the father of her unborn child being identified, and a hasty marriage arranged for Sundari with this seedy individual.

It may be difficult to make an inventory of the conventions mocked by *Tarle Nan Maga*, but endogamy, parents as figures of moral authority, and feminine virtue are a few which are pertinent from my viewpoint. Perhaps more importantly, the film dispenses with the notion that the exemplary subject should be upright and dignified, an aspect that finds little correspondence in Hindi cinema—even in *Kaminey* (2009). As I have argued elsewhere,[3] *Kaminey* celebrates enterprise in an era in which competition is unregulated, and the protagonists follow a new code considered appropriate to their times. In other matters,[4] *Kaminey* is conventionally moral in its thrust. This is not true of *Tarle Nan Maga* in which every convention is lampooned and there is no code of ethics to replace the one abandoned.[5]

As important aspect of films like *Tarle Nan Maga* is the low kind of Kannada they employ in their dialogues and titles. 'Tarle nan maga' translates as 'my roguish son' but there is a touch of illegitimacy in the fatherly declaration that makes the phrase ambiguous. There are other films employing a deliberately low language, like P.N. Ramachandra Rao's *Bombat Hendthi* (1992), the title of which translates as 'terrific wife' but with a touch of lewdness in it. Overall, it may be said that these films exhibit the same disregard for the Kannada language that they show towards the moral codes of Kannada cinema. While the use of high Kannada in *Sri Krishnadevaraya* was principally to uphold the language as a sacred object for the people of the linguistic state, films like *Tarle Nan Maga*—with their 'gutter' Kannada—do the opposite. They do not single out the Kannada language for derision but their attitude towards all conventional loyalties reflects on the language as well.

It would be unfair to deny that *Tarle Nan Maga* is intelligent and parts of it are hilarious—notably the 'childhood' sequence with the heavily mustachioed Jaggesh is shorts mimicking a schoolboy. There is also determination in the film's efforts to break with the past of Kannada cinema. If one were to interpret Kannada film convention in political terms as 'favouring status quo', *Tarle Nan Maga* might even seem 'subversive', or at least 'irreverent'. But this argument would not be valid because of the film's tendency to titillate. Its mischief is boisterous rather than pointed and it is politically innocuous. Rather than being cynical or nihilistic (easy adjectives to attach to parody), *Tarle Nan Maga* appeals to one's sense of moral expediency. Like *Ganeshana*

Maduve, Tarle Nan Maga is designed as a film in the making, with a self-mocking opening that includes 'interviews' with the characters. This aspect is important and will be examined later in the chapter.

That the negation of ethical conventions in 1990s cinema is a trend is suggested by other films which are not parody. In S. Narayan's *Chaitrada Premanjali* (1992), the male protagonist's father is referred to slightingly[6] as a philanderer who 'salivates at the sight of women'. The protagonist slaps his devoted servant and the woman he loves at the smallest pretext, but the film refuses to drop the pretense that he is exemplary. The dialogue is distastefully provocative; the villain talks of arranging a fake marriage for his son with the heroine, so that he can 'have his pleasure without the attendant obligations'. If this wife is difficult, the father even proposes that setting her ablaze is a solution. In Nagathihalli Chandrashekar's 'thriller' *Baa Nalle Madhuchandrakke* (1993), a poet kills his beloved wife on their honeymoon for having had a sexual relationship with the driver of the college bus. This driver has only a small part in the story and no grounds are created for the 'affair'. But the general implication is that women are not fastidious in their relationships.

In the 1980s, there are references to politicians—*Anand* and *Premaloka* specifically—but the portrayal of politicians in the 1990s is inevitably negative. More importantly, while the corrupt politician is a single MLA in *SP Sangliana* (1988) he is represented by ministers in Bangalore in *SP Sangliana 2* (1990). While the protagonist's father in *Anand* could 'cleanse politics' in Bangalore and the chief minister's daughter in *Premaloka* could set her heart on the hero, Bangalore's politicians in the 1990s are involved in illegalities of various sorts. There is certainly skepticism about the goodness of the politicians in *Anand* and *Premaloka*, but this is transformed into open disgust around 1990. There is perhaps an association between the happenings in politics and the decline in moral values in 1990s cinema.

The Congress came to power in 1989 after factional fighting within the Janata Party and Chief Minister Veerendra Patil was widely respected but, within a year, he was replaced by S. Bangarappa whose name soon became synonymous with corruption. It was widely believed that leaders in the Congress (I)—on

Rajiv Gandhi's initiative—had deliberately conspired to remove the chief minister who had done well to restore the health of the state's finances within a short period.[7] Also blamed was the liquor lobby, against the interests of which Veerendra Patil had acted.[8] When Bangarappa assumed office he was hardly a consensus candidate but he was placed there because Rajiv Gandhi believed he would be more amenable to fulfilling the directives of the high command, and also to providing funding to the Congress party. Where Veerendra Patil had instituted proceedings to bring civil servants accused of corruption to book, many of the very same civil servants were given important posts by Bangarappa and the corruption cases withdrawn. The Inspector General of Pclice (IGP) under Veerendra Patil, who had planned and executed raids on corrupt colleagues, was given an insignificant posting. The chief secretary who said that the chief minister was 'untrustworthy' was suspended. When the central government struck down the suspension order, the former chief secretary remained without a portfolio.

When Veerendra Patil was unceremoniously sacked it had been alleged that the liquor lobby had spent Rs 200 crore to have him removed because he plugged loopholes in the excise department. Bangarappa's proximity to the liquor lobby suggested that he would act in the interests of the lobby; once installed as chief minister, his patronage of the lobby was transparent. This was done openly and, despite Bangarappa having no history of loyalty to the Congress Party, he remained in power. This was possible because of Bangarappa's ability to raise funds for the party.[9] While chief ministers Devaraj Urs, Ramakrishna Hegde, and Gundu Rao (who had corruption charges against them and were all highly controversial) were seen as arrogant, devious, and hedonistic, respectively, Bangarappa was seen only as brazen—with no attendant qualifications—and quickly became the butt of satirical treatment in the media. Newspaper cartoons at the time satirized local corruption (with Bangarappa as its emblem)[10] more than they had ever done before.

The 'public sentiments' of a past moment are difficult to identify and attributing them to the doings of a chief minister is a problematic undertaking. Still, while there was no dominant political discourse in the public space, Bangarappa's reign as chief minister led to heightened public cynicism because of the openness of his dealings. Satire carries with it an admission of political helplessness perhaps because we laugh away things that we cannot remedy. Satire and parody are evidently related; if cultural texts are covert or overt representations of social life, satirizing a social situation finds correspondence in the parody of a cultural text—parody is perhaps to a cultural form what satire is to a social situation. Both have their origins in discontent, one with social life and the other with cultural convention.

'Easy Women'

In the last chapter I made some observations about the treatment of women in Kannada cinema owing to the absence of women's emancipation as a component of the modernity introduced into princely Mysore. Women's emancipation was a key factor to inform post-colonial modernity in India—due to the nineteenth and early twentieth century reform movements largely in Bengal—and this is imprinted upon Hindi cinema. But there is another aspect to the Kannada cinema of the 1990s that needs examination and this is the notion of feminine promiscuity that all the films described in the last section introduce. Even when the woman protagonists of these films are blameless, their names are sullied by the exemplary men who love them and this is not a motif from the earlier cinema. For instance, even though Ananthalakshmi/Shruti in *Ganeshana Maduve* is hardly licentious, the male protagonist finds it easy to besmirch her character—as well as that of another girl who also loves him—to avoid a marriage. While *Tarle Nan Maga* touches a new low in its depiction of feminine character, *Baa Nalle Madhuchandrakke* and *Chaitrada Premanjali* are offensively blunt that women are objects to be used and/or disposed of at the man's convenience. If the heroine in these films (except in *Baa Nalle Madhuchandrakke*) is blameless, the general attitude exhibited towards women still reflects upon them by association. The 'vamp' is not conspicuous in the earlier Kannada cinema[11] but even when she is present—as in *Anubhava*—her conduct is not made to reflect upon women in general as happens in these films.[12] Considering the high premium once placed upon the woman's character, this is a representation that needs enquiring into. We may perhaps begin the enquiry by

recalling the heterosexual relationship which was once considered exemplary between the man and the woman in Kannada
cinema.

In the introduction I explained how the relationship between
the husband and wife allegorized the relationship between the
monarch and his subjects, and dharma was the code that both
needed to follow. The husband would fulfil his obligations while
the wife—like their children—would be obedient and submit to
him. The motif of the monarch leaves Kannada cinema—with
the mythological film and the historical retaining them till
they disappear as genres in the 1980s—but the motif of the dutiful woman/wife remains strong. In *Bandhana*, for instance, the
husband is despicable but the wife is firm in her loyalty to him.
Nanjundi Kalyana is about the steps sometimes required to turn
a wife into the 'exemplary' kind.

In an earlier chapter I also observed that from the 1970s onwards
one needs to interpret the films with Rajkumar and those without
the star in different ways. This is because Rajkumar becomes,
increasingly, an emblem for the region while the other actors'
presence cannot be understood in the same constant way. An even
more stable 'constant' in Kannada film narrative is the woman
protagonist. While the Hindi film heroine goes through a range
of avatars from the 1950s (dominated by the 'modern' woman) to
films like *Rang De Basanti* (2006) (in which she is British and
represents the global west[13]), the Kannada film heroine (barring a
few exceptions like in the films of Puttanna Kanagal), conforms
to the image of the loyal, virtuous, and submissive woman, and
her constancy suggests that she is emblematic of another notion—
rather than simply being a family ideal.

Since, in the earliest representations, the wife stood for the subjects of the princely state, there is the likelihood that the woman
protagonist continues to represent the constituents of the region
in later cinema. It should be noted here that mildness, loyalty,
tolerance, and lack of aggression are broadly thought to characterize the Kannadiga,[14] and these have been the characteristics of the
heroine. If Rajkumar provided a proud self-image that the region
wished to be identified by—in films like *Kasturi Nivasa* and
Bangarada Manushya—the virtuous, tolerant, and pliable woman
protagonist in the Kannada film is perhaps the partly self-depre-
cating image of the constituents of the region. Overall, I propose

that the relationship between the man and woman (or husband and wife) roughly corresponds to the one between the region and its constituents. Until the mid- to late 1980s this submissiveness still has dignity attached to it but it begins to acquire negative connotations thereafter. The lowering of the Kannada language spoken in films to a 'gutter' level concurrently also suggests an association: the demeaning of women in the Kannada films in the 1990s was caused by a lowering of the self-image of the Kannadiga, which also reflects in the lowering of the language. The lowering of the self-image may have been the result of local politics in which politicians openly disgraced themselves without being made accountable to the constituents of the region, who remained helpless. This perhaps led to public cynicism over whether the political choices that the public was making in the region had any significance at all. Was their characteristic tolerance such a good thing, they may have wondered, or were they merely pliant? If the constituents of the region were once happy to see themselves represented as the loyal, submissive, and tolerant woman/wife of Kannada cinema, local politics in the democratic era may have caused them to wonder if these were virtues, or even if the qualities should not be despised. This process perhaps began even in the late 1980s—during Ramakrishna Hegde's acrimonious second term.[15] But Bangarappa distinctly exacerbated it. Veerapa Moily, who succeeded Bangarappa, had a much cleaner image but his period was marked by dissident activity and balancing acts[16] and he was unable to change the way politics was regarded.

'Unworthy Masters'

The denigration of women has just been read as a lowering of the self-image of the constituents of the region owing to the happenings in the local political arena. This relies primarily on the premise that since the relation between the woman and her man once allegorized the relationship between the subject and the monarch, the constituents of the region, as members of the polity, are represented by the 'woman' in her relationship with her 'master'. While the films discussed hitherto focus on the 'pliability of the woman' but do not include her 'unworthy master' in the discourse, there are several films in the period 1990–6 in which the motif of the woman forced to submit to an unreliable man come to the fore. All these films begin by creating a bond of love between

the woman and the exemplary male protagonist but then introduce another male figure intent on pairing with the woman.
The exemplary male is then made to step aside and expose the
woman to danger and this causes uneasiness in the spectator,
the uneasiness created by the prospect of someone without
recourse being forced to submit to a master who is unworthy.

To examine the films briefly, P.H. Vishwanath's *Panchamveda*
(1990) deals with the love of a middle class boy and the daughter
of a landowner. The male protagonist has come to the village
pretending to be his rich friend who is betrothed to the girl but
is not inclined to marry her because his heart is given to another
girl. The two fall in love but, at this point, the rich friend loses
his girl and therefore decides to exercise his right over the heroine
despite knowing that his friend loves her. The girl is married off
to the rich boy and marital rape is imminent but the two protagonists kill themselves to save her from the wrong man. In
S. Narayan's *Chaitrada Premanjali* (1992), the woman's father
forces her to marry the man who has tried to rape her, instead
of the protagonist who has just rescued her from him. In T.S.
Nagabharana's *Akasmika* (1993), the male protagonist saves a
woman from a man who is running women for the flesh trade. The
woman falls in love with him but the villain reappears and takes
her away by force. In T.S. Nagabharana's *Janmada Jodi* (1996), the
villains have the heroine forcibly married to a village idiot because
they know of her love for the male protagonist, who has opposed
their designs. In S.V. Rajendra Singh Babu's *Doni Sagali* (1998),
the man chosen by the heroine (Soundarya) over a worthier suitor
is already married. As can be seen, the films make the unworthy males despicable and arouse our apprehension. It should be
noted that in *Nagara Haavu*, the male protagonist Ramachari's
sweetheart is married to a reprobate but the film dwells only on
Ramachari and we do not feel apprehension for the woman as we
are made to feel in these films.

The 'Community' and Bangalore

As already touched upon several times in the course of this book,
the attitude of Kannada cinema towards Bangalore has been characterized by ambivalence. In the films dealt with in the last
section, Bangalore appears to represent the community in most
cases. A question that may be asked here is whether it is Bangalore

that figures in the films or the 'city' (as abstraction). What actually happens is that there are several emblems associated with
Bangalore that are unmistakable in these films—the Kempegowda
Bus Terminal in *Tarle Nan Maga* and 'pub culture' in *Ganeshana
Maduve* were as iconic of Bangalore in the local consciousness of
the 1990s as Hotel Ashoka was in 1972, when *Nagara Haavu* had
the woman protagonist 'delivered' to clients there. Of the films
dealt with hitherto in this chapter, *Beladingala Bale, Utkarsha,
Nishkarsha, SP Sangliana 2, Shruthi, Ganeshana Maduve, Tarle
Nan Maga*, and *Bombat Hendthi* are set in conspicuously Bangalore
although only a few of them see a 'community' in the city. To
understand how this Bangalore 'community' is constituted, it
may be useful to reexamine a few of these films.

We acknowledge a community being represented when people
from different families and backgrounds are seen united by a
legitimate purpose, for example, participating in ceremonies as in
Hum Aapke Hain Koun ...! (1994), or in defeating the English at
cricket, as in *Lagaan* (2001). The villagers in *Bhoothayyana Maga
Ayyu* are a community united against the wicked moneylender.
The five protagonists in *Shruthi* are migrants to the city and are
intent on finding success together as musicians. Since the five
do not return to the original homes we may presume that they
form a stable new community in Bangalore to which they owe
allegiance, a community of migrants. That this is a community
separate from entrenched Bangaloreans is suggested the break-up
of the romance between the woman protagonist Shruthi (played
by Shruthi) and a rich local, after which she lives as a 'friend' with
the four men. P.N. Ramachandra Rao's *Bombat Hendthi* (1992)
also posits migrants as a community through a plot dealing with
four friends seeking success in the city.

In *Ganeshana Maduve*, Ganesha is also a migrant because his
parents live outside the city, there is another single woman, and this
suggests that the others in the vattara are also like him although
we cannot be certain. The people in the vattara in *Ganeshana
Maduve* are a community in as much as they are united against
the landlord but the difference is that the one in *Ganeshana
Maduve*, because it is dominated by comic actors such as Musuri
Krishnamurthy (who attained notoriety by playing reprobates), is
conceived partly as parody. This becomes apparent when the film
is compared to H.S. Rajashekar's *Hrudaya Hadithu* (1991) which

makes a more laudable community out of medical students—but from Mysore. A more obvious parody of the community than in *Ganeshana Maduve* is contained in *Tarle Nan Maga* in which the protagonist Santhosh and his degenerate/criminal friends,[17] in whom he confides most of his anxieties about love and marriage constitute a 'community'. Since the friends are undifferentiated, I propose that they are representatives of a social type which is identifiable—like medical students—that is, they represent a community of some sort. They constitute a community but a community conceived largely as parody because bringing them together is not a legitimate aim but lasciviousness and a desire to participate vicariously in Santhosh's 'romance'.

Overall, Bangalore as a space does not appear amenable to representing the 'community' and it becomes convincing only when the community is represented by non-Bangalorean Kannada migrants, with loyalty to their own kind rather than the city. The mid-1980s were a period in which there was large scale migration from within Karnataka into Bangalore and the language equation in labour shifted in favour of the Kannadiga[18] in industry. This motif of migrants as a community becomes much stronger in later Kannada cinema after 2000.

Bangalore is located on a semi-arid plateau around 1000 metres above sea level with no major rivers running near the city. From its rather humble origins, it gained importance in 1807 when the British arranged with the government of Mysore for a regiment of European cavalry and another of infantry to be based to the north-east of the city with administrative offices in the fort, south of the old city. The importance of the cantonment increased when the British intervened to wrest power from the king and his advisors in 1831 on grounds of the prevailing corruption. The state came under the administration of the British commissioners and government offices were relocated to Bangalore, the king being relegated to a strictly ritual position in Mysore. The relocation of government offices and the presence of the garrison meant that there was an influx of service providers from all over southern India—especially Urdu-speaking Muslims and Tamil speakers. The migrant populace concentrated around the cantonment area, while the city area was mostly Kannada-speaking like the majority in Mysore state.[19] A linguistic gulf separated the two since the cantonment housing the garrison was deliberately kept apart by the British from the city.

With the linguistic reorganization of the states in 1956 Bangalore became the capital of Kannada-speaking Karnataka though it was only a few hours away from Tamil-speaking Tamil Nadu, Telugu-speaking Andhra, and Malayalam-speaking Kerala. As the two sections of Bangalore grew into each other, the city exhibited an unusual degree of cosmopolitanism. While in Karnataka as a whole 66 per cent of the population had Kannada as their first language, in urban Bangalore itself, only 37 per cent spoke it as their mother tongue.[20] Another factor of great importance was the growth of education in English. The commissioners had supported the establishment of the first English medium school in 1842, but over a period of time private schools mushroomed in the city with over 90 per cent of the secondary schools being privately run in the 1990s. As against the Kannada-medium government schools, the private schools were mostly English-medium. The association of Bangalore with English is satirized in the first segment from *Tarle Nan Maga* when a beggar speaks cultivated English to a television reporter.

Bangalore became a hub of the public sector with the establishment of four large industries by the central government after Independence. There was already a scientific establishment in the Indian Institute of Science (IISc) and there were several engineering colleges capable of providing the industries with an educated workforce. The more pertinent factor is however that until well into the 1960s these public sector industrial units had predominantly Tamilian and Keralite employees and the mother-tongue of the employees was a burning issue as late as 1981.[21] Overall, Bangalore was hardly suited to serve as an emblem for a Kannada speaking community and the element of parody in the 'Bangalore communities' in *Ganeshana Maduve* and *Tarle Nan Maga* suggests it. The low Kannada used in Kannada films like *Tarle Nan Maga* is also associated with Bangalore's lumpenized classes, which is why I referred to it as a 'gutter' rather than a 'street' Kannada. Unlike Hollywood films in which swear words punctuate the speech but there are also other kinds of language (for example, technical, legal), the language here is consistently low. The concurrent rejection of the earlier cinema's moral codes, the vulgarization of the language employed and the turning to Bangalore to simulate the Kannada community suggest this: that there is an apparently lowering of Kannadiga self-esteem in the 1990s. The film *Akasmika* (1993) does its best to address the issue seriously using the same motifs as these films—the woman's virtue, the Kannada language, and Bangalore.

Akasmika

Many of the aspects just commented upon find reflection in a deeply melancholic way in the last film starring Rajkumar as the male protagonist, T.S. Nagabharana's *Akasmika* (1993). Rajkumar's films have always been the most reliable indices of the region's spiritual condition at any given moment and *Akasmika* is not an exception. The film begins with a police officer visiting a Christian grave (of 'Clara N. Murthy') when a passing train sets him off on a reverie, and the story of much of the film commences in flashback. The protagonist is Narasimha Murthy (Rajkumar) and he is on a train from Talaguppa in Shimoga district when his compartment is shared by a young woman named Indira (Geetha) and her escort, a man named Vyasaraya (Vajramuni). The girl is due to join a drama company and her companion is conducting her there. It soon comes out that Vyasaraya is in a girl-running racket and Indira is a poor girl from a village in the district who has been trapped and is being coerced into the flesh trade. Narasimha Murthy rescues her and it is apparent that the girl is in love with him but Vyasaraya reappears and abducts her again.

The second part of the film deals with a Christian woman named Clara (Madhavi), who is a hopeless alcoholic because of a trauma she underwent. She caught her fiancé in bed with her best friend and that led her to her present condition. Narasimha Murthy is caring, he makes Clara live once again and marries her, although he has not got over the earlier tragedy with Indira. His marriage is made possible through the mediation of three friends who also help in getting his mother's concurrence. Unfortunately, Clara dies in an accident during their honeymoon and Narasimha Murthy is left alone as he was before he met Clara.

In the third part of the film, Narasimha Murthy is abruptly a police officer in Bangalore, a fact not hinted at earlier—at least after the opening segment. Narasimha Murthy is engaged in a determined battle against all those who are disrespectful towards women. His resolve is demonstrated when he has two young eve-teasers severely beaten for being casual about women. The officer is so obsessive about feminine honour that he will not tolerate them being abused even in the abstract. In fact, there is a sequence in Bangalore in which he attacks a citizen for addressing someone else as a 'sooley maga' which roughly translates as 'son of a bitch'. As may be expected, Narasimha Murthy's target is Vyasaraya and his unfinished task is tracing Indira, whom he has never forgotten despite his interlude as a married man. After visiting Indira's impoverished family, Narasimha Murthy has come to know that the deceit was made possible by an immoral local woman, now lodged in Bangalore Central Jail. From the woman he finds out that Vyasaraya had two partners, Thimmaraju and Kataiah. Narasimha Murthy locates Kataiah and gets him to confess by snatching his daughters. Under torture Kataiah (Thoogudeepa Srinivas) reveals that Thimmaraju died several years ago but Vyasaraya is now in Hubli, still running women for brothels.

The last segment of the film is shot around Hubli, which is new for Kannada cinema—which has been averse to areas outside the former princely state.[22] Narasimha Murthy visits the brothel being run by Vyasaraya but finds him absent. Vyasaraya is apparently taking the train to Bangalore the same night. Narasimha Murthy does not find Vyasaraya on the train but he is witness to a commotion later that night. When he investigates, he finds that Vyasaraya and his goons are pursuing a woman, who turns out to be Indira. Vyasaraya is run over by a train in the ensuing fight and Narasimha Murthy is reunited with Indira.

If *Tarle Nan Maga* mocked most of the moral conventions of earlier Kannada cinema, *Akasmika* tries to bring back at least two of them—the sacred mother and the concern for feminine honour. Endogamy is the one issue that it does not reintroduce. While many of the films dealt with in this chapter are bereft of interpretable signifiers, *Akasmika* is teeming with them. The first aspect of the film that needs commenting upon is the rage it enlists on behalf of the male protagonist, and another is the abrupt way in which he is made a policeman.

Where the early part of the film is taken up with portraying Narasimha Murthy as an ordinary citizen unable to deal with corrupt social life, he appears almost vengeful in uniform in the later part. The motif of the 'demeaning of women' ties up with the one pertaining to the citizen's helplessness because I identified the citizen's helplessness at local corruption as indirectly causing women to be denigrated in 1990s Kannada cinema. The police officer played by Rajkumar, while being a staunch protector of women, also speaks out against the demeaning of the language by the 'gutter' Kannada spoken—in Bangalore. The Hubli sequence begins with a celebrated song *'Huttidare Kannada nadinalli hut-tabeku ...'* (If one is born, one must be born in the Kannada land ...) and the insinuation is perhaps that Kannada language is safer in Hubli than in corrupted Bangalore. Bangalore's corruption is emphasized when Kataiah and Vyasaraya both have their roots in the city. The film gives us such a harsh portrayal of the local situation in Bangalore that one finds oneself even relishing the beating and the torture sequences involving Narasimha Murthy and offenders. Since the police represent the authority of the central state, this strange contentment may be comparable to the relief a beleaguered citizen might feel at central intervention when law and order has broken down locally. Narasimha Murthy's ruthlessness at snatching Kataiah's daughters does not cause disquiet. Vyasaraya being torn apart by the train at the conclusion actually gives satisfaction. It should be emphasized here that the invoking of central authority in the film does not imply that the centre is morally unimpeachable but only that it is the ultimate arbiter. The nation was the higher object of loyalty in the earlier cinema and the same discourse continues here. It is apparently not for Kannada cinema to judge the nation state.

I earlier traced the trajectory of the sacred mother in Kannada cinema and tried to show that she represented remembered Mysore. The mother disappears from cinema in the 1980s when the memory of Mysore fades away. Her reappearance in *Akasmika* is perhaps simply as an object of loyalty befitting the virtuous hero. It is significant that when the 1980s protagonist played by Rajkumar was not heroic—as in *Halu Jenu*—the mother figure was conspicuously absent. Narasimha Murthy is associated with both the central state (as policeman) and the language (because of the song sequence in Hubli). The mother may therefore be emblem for both nation and language which, in any case, are not in conflict. *Akasmika* can, in fact, be read as a sincere attempt to imagine an inclusive community based on language because of its extraordinary privileging of Hubli in the narrative, for which purpose it is enlisting the central state as an ally. The statue of Kittur Chennamma, a *national* heroine, in the song sequence also suggests this. The contamination of the local space constituting the region is perhaps so severe in the 1990s that it cannot be trusted to uphold the language and the central state may be more reliable.

Another interesting motif not explored hitherto is the one pertaining to the protagonist's three friends who arrange his marriage to Clara.[23] Not only do the three communicate in the coarsest way possible—gesturing vulgarly and vicariously at every opportunity—but Narasimha Murthy barely hides his aversion for them. His mother, on the other hand, appears to regard them affectionately as though her position as 'mother' makes this a requirement. The general sense to be got is of a mother who must love her children equally without being attentive to whether all of them plainly deserve her love. Narasimha Murthy's three friends conduct themselves in the way Santhosh's friends in *Tarle Nan Maga* and the three corrupt politicians do in *SP Sangliana 2*—grossly and inevitably talking/gesturing with innuendo. While *Tarle Nan Maga* tries not to direct us into distaste for Santhosh's degenerate friends, *Akasmika* tries to be different.[24] At the very least, the film is ambivalent about the 'communities' posited by Kannada cinema in the 1990s, which are marked increasingly by moral impropriety and coarseness towards the language. This becomes apparent if these friends are compared to the group in T.S. Nagabharana's *Janmada Jodi* (1996), in which they are well-mannered rustics who speak Vokkaliga Kannada.

Akasmika is different from the other films dealt with in this chapter. It has a gravity that the other films lack because it addresses the issue of the region seriously. Where the other films only react instinctively to the cultural problems arising out of the extinguishing of remembered/imagined Mysore in the popular consciousness, *Akasmika* tries to erect another object of loyalty in its stead, a region constituted by the spoken language and more inclusive. This is rendered possible because of the presence of Rajkumar, the only actor having the required significance for a renewal of the region. That endogamy is abandoned also means that the narrow object of loyalty that once served Kannada cinema is no longer pertinent—if Kannada cinema is to address a more inclusive community.

Lastly, 'Narasimha Murthy' is a Brahmin name. The notions of 'Brahmin' and 'hierarchy' are dead around 1990 and non-vegetarian food—taboo at one time—is routinely invoked. *Akasmika* reintroduces the notion of the 'Brahmin'[25] but perhaps without much vigour because the representation does not gain much popularity in Kannada cinema.

The motif of Filmmaking

An unusual occurrence in the 1990s is the fact that a large number of films are either 'framed' as stories being related by filmmakers or involve the process of filmmaking in some way. *Ganeshana Maduve* (1990) begins with the director Phani Ramachandra addressing an audience and then relating the story of the film as cinema. *Tarle Nan Maga* (1992) begins with an unseen television interviewer/documentary filmmaker talking to the protagonists of the film before allowing their story to unfold. Upendra's *Shh!* (1993) involves a film crew shooting in an estate in the Malnad region of Karnataka. In Sunil Kumar Desai's *Nammoora Mandara Hoove* (1996), a filmmaker from Bangalore goes to Karwar to scout around for a film project. Upendra's *A* (1997) is the story of a firebrand filmmaker who is betrayed by the actress whose career he helped to launch and includes other motifs like film world happenings and parties, filmmaking, and the film within the film.

The motif of filmmaking in world cinema has been employed when the issue explored is the nature of reality—subjective reality as in Federico Fellini's *8 ½* (1963), inter-personal truths as in Francois Truffaut's *Day for Night* (1973) and Jean-Luc Godard's *Contempt* (1964). If all works of art try to seek out 'truths', films about filmmaking are preoccupied with getting beneath appearances. Two celebrated Indian films about filmmaking are Guru Dutt's *Kaagaz Ke Phool* (1959) and Mrinal Sen's *Akaler Sandhane* (1980). Both these films explore the notion of the 'truth'—aesthetic truth in Guru Dutt's film and political truth in Mrinal Sen's. It would therefore seem that 'reality' and 'truth' are the notions generally implicated in films about filmmaking. This may be because of the understanding that cinema—by its very nature—calls into question the relationship between illusion and reality.

Coming to the Kannada films, *Ganeshana Maduve* is more realistic than any popular Kannada film of the 1980s in its depiction of the milieu. *Tarle Nan Maga* virtually announces that families are not as they were once shown in Kannada cinema and tries to portray them afresh for the times. The film's break with the past of Kannada cinema is, in a sense, in the service of the 'real'. The language of *Tarle Nan Maga* is low but this 'low' language is also an attempt to show us how people actually talk on the street. If the difficulty is that the film lapses into another kind of illusion, an uglier one, *Tarle Nan Maga* at least begins by upholding the ugly 'real' over the deliberate artifice of film convention.

There are two aspects that pertain to the films about filmmaking in Kannada cinema. All of them have some 'truth' to communicate that goes beyond film convention. Sunil Kumar Desai's *Nammoora Mandara Hoove* takes the camera to a part of Karnataka outside former princely Mysore—Uttara Kannada district—and attempts to capture its panoramas as well as its culture. This may be the outcome of wanting to define an inclusive community as *Akasmika* also did. *Nammoora Mandara Hoove* is a love story about a filmmaker from Bangalore, Manoj (Shivaraj Kumar), falling in love with a local girl, Suma (Prema), who also is also loved by a local boy, Praveen Bhatt (Ramesh Arvind), who is the filmmaker's classmate. By having Suma consent to marrying Manoj rather than Praveen but with the two classmates remaining friends, the film tries to knit spaces and posit an inclusive region. Not only is endogamy deliberately set aside but so is caste—while Suma is a Brahmin (Suma's brother Pramod wears a sacred thread like Praveen), Manoj is apparently not.

The second aspect of the Kannada films about filmmaking finds a place mainly in Upendra's films *Shh!* and *A*. This aspect has to do with portraying the actual conditions prevailing in the film industry, attempting an exposé of some sort. *Ssh!* is about a film crew shooting in the Malnad region and features film director Kashinath, who attained notoriety for his low-budget sexploitation films beginning with *Anubhava*, starring himself in the lead role. *Shh!* has sequences in which Kashinath's capacity for sexual innuendo are invoked. Before we examine the most outrageous of the films—Upendra's *A*—it should be noted that this 'exposé'

aspect of some films suggests low self-esteem for the film industry; the films virtually declare that their low preoccupations are
due to the kind of milieu that produces them.

Upendra's *A* begins as a film within a film called '*A*'. A lunatic
escapes from the asylum believing he is god. After killing a policeman and stealing his revolver, he kills an impoverished drunkard
who is assaulting his wife, and also the wife—when she mourns
her husband. He takes a rich man's car and makes the rich man
and his daughter administer to a poor cart-puller after forcing the
rich man to give away half his house to him. The film '*A*' ends
abruptly with the same man and a beautiful woman in a hovel
burning to the ground, the man having apparently bitten off the
woman's cheek.

The screening of the film '*A*' is being watched by a woman
representative of the 'Chicago International Film Festival', who
is told that the middle portion of the film has been excised by the
censors and only this portion remains. The representative of the
'Chicago International Film Festival' is so impressed by what she
has seen that she asks to meet the director Surya (Upendra) and
complete the film. Surya, unfortunately, is now an alcoholic and
quite incapacitated. We learn that this is because Chandani, the
female lead of '*A*' and his protégé, subsequently betrayed him. She
is the reigning queen in filmdom now and he, virtually a beggar,
but his passion for Chandani cannot be quenched. She is wealthy
and unapproachable but Surya will do anything to get her love—
even kill himself.

The story of Upendra's *A* is impossible to summarize and I
will therefore only provide an impression. The general thrust of
the film is that Surya is initially a cynic/pragmatist who believes
that only self-interest directs people until Chandani teaches him
the power of love. But when he has learned about 'love' Chandani
has learned of self-interest. She therefore sets up as a procurer of
women for politicians and becomes immensely rich. When Surya's
own family is accused falsely and jailed—for being in the flesh
trade—Surya makes films again and is successful. Surya is also
constantly repelling the advances of the woman representative of
the 'Chicago International Film Festival', although she imagines
herself with him in all kinds of amorous activity—duly visual-
ized in the film. The film ends as the film within the film had
ended—Surya trying to set Chandani ablaze after smothering her

in currency notes, but also after Chandani demonstrates conclusively that she loves him.

There are two aspects to the 'truths' proposed by the film and apart from the murky life of politicians the main aspect has to do with the film industry being a den of vice. Making an association between the Indian film industry and crime is not novel because films like *Aar Paar* (1950) and *Kala Bazar* (1960) do it much earlier. *Kaagaz Ke Phool* itself hardly eulogizes the film industry. But the question to be examined is why Kannada cinema should do it in the 1990s because vice in the industry could have hardly begun as late as that.

I proposed, earlier, an association between the pursuit of the 'real' in Kannada cinema (the 'peeling away of convention') and the motif of filmmaking. I have also tried to establish a connection between the abandonment of convention in films like *Tarle Nan Maga* and the end of the imagined region. Since it would be dishonest to be concerned about the 'real' but also not present a 'true' picture of one's own field, these films present a deliberately low picture of the industry. But the films are also conscious of their own lowly stature. Their posture is that since social life is irremediably corrupt it is best to take advantage of it. They, therefore, make themselves as vulgar as possible, as though it might be improper for them to aim anywhere but low, that is, inappropriate to take their own visions seriously.

Many of the conventions of Kannada cinema arose in princely Mysore; but with Mysore politically defunct, they still assisted in imagining it. But with the imagined region dead, what use can cinema have for convention? To abandon the conventions for their artificiality is one way out—to peel away the artifice and capture the ugliness glossed over hitherto.

The social reality in the milieu deserves the basest abuse, consequently, not because it is so corrupt but because the region, having been extinguished even in the public imagination, it is not overlaid with meaning and is therefore 'empty'. It can be argued that where the glossier films of the 1990s—*Nishkarsha*, *Beladingala Bale*, *America! America!* and *Amruthvarshini*—are extravagant exercises without much interpretable content—because whatever 'meaning' sustained Kannada cinema does not exist—Upendra's ventures into 'realism' like *Tarle Nan Maga* and *A* actually acknowledge the new emptiness.

Watching Upendra's *A* can be an exhausting experience not only because it is so incoherent but also because of its aggressiveness. The film creates the sense that there will be no restrictions upon what the spectator will see[26] and causes the uneasiness that bathroom graffiti causes. With all conventions set aside, anything is theoretically possible and the filmmaker is apparently producing the cinematic equivalent of 'everything made possible'—in the worst sense. Interestingly, *Shh!* and *A* try to build communities around filmmaking—the members of the crew guided by the filmmaker—but the guiding hand is so sickened by itself that the community built around it can only appear a parody—of the community as it might have been.

Living in Bangalore

Earlier, I explored the notion of Bangalore as a community in 1990s cinema and concluded that its linguistic heterogeneity prevented the city from featuring as the seat of a viable community. Only when the community is represented by non-Bangloreans and migrants does a stable community become signified as in *Shruthi*. But another aspect related to Bangalore pertains to its image in the 1990s. Despite the ambivalence with which Kannada cinema has always treated Bangalore there is a gradual sense to be got from 1990s cinema that the city is becoming a glamorous space. While films like *Utkarsha* (1990) see Bangalore as glamorous quite early by showcasing the up-market areas and five star hotels, the general representation of Bangalore in the 1990s—*Ganeshana Maduve, SP Sangliana 2*—does not emphasize its glamour as do later films like *Beladingala Bale, Nishkarsha,* and *Amruthavarshini.* Although *Nammoora Mandara Hoove* is set in Uttara Kannada district, the protagonist and his friends were once together in Bangalore and there is the sense that the space in which they studied is a glamorous one, not the least because of their apparent sophistication. Even within Upendra's oeuvre—not known for showcasing glamour—there is an exhibition of opulence in the basically cheesy *A* that is not seen in *Tarle Nan Maga.*

This opulence is also conspicuous in *America! America!,* which is about the sophisticated young children of rich plantation owners, who might have got their education in Bangalore city. The husband being a software engineer settled in America suggests the same thing because in the mid-1990s Bangalore had become well-known internationally as a hub of the IT industry and often referred to as 'India's Silicon Valley'.[27] The growth of the service sector may have had a cascading effect because this led to a boom in the other areas—such as construction, etc.—which boomed in the late 1990s. Although opportunities in the public sector—once Bangalore's most important industrial sector—were shrinking, there was migration to the city because of the growing informal sector. There was a huge generation of wealth in the city in the 1990s with significant capital accumulation in the informal sector also being possible.[28] Even compared to a city like Madras, Bangalore provided greater opportunities. Both men and women migrants found that Bangalore offered them much greater possibility of mobility so they could remit money back home.[29]

But if the portrayals of Bangalore in Kannada cinema as a glamorous space are characteristic of the mid-1990s the situation does appear to change by the end of the millennium. N. Omprakash Rao's *AK 47* (1999) gives us a more alarming picture of the city. In this film, Ram (Shivaraj Kumar) is the son of bank executive named Jagannath Rao (Girish Karnad). The film is in two parts with the second part set in Bombay being mainly in Hindi. The protagonist gets accidentally implicated in terrorism and is then accused when chief of police Yeshwant Sinha (Om Puri) is assassinated by the henchman of a terrorist named Dawood, whom Ram kills. While this part of the film gives us a picture of Bombay as a lawless space—often under curfew—my own view is that it is derived from Hindi films like *Bombay* (1995), and is mainly used to attach a heroic image to the male star. The motif of terrorism, I suggest, has also not been pertinent to Kannada cinema. The segments set in Bangalore, from my viewpoint, are those which are more useful to interpret.

Ram is courageous but impetuous, and the film has Bangalore sequences in which he is drawn to fighting hoodlums. Significantly, he is a Brahmin and speaks Brahminical Kannada, while the hoodlums speak the abusive Kannada made popular chiefly by Upendra's films. The difference between *AK 47* and films like *Tarle Nan Maga* is that the low Kannada here is threatening because the hoodlums arrive at the protagonist's home on the occasion of his thread ceremony and Jagannath Rao humbly seeks their pardon for Ram's acts. It would be easy to see the low and Ram's Brahminical Kannada as indicative of caste but the abusive Kannada does not have hierarchical connotations—as rustic Kannada would have had. Considering that it is also peppered with Hindi swearing, it can be argued that the abusive Kannada in *AK 47* is spoken by a threatening community of non-Kannadigas. This is different from its significance in *Tarle Nan Maga* and *Bombat Hendthi*, where it has comical connotations. The motif of the 'Brahmin' means what it once did in Kannada cinema—that Jagannath Rao and Ram represent the region. It is also significant that Ram and the hoodlums first come into conflict during Holi, a festival not celebrated as fervently in Karnataka as in north India. The festival hardly carries the implication of a threat in Hindi cinema—where it is always celebratory—that it carries in *AK 47*.

The first part of *AK 47* is perhaps indicative of the threat to the regional identity in Bangalore from non-Kannada communities largely composed of migrants from outside the region. In 1991 and 1994 there were anti-Tamil and anti-Urdu riots in which twenty-three and twenty-five people were killed, respectively,[30] and it is evident that the issue of the non-Kannadiga migrant had become an even more crucial one in 1999—because Kannada cinema had not exhibited the above motif earlier.

Economic Liberalization (1991–2)

An influential development in Indian economic history was the extensive economic reforms proposed in June 1991 and February 1992 by the P.V. Narasimha Rao government. The collapse of the Soviet Union and the socialist economies had, apart from disrupting a convenient barter system for Indian goods, also removed the only alternative model to the capitalist market. There could no longer be significant opposition within India for a comprehensive loosening of state control over the economy, and business and industrial interests therefore found new political allies. Prime Minister P.V. Narasimha Rao and Finance Minister Manmohan Singh were not politicians with strong constituencies but their perceived 'weakness' actually worked in their favour.[31] The killing of Rajiv Gandhi in 1991 left politics a 'level playing field' in India. A vulnerable government with few economic options initiated the economic reforms of 1991–2 but the 'inevitability' of the reforms was widely accepted; the perception that the government was 'helpless' actually lent the reforms legitimacy. In effect, therefore, the reforms represented an official and decisive break with

'Nehruvian socialism', which had been the 'grand narrative' influencing mainstream Hindi cinema. The film generally taken to represent the commencement of the new economic era in Indian popular cinema is Sooraj Barjatya's *Hum Aapke Hain Koun ...!* (1994).[32] It took more than two years for Hindi cinema to transform but the effects were far reaching. Some of the effects of the economic measures upon Hindi film narrative are:[33]

1. Hindi cinema did away with the poor as principal subjects of film narrative and began focusing exclusively on the rich— as in *Hum Aapke Hain Koun ...!*
2. The economic liberalization was interpreted as the state withdrawing from the public space. Since the state vacated film narrative, the stories became simpler. Films tried to compensate by focusing on spectacle—ritual as in *Hum Aapke Hain Koun ...!* and foreign locations as in *Dilwale Dulhania Le Jayenge.*
3. The nation was represented as an abstraction without the state being implicated in the film narrative. Allegories of the nation flourished as different kinds of communities—a happy family in *Hum Aapke Hain Koun ...!*, a school in *Mohabbatein* (2000), the household of a musician-guru in *Hum Dil De Chuke Sanam* (1999), and a cricket team in *Lagaan* (2001).
4. The state withdrawing from its own institutions led to the police being represented as unfettered by the law—as in *Satya* (1999). Gangland wars became a metaphor for unregulated competition, with the police behaving as private agencies.
5. With there being no possibility of social conflict between classes in film narrative, conflict was pushed to the boundaries of the nation. This registered as 'patriotism' in films like *Border* (1998) and *Lagaan* (2001).

Since Hindi cinema responded to the economic liberalization measures only in 1994, it would be reasonable for us to look for similar effects upon Kannada cinema around the same period. This is perhaps not as easy as it sounds because one of the characteristics of 1990s Kannada cinema is the depletion of signifiers and that, as I observed in the last chapter, is also a characteristic of Hindi cinema after *Hum Aapke Hain Koun ...!* The depletion in signifiers ('the new simplicity') in Hindi cinema was due to the nation state not figuring in film narratives as an element while a comparable phenomenon arose in Kannada cinema due to the region not being represented in film narrative because of the end of Mysore—even as a remembered community. This means that there is hardly as sharp a division in the Kannada cinema of the 1990s as there is in the Hindi cinema. A chronological rearrangement of the films of the 1990s discussed hitherto into two groups, with the second group beginning in 1994 may, therefore, be helpful. The justification is that the broad differences in the characteristics predominant in each group may furnish us with clues. This cannot be conclusive because these are only a few films out of an enormous number made. Still, the films were not chosen to argue out or support a point but on their general importance to Kannada cinema and the differences noticed are hardly inconspicuous.

Group A (before 1994)

Panchamaveda (1990), *SP Sangliana 2* (1990), *Shruthi* (1990), *Utkarsha* (1990), *Ganeshana Maduve* (1990), *Muthina Hara* (1990), *Hrudaya Hadithu* (1991), *Chaitrada Premanjali* (1992), *Tarle Nan Maga* (1992), *Bombat Hendthi* (1992), *Baa Nalle Madhuchandrakke* (1993), *Ssh!* (1993), *Akasmika* (1993).

Group B (1994 and after)

Nishkarsha (1994), *America! America!* (1995), *Beladingala Bale* (1995), *Nammoora Mandara Hoove* (1996), *Janmada Jodi* (1996), *A* (1997), *Amruthavarshini* (1997), *Nishabda* (1998), *Doni Sagali* (1998), *AK 47* (1999).

The difference between the two groups is not huge, which suggests that economic liberalization had less of an impact upon Kannada cinema. But overall, there is a greater sense of the community to be gained from the Group A films above. Upendra's film *A* is not an exception because while in *Ssh!* the crew members have names, those in *A* do not. The director, Surya, is usually shown alone in *A* except in the shooting sequences while in *Ssh!*, they form a community even when there is no shooting in progress and interpersonal relationships are suggested. In *AK 47*, as I have already shown, the 'community' is threatening.

The glossy representations of Bangalore has already been commented upon and the sense that films of the 1990s—because of their 'emptiness'—are more easily adaptable into other languages is more true of Group B, in which there is less sense to be got of the community. Another aspect marking out the two categories is that abusive Kannada appears to go out of fashion in later cinema[34]—as do the negative portrayals of women. This, however, does not mean that the old virtues upheld by Kannada cinema are brought back, as in *Akasmika*. Even in *AK 47*, the father who could have represented these virtues, is presented as strict and forbidding—rather than as a moral beacon to the protagonist.

If the region is consistently weak in the 1990s the nation is significantly weaker after 1993. *Muthina Hara* brought back nationalist sentiments only in a doubtful way but the Indian state (through the emblem of the police) is strongly inscribed in the narratives of several films before 1994—*SP Sangliana 2, Akasmika, Utkarsha, Baa Nalle Madhuchandrakke,* and *Ssh!* Among the later films only *Nishkarsha* and *AK 47* feature the police in a central way. It is significant that the police feature in only the Bombay part of *AK 47*, as though it would be unsuitable for them to be given importance in Bangalore. The near absence of the police in *Nishabda* despite it being a crime/action story is also significant.

When we examine the representations of the region and the nation in Kannada cinema, we understand that they are not treated in the same way. While the region in Kannada cinema is often treated as an abstraction—for example, represented as a community or a space, personified as the mother, or even symbolized through a traditional practice (endogamy)—the nation is, by and large, inseparable from its authority. In the Kannada mythological film, for instance, the nation is represented as god and the conflict in films like *Bedara Kannappa, Babruvahana,* and *Bhaktha Prahalada*, inevitably arises from god's authority being questioned or flouted until it is reaffirmed. Whenever a Kannada hero plays an agent of the law—as in the CID 999 films and *Antha*—it is because the region has shared the nation's authority at that moment. After the economic liberalization of 1991-2, when the state withdraws from film narrative in Hindi cinema, in Kannada films, correspondingly, the state finds itself absent or weak. The primary difference from Hindi cinema is that in Kannada cinema there are few other ways of implicating the nation in the narrative, except though its authority. That is why the ex-army protagonist of *Nishabda* takes recourse to private action when his younger brother is murdered, instead of going to the law. The implication here is of someone who once served the nation not protected by the state after 1991–2.

I have already speculated about the use of low Kannada and the demeaning of women in Kannada cinema of the early 1990s, and associated them with the lowering of the self-image of the constituents of the region. I would like to argue now that the self-image of the region and its constituents is not autonomous but defined only in relation to the nation. The proud self-image of the region as the 'modern Brahmin' in *Kasturi Nivasa* was defined deliberately in relation to the Nehruvian modern, which was 'inferior' because of the decadence associated with it.[35] The Kannada films of the early 1990s that suggest a lowering of moral standards usually invoke the nation. In *SP Sangliana 2*, the actual IPS officer known to be from outside the region contributes in the discourse, and the region is held up to the nation through him. *Tarle Nan Maga* arranges for a fake policeman to intervene when the father is a dowry seeker, and by doing this it is suggesting that the mere summoning of state intervention will be adequate to see a discernible improvement in moral standards. *Akasmika* also suggests 'state intervention' to raise moral standards in the region. The fact that policemen are witness to events, or hear confessions, that imply low morals among women in *Baa Nalle Madhuchandrakke*, *Ssh!*, and *Utkarsha* supports my proposition.

Since the representation of the nation in Kannada cinema is intimately tied up to its authority, that is, as the nation state, the perceived withdrawal of the state from the public space beginning with 1991–2 had, perhaps, the effect of removing the single arbiter who might have judged the constituents of the region. There is, consequently, generally less demeaning of women, less vulgarity, and low language in the later films of the 1990s, although these films are also 'emptier'. Even within Upendra's oeuvre, the emphasis on 'love' rather than the milieu (as in *Tarle Nan Maga*) leaves *A* more empty of signifiers. The same explanation can perhaps be offered for the lower incidence of 'communities' in the later films of the 1990s. Communities, in a sense, try to be microcosms of the region,[36] which exists only as a constituent of the nation. With the nation not signified, communities lose their pertinence. With neither the region nor the nation having a significant presence in Kannada cinema of the late 1990s, H.D. Deve Gowda's ascension to the post of prime minister in June 1996 is not even registered by Kannada cinema—although his period as chief minister was marked by a clearer understanding of local issues and he did not try to go back to the 'dominant caste politics' of an earlier era.[37]

As we come to the end of this chapter we understand that with the end of imagined Mysore in the 1980s there is no stable notion of the region to replace it, although there are attempts to define a 'community'—composed of migrants to Bangalore (as in *Ganeshana Maduve* and *Shruthi*), or a more inclusive one with language as the consideration (as in *Akasmika*). Bangalore always had an ambivalent position in Kannada cinema but with its newly found economic importance in the 1990s, narratives move there although aware that its linguistic heterogeneity leaves it an unsuitable emblem for the region. The transformation of the meaning of the nation because of the economic liberalization of 1991–2 also complicates matters here. Bangalore being more important to both the region and the nation in the new millennium than in the earlier decades because of economic factors, it will evidently play a large part in the shape taken by Kannada cinema as it emerges in the global age.

5. The Curse of Bangalore
2000–8

A Recapitulation

Since I have come to the last decade of Kannada cinema, it may be helpful to recapitulate, briefly, my findings with regard to the shape taken by Kannada narrative from the 1930s onwards, up till the new millennium. To begin, Kannada cinema originated in the princely state of Mysore and was less 'post-colonial' than Hindi cinema because Mysore was under indirect rule before 1947. Since the colonial encounter was weaker, it remained a more 'Hindu' cinema than the Hindi cinema contemporary to it. The principal way in which this is manifested is in caste hierarchy, furnishing it with its most important motifs. The family itself is hierarchically organized with the man roughly holding the position of 'master' in relation to the woman. Kannada cinema also did not attempt to be a 'secular' cinema by including the token Muslim as many Hindi films of the 1940s and 1950s do—and there is no Kannada genre corresponding to the Muslim social. The fact that family relationships were established through marriage networks within each caste in former princely Mysore resulted in endogamy being the favoured means of contracting marriages in the Kannada film and the Hindu joint family being valorized for several decades.

With the linguistic reorganization of the states in 1956 the Kannada-speaking regions were unified but Kannada cinema continued to address the region corresponding to former princely Mysore. That former princely Mysore took nearly two decades to become culturally integrated with independent India is suggested when Kannada cinema of the 1950s and early 1960s exhibits few of the motifs cf Hindi cinema of the period but favours the mythological film.

Going on to the significance of the motifs exhibited by Kannada cinema, the mythological film is essentially a way of allegorizing the position of the region vis-à-vis the nation. Since king and country are identical to the subjects of a monarchy, the region is represented as a king or a prince in Kannada cinema well until the 1980s, and the nation as divinity. When the citizens of prosperous Mysore are apprehensive about the effects of the merger of the poorer Kannada-speaking areas with their own territory, Kannada cinema exhibits the motif of the prince or king cursed with poverty but who submits to it through his devotion to god and gains a community in the process. The relationship between the king and the gods is however not always one of submission because the region also has claims upon the nation. This shows itself again and again—in the 1960s and later—when the two come into conflict (for example, *Mahishasura Mardhini*). The mythological continues until the 1980s and another comparable genre, the historical film, also becomes popular in the 1960s. Where the mythological film deals with princes and gods, the historical film usually has a smaller and a greater monarch (for example, *Vijayanagarada Veeraputra*), with devotion to the greater monarch being primary. The mythological and the historical films are partly indices of the relationship between the region and the nation but they also depend on memories of princely Mysore remaining strong in the popular consciousness. The memories gradually fade away and the two genres die out in the 1980s.

The late 1950s also sees the 'social' (or the domestic melodrama) becoming important as a genre, with 'Nehruvian modernity' being an important notion. But unlike in the Hindi film in which 'modernity' is viewed ambivalently, Kannada cinema does not regard it as a threat. Where good modernity is represented by the doctor in Hindi cinema, Nehruvian modernity in *School Master* is represented by the school teacher, who does not fight backwardness but corruption. Nehruvian modernity is not an important notion in Kannada cinema because the modern had been ushered into Mysore by forward looking dewans like Sir M. Visveswaraiya in the 1920s but it is still associated with the central state. When the region feels itself distant from the nation (as around 1970) the 'Mysore modern' is separately invoked (for example, *Kasturi Nivasa*) and shown to be superior to the Nehruvian modern. The region makes a claim upon modernity and the pertinent films include those with Rajkumar in the early 1970s and the first Kannada art film, *Samskara*.

From the 1970s onwards, Rajkumar, who is already the key male star in the 1960s, begins to provide the region with a proud self-image. Unlike Madras Presidency where there was political polarization because of the Dravidian movement, princely Mysore had no corresponding political movement; when the Congress assumed power in 1947 it did not even have a political agenda. This led to one party rule in Mysore after 1947 and the absence of political polarization also reveals itself in cinema. The values for which the 'ideological hero' stands in Tamil cinema were a direct consequence of the political polarization created by the anti-Brahmin movement. Since there was no such polarization in Mysore, the values for which Rajkumar stands are apolitical and the character he usually plays is best termed the 'ethical hero'. While the ideological hero's enemies are political categories—moneylenders, landlords, priests, etc.—the ethical hero's adversaries—owners of nightclubs, counterfeiters, quack doctors, ungrateful nephews—cannot be so described.

With the rise of Indira Gandhi and the ascendancy of her representative Devaraj Urs in greater Mysore (renamed Karnataka in 1973), the region feels closer to the nation than ever before. Devaraj Urs went even further in populism than Mrs Gandhi and his land reforms policies had huge consequences. It is therefore a period in which there is a dominant political discourse in the public space which registers in Kannada films like *Bhoothayyana Maga Ayyu*. This is also the period in which the Kannada art film movement flourishes. But while *Samskara* addresses the region, the art cinema which comes later in the 1970s (*Chomana Dudi, Ghatashraddha*) is more pan-Indian and takes its place in the Indian art film movement. The art cinema in Kannada today—with nationally recognized filmmakers like Girish Kasaravalli and Kavitha Lankesh—also holds itself up to the nation rather than the region. It addresses a pan-Indian art film audience and therefore has a smaller local significance.

After Mrs Gandhi's defeat in 1977 there is an increasing disconnect between the region and the nation. The 1970s are the years in which Kannada popular cinema adapts major works of Kannada literature in a significant way. With Mysore defunct as a political entity, imagined Mysore still exists in literary works—and can be summoned—but this ceases by 1980, when Mysore fades from public memory. Endogamy and the joint family remain the last cultural relics of Mysore still present in cinema and they recall Mysore when employed as motifs in films like *Na Ninna Bidalare*. Also significant is the figure of the mother who is venerated especially in the films with Rajkumar because she embodies Mysore—as the mother embodies the nation in Hindi films like *Mother India* and *Deewar*.

The 1980s was, for the nation, a period in which divisive forces had gained ascendancy. Some motifs exhibited by Hindi cinema—especially the beleaguered state as represented by the weakness of the police—are found in Kannada films like *Antha*. These motifs in Kannada cinema do not survive the decade—as they do in Hindi cinema—but disappear after the first few years of the 1980s. The 1980s also mark the demise of Mysore as an imagined community with endogamy and the joint family leaving Kannada cinema—or parodied in films like *Haalu Jenu*. After the Devaraj Urs era there is no dominant political discourse in the public space constituting the region; with Kannada films abandoning most of their earlier conventions there is a 'young' cinema (*Premaloka*), which is singularly bereft of signifiers. Kannada cinema also attempts to substitute Mysore with other communities and other objects for veneration but without success. To elaborate, as long as Mysore—although politically defunct—existed in the imagination of the public it is signified variously—for example, through the village, the joint family, the practice of endogamy, or the venerated mother figure. In the late 1980s most of these signifiers have departed from Kannada cinema. Cinema therefore attempts to erect other communities and objects of loyalty in its stead, but these remain unstable. The 1980s sees Kannada cinema at the beginning of its decline, perhaps, because it is uncertain about the 'region' it is addressing, the social experiences it is narrativizing, and the pertinence of the conventions it is following.

With Mysore—the original region addressed by Kannada cinema—defunct even as an imagined space, the conventions owing to its origins apparently mean little. The sense that all convention is irrelevant permeates Kannada cinema in the 1990s, showing itself in a new kind of 'realism' (for example, *Tarle Nan Maga*) that abandons the former graciousness—chiefly the kind that Rajkumar represented. There are films about filmmaking in the 1990s that try to 'peel away' convention but what comes up is only a new vulgarity—especially with regard to women. A persisting convention is the relationship between the man and the woman which endorses the earliest representations. As noted, the exemplary relationship between the man and the woman in Kannada cinema once allegorized the relationship between the king and his subjects and this means that the heroine of Kannada cinema is more submissive than her Hindi counterpart. After the end of monarchy, the figure of the submissive and accommodating woman still contributes to the self-image of the constituents of the region. The exemplary relationship between the man and the woman also finds correspondence in the one between the region and its constituents in a loosely allegorical way. While the woman's 'submission' was generally looked upon as a mark of her goodness, it begins to have negative connotations from the late 1980s onwards. The reason is perhaps the marked deterioration in public life when Karnataka was ruled with even brazen indifference to ethical propriety without the region's constituents resisting. The denigration of women in Kannada cinema and the use of low Kannada perhaps respond to this because both aspects point to a lowering of the constituent's self-image.

Although the Devaraj Urs era is generally regarded as a period in which there was a huge increase in corrupt practices, Urs was still responsible for other measures which are considered progressive. The Bangarappa era (1990–2) was different in as much as the chief minister simply acted as fundraiser for the Congress without doing much else besides. I have already elaborated upon the possibility of the woman's qualities standing for those of the region's constituents, and there is a suggestion in some Kannada films of the 1990s that women are not fastidious about their men, absurdly pliant rather than 'good'. The explanation offered for the use of abusive Kannada is that since classical Kannada (largely in the mythological and historical films) furthers the cause of regional nationalism, abusive Kannada, conversely, points to low regional self-esteem. The association between these aspects and the local political leadership is perhaps only speculation but to support it, there are also several films in the 1990s in which good women are attached to despicable men—or 'unworthy masters' as Kannada cinema might have it. Also to be noted is the motif of local politics obstructing the nation state in *SP Sangliana 2* (1990) and *Nishabda* (1998) in which local politicians have police officers in their grasp. In both these films, recourse is finally to be obtained only through someone associated with the nation— the ex-army officer in *Nishabda* and IPS officer Sangliana in the other film.

The economic liberalization of 1991–2 does not strongly affect the Kannada film but the low self-image of the region's constituents is less apparent in the later 1990s. The possible cause is that the self-image is not autonomous but places the nation state in the position of arbiter and, after the economic reforms, the state is perceived to be withdrawing from the public space. But the departure of the nation state from the film narrative and the continued absence of the region in the shape of a stable community sees Kannada cinema emptier of signifiers and prone to exploiting the glamour of Bangalore in a new way (*Beladingala Bale*).

While most films of the late 1990s tend to use the city as a glamorous space, *A K 47* points to the demographic composition of Bangalore as likely to be the cause of a threat. Kannada cinema, as already brought out, has always regarded Bangalore ambivalently. This is because Bangalore was associated more with British rule than with princely Mysore, and it later also became the site of huge investment by the central government through public sector enterprises and institutions. This is perhaps why Bangalore has positive connotations when the region felt itself closer to the nation (*Jedara Bale*) and negative when it felt itself distant (*Pattanakke Banda Pathniyaru*). Since Bangalore is an alienated space—while being in former princely Mysore it had few affinities with it—it did not acquire an iconic presence for Kannada cinema although the Kannada film industry is located in the city. Bangalore plays a greater role in the Kannada film after 2000 and it is in the context of the past representations of the city that we examine its implications now.

'The Way We Might have Been'

Vishnuvardhan, the leading male star in Kannada cinema after Rajkumar retired in the 1990s, attempts to do in Seshadri's *Yajamana* (2000) what Rajkumar did in *Bangarada Manushya* (1972). This film is about a pious villager, Shankar, who makes huge sacrifices for his family—consisting of his mother and three younger brothers. He declines to marry the woman he loves because he finds her resenting the attention he is giving to his siblings and this is despite the wealth that the marriage will bring him. The story of an individual's sacrifice for his family usually leads to tragedy as in *Bangarada Manushya* with the beneficiaries being ungrateful but *Yajamana* is triumphantly different. In fact, the film relies on the strategy of creating circumstances where our expectations of tragedy are constantly belied.

Shankar's oldest brother is betrothed to his childhood sweet-heart, whose father Rajeev was helped out by Shankar. When the two are of marriageable age and Shankar goes to the city to meet Rajeev, he finds the latter rich and arrogant. As chance will have it Shankar's brother becomes a cook in Rajeev's house and is ill-treated by his former sweetheart, but singing their childhood song is enough for the girl to understand her errors and the two are married, after which the girl conducts herself admirably. The second brother becomes a policeman and is required to arrest Shankar who is falsely accused of defalcation. Instead of arresting him, the brother resigns but his resignation is not accepted—and the charge is also forgotten. The third brother graduates with distinction as a doctor. When the visiting Shankar is ill-treated by the college watchman for being a villager, rather than being ashamed of him, the doctor-brother has Shankar brought on to the podium and felicitated. Shankar's adversaries invariably learn their errors and arrogant people become unassuming. Although the story abounds in crises, none of them comes to much individually, and family togetherness is affirmed without much exertion on any-one's part.

At first glance, *Yajamana* seems to be employing many of the motifs of Kannada cinema of the 1970s largely because it eulogizes the joint family. There are, nonetheless, differences and the first is that it is Shankar, rather than his mother, who is at the film's moral centre. In fact, his mother admits that there are aspects of conduct that she can learn from her son. Second, Shankar does not tower above the others of his own generation and he is only the first among equals, three others being the fathers of the girls his brothers marry. The protagonist of *Bangarada Manushya* had the position of a patriarch and towered above everyone else because he allegorized remembered Mysore—or its modernity as represented by Visveswaraiya and Shankar in *Yajamana* is apparently different.

When *Yajamana* begins Shankar's brothers are children and the family becomes a 'joint family' only when they marry, and this is different from *Bangarada Manushya* and *Chandavaliya Thota* (1964) in which the family is a joint family to begin with, but is later put under threat. *Yajamana* is therefore not about the threat to the joint family but about a joint family being created against all odds. Also, considering that Shankar in *Yajamana* is conciliatory when ascendant—even with those who have wronged him—he is apparently trying to build a community with his own joint family at its core—extendable to embrace a network of goodwill.

To examine the impediments standing in the way of the 'community', Shankar is not represented as 'poor' but as a villager without 'sophistication'. His house is not small but is intended as the archetypal 'village' dwelling. The oldest of Shankar's brothers is unlettered and is only a waiter—and briefly a cook—but the English-speaking girl who once mocked him takes up her position as dutiful daughter-in-law in his household though he remains a waiter. When he succeeds at business later, the material aspect of his success is not highlighted. It is not money which is made the issue but education and sophistication. Two of Shankar's brothers are educated and while we expect them to desert him, they stay on and acknowledge him as their ideal. The film is evidently concerned with *why education and 'sophistication' need not be a threat to the community*. It is perhaps when 'sophistication' and education are real threats that such a message will be most welcome.

Comparing the film to *Bangarada Manushya*, we find that where Bangalore was the threat that changed family circumstances for the worse in that film, the city is notably absent in *Yajamana*. Shankar's younger brother gets his education in

Mysore and the Mysore palace features in several song sequences but Bangalore is discreetly absent. Rajeev goes to the city' and not to Bangalore although the party scene in which everyone speaks English smacks of Bangalore as does the episode in which the comic character hurries to an English film to 'improve his general knowledge'. I would like to argue that since the film is about people being placed in materially favourable circumstances but their natures not changing for the worse, it would have been inconvenient to have Bangalore as an element—because the city *is* seen to change people in that way. Bangalore's absence is striking in *Yajamana* and the film can be interpreted as a wistful reflection on how people might have been—were it not for Bangalore's looming presence. Bangalore is perhaps the seat of the education and 'sophistication' that threatens the community—one that has still to be constructed. The sense that the community has still to be is consistent with my conclusion in the last chapter that after the end of imagined Mysore, Kannada cinema was still to find a community. But why Bangalore should be a threat here needs to be examined.

As already brought out, Bangalore has never been perceived as a wholeheartedly Kannada city. More importantly, Bangalore's elite—even when Kannada-speaking—has tended to gather around the cantonment side of the city and this 'colonial' hangover has frequently invited the irony of Kannada litterateurs and cultural figures.[1] Since Bangalore's elite had always been 'colonially inclined', why should Bangalore become such a threat around 2000? The answer is perhaps that the IT industry made a huge difference to the wage levels seen in Bangalore in the late 1990s. Since Bangalore had a surplus of skilled manpower and there were a large number of engineering colleges, the 1990s saw the city being transformed from a 'low wage backwater' to something quite different.[2] In the initial period at least, much of the recruitment by Bangalore's IT companies was done locally. In the late 1990s, the wages in the IT industry were up to near US levels,[3] a fact which would have been incomprehensible to people outside it. Perhaps more importantly, high wages were associated with the English language. It will not be farfetched to say that the late 1990s created a situation in which there was a schism in the Kannada-speaking community around Bangalore with those who were English educated becoming phenomenally better off than those who were not.[4] Bangalore, to the constituents of the region, apparently took a turn for the worse in the late 1990s. Consequently, if *Shruthi* (1990) portrayed the entrenched Bangalorean as rich, arrogant, and hostile to others in the region, *Yajamana* goes further: it excludes Bangalore from its domain when it attempts to envisage a new community through a joint family constituted by equals.

When Bangalore appears after 2000, it is often the site of snobbishness as in Ashok Patil's *Joke Falls* (2005). The film reworks Hrishikesh Mukherjee's Hindi comedy *Chupke Chupke* (1975). Ananth Patil (Ramesh Arvind), who is a professor of botany in Mysore, marries Sulekha whose brother-in-law Joshi (Datanna) is due to become a high court judge in Bangalore. Joshi pretends to be a lover of 'pure Kannada' but his speech cannot do without a huge proportion of English. He regards academics as social inferiors and the comedy comes from Ananth Patil taking up employment as chauffeur to the brother-in-law and pretending to be Sulekha's lover. Interestingly, apart from the snobbish person in the film being Bangalorean and (by virtue of being a judge) associated with the state, the characters travel to and fro between Mysore and Bangalore but the only icon we see of Bangalore (and repeatedly) is Cantonment railway station, which does not lie on the Mysore-Bangalore railway line.

Informal Power against the State

The next development of importance in the recent history of Bangalore is perhaps the Congress returning to power in 1999, with S.M. Krishna at the helm. Before we look into this however, it is necessary to examine another youth film, Puri Jagannath's *Appu* (2002)—previously made in Tamil and Telugu. This film is constructed around a new kind of hero for Kannada cinema, a youthful hooligan given to fighting and skirmishing. *Appu* was the launch vehicle for Puneeth Rajkumar as a hero just as *Anand* had launched his older brother Shivaraj Kumar in the mid-1990s. The protagonist of the film is Appu, a student in Bangalore who is admired for his tenacity and toughness. In the first part of the film he is assaulted by adversaries but his life is saved by a girl who later becomes his classmate. Appu decides to marry her even before he has set eyes on the girl but she is the police commissioner's daughter. Appu has a father who objects to his unruly ways and just when we take him to be the well-placed patriarch, we learn that he is a police head constable, a sycophant plying the commissioner with home-cooked food. Appu does not reconsider marrying the commissioner's daughter despite the girl being above his station and disliking him. He therefore systematically harasses the girl—until she falls in love with him.

Appu has several aspects of significance and the first is the singular disdain it shows for the police. Appu's first brush with the police occurs when he and his friends are stoning a cinema for not providing them with tickets. The film in question stars Rajkumar and Appu is the president of the Rajkumar Abhimanigala Sangha, a fan association. This is an actual fan association and wields considerable informal power in Bangalore city, having attained some notoriety for its targeting the non-Kannada subaltern classes in street violence and riots.[5] But Appu's conflict with the police begins when the commissioner's daughter complains to her father of his annoying conduct. Appu is therefore tortured, but in vain because he refuses to give her up. When the girl begins to love Appu, her father employs some rowdies to have him liquidated, but also unsuccessfully. In the last sequence the commissioner tries to get his daughter married off to another IPS officer but Appu mobilizes 'public opinion' and effectively prevents it. The film concludes with the DGP admonishing the commissioner for his doings and Appu going off nonchalantly with the girl.

Appu is disquieting because the protagonist is portrayed as exemplary but acts in ways that are difficult to justify. Appu, while constantly being admonished by his father, has his mother's wholehearted support which, given the mother's traditional role in Kannada cinema, suggests the film's endorsement of whatever he is doing. Apart from his stoning of the movie theatre, Appu climbs up to the girl's bedroom, straddles her, shows her a knife, and then reassures her that he is there to wish her on her birthday. While he is openly contemptuous of the police, there is also the suggestion that the lower ranks are preferable to those in the IPS, although these higher officials are more 'sophisticated'. The inspectors and sub-inspectors understand him, use his services, and even employ Appu as an informer, but the IPS officer—even while appearing fair—heaps false accusations upon him and personally tortures him. In *SP Sangliana 2* (1990) the upright IPS officer was contrasted with lower-ranking officers who are either corrupt or easily intimidated, and *Appu* seems to be doing the opposite. There is a sense here of lower-level policemen being more sympathetic because they are local while the higher ranking ones dutifully serve the partisan state.

While dealing with the film *Yajamana* earlier in this chapter, I tried to show how Bangalore was regarded as alien by the constituents of the region because of the schism created by its 'sophistication' and wealth. This was perhaps accentuated during S.M. Krishna's period (1999–2004) as chief minister when the government initiated a series of measures by which the state could attract new capital, enter into partnership with private enterprise to develop the city and manage its services. The government instituted an advisory body named the Bangalore Agenda Task Force (BATF) from figures associated with industry to improve the quality of life in the city through deepening and strengthening a public-private partnership. It has been noted by commentators that the BATF was also entrusted with 'institutionalizing upgraded service-delivery mechanisms by amending the legal framework', that is, it would shape the legislative functions of the government.[6] It has also been suggested that the new initiatives favoured the elite because of the emphasis on 'roads rather than public transport; garbage and pollution rather than public housing; mosquitoes and public toilets rather than public health'.[7] The city's housing schemes also favoured low-density, low-rise, and privately-owned housing, and the issue of providing mass housing to meet the growing demands of the people with lower incomes was not addressed.

S.M. Krishna was originally elected from Mandya district but by the end of his period as chief minister he was more popular among entrenched Bangaloreans than in the rest of Karnataka and he shifted his constituency to middle-class Bangalore. It is difficult to interpret the motifs in *Appu* more than broadly (the film is a remake) but its success means that it touched a chord. The Congress government had won the popular vote in 1999 but it did not act as a popular government might have acted. S.M. Krishna was presented as an icon of 'economic reform'[8] and what this meant locally was perhaps that he had followed P.V. Narasimha Rao's example of the early 1990s. He conducted himself as a CEO might rather than as an elected political leader should.

Mainstream Hindi cinema, which was once a broad-based cinema, became progressively, after 1991–2, a cinema of the affluent classes from metropolitan cities. My reading of Kannada cinema shows that it has had those outside Bangalore as its constituency; when dealing with the city, it is the newly arrived migrant in Bangalore with whom its sympathies usually are. Kannada cinema during 2000–2 perhaps sees the initiatives of the Congress government as it might have been seen 'from the other side'—not by those who benefited by it but by those who found themselves threatened. To the segments shackled by state intervention the 'withdrawal of the state' is opportune, but to the other side, it tends to mean their alienation from political power.[9]

When the protagonist opposes the police in *Appu*, he is perhaps harnessing a deep resentment in Kannada film audiences towards the state but his triumphant note is not typical of Kannada cinema. More typical are the films in which the police are brutal adversaries but the protagonist, instead of prevailing over them without difficulty as in *Appu*, is doomed to tragedy and death. Examining some these films reveals how uncharacteristic Appu's optimism and bravado are in the Kannada cinema of the new millennium.

Street Violence

It is difficult to say when it actually began but P.N. Satya's *Majestic* (2002) is perhaps the film that initiated the genre, which usually advertises itself through posters where the protagonist wields a weapon—a chopper, a razor, a chain, or a knife, and signals his belligerence. Some other films are Mudduraj's *Kitti* (2004), Ravishankar's *Durgi* (2004), Prem's *Jogi* (2005), and Soori's *Duniya* (2007). In *Majestic*, a boy lives in a rustic milieu with his drunkard father, his long-suffering mother, and his ailing baby sister. Since the child needs medical attention and the man has spent the family income on drink, the boy sees his mother selling herself—but still unable to save her daughter's life. When the father returns from one of his binges and finds the dead child, he is unrepentant and remains intent on laying hands on his wife's earnings. This incenses the boy so much that he stabs his father to death and escapes to Bangalore. In Bangalore, the boy becomes handyman to a corrupt policeman named Randhir (Jai Jagadeesh) and is given the name Daasa ('slave'). But Daasa (Darshan) learns the ropes and grows up to be a dreaded hoodlum. He has his own gang and is feared by his underworld rivals. He is an extortionist, a paid killer, and undertakes unlawful activities of all kinds on behalf of 'clients'. The turning point is when he needs to stop a romance between a rich boy and a slum girl. The girl has a classmate named Kiran and this plucky girl virtually drives away Daasa's henchmen when they try to break up the romance. Daasa seeks to subdue her and after considering various alternatives, decides to change his appearance and feign interest in her. The inevitable happens and the two actually fall in love although the girl remains unaware of his antecedents. Daasa (as Prajwal) also finds himself undergoing a moral transformation. We now come to learn that Kiran is the policeman (now DCP) Randhir's daughter. When Randhir discovers that his daughter's boyfriend is actually Daasa, he tells her everything about his former protégé. Kiran accosts Daasa and will not hear his protests that he is transformed. In the last part of *Majestic*, Randhir's well-meaning mistress reveals to Kiran the kind of person her father really is but by then, Daasa has decided to kill her and take his own life. He stabs Kiran, learning too late that she still loves him. The film ends with Daasa also shot down by DCP Randhir.

A motif that *Majestic* shares with other films from the mould (for example, *Jogi, Durgi, Kitti,* and *Duniya*) is that Bangalore figures in all the films as a lawless space and the viewpoint is that of the Kannada-speaking migrant. Second, not only do the films identify with a Kannada migrant but they also regard his/her integration with the city as impossible. The protagonists of *Durgi* take up residence in Bangalore in a colony named after a woman from a small town ('Mandya Mangamma') and become part of the community there. Migrants in temporary dwellings constitute a special community to the protagonist of *Jogi* even when he rules gangland. This inability to integrate is given emphasis when the possibility of romance (with a woman from the city) is deliberately underplayed.

A crucial requirement in my analysis has been to identify/characterize the community represented in the film and the Hindi gangster film *Satya* (1998) may be useful here because that film is also about a migrant joining the city underworld and gaining prominence. The difference between the two films lies in the protagonist of *Satya* rising in stature and acquiring power. The protagonists in both *Majestic* and *Satya* come into contact with the police but while Satya connects with them at the highest level (and plots the killing of the police chief), Daasa deals with underlings who still tower above him. I will argue that in a narrative that charts the rise of a heroic individual from humble origins to stature, the limit placed on the stature he/she attains is broadly indicative of the limits to which his/her community may rise. If Daasa's community is associated with the region[10] the film is placing a small limit on what is achievable by it. The film is set in a city known to be glamorous, but it locates its action in the rundown areas (in the 'city' and not in the 'cantonment') as if a constituent of the region cannot be equal to the glamour of Bangalore.[11] The film is deliberately carving out an unglamorous city out of Bangalore to fit the image of its protagonist and this is singular because Daasa is presented as heroic.

Duniya came five years after *Majestic* and its similarity to the earlier film indicates how stable the motifs are. This has a parallel in Hindi cinema when many of the motifs introduced by economic liberalization remain forever because the social/economic process itself is not reversed. *Duniya's* protagonist Shivalingu (Vijay) works in a quarry and comes to Bangalore when his mother is critically ill. When she dies and he has to bury her, he is drawn into a gang by a need for money. Shivalingu also meets Poornima, an orphan, and the two take up residence in an abandoned bus with the help of Sathya, a good-hearted drunkard. Particularly important is an assistant commissioner of police Umesh Kumar who liquidates grovelling gangsters in 'encounters' when they gain in importance. The film concludes with Shivalingu and Poornima consuming poison rather than surrender to the assistant commissioner and his constables.

Shivalingu, based on his occupation as a stonecutter, can be identified as a dalit but the film de-emphasizes caste associations as Poornima is vegetarian and apparently born into an upper-caste. Shivalingu himself cheerfully admits that he has eaten every creature from dog to lizard while working in the quarry. *Duniya* is even more extreme than *Majestic* in as much as Shivalingu's valour is useless to him, money hardly comes his way, and he does not rise in stature at all. The first time he earns anything is when the boss gets him to assault one of the members of his own gang—for fun. The second occasion is when this gang member wants 'revenge' and pays Shivalingu to submit to a thrashing.

The gang itself is composed of a handful of layabouts in one of the seedier quarters of the city—Srirampuram—known as the home of Bangalore's 'rowdies'. The gang is not engaged in any lucrative trade, and if their leader Prabhi has grown enough to be outside the policeman's reach, it is because of his elder-brother Raghupathy, a small-time politician. The drunkard Sathya is their mascot and he spends his time playing the clown in the market, donned in the ceremonial turban associated commonly with Old Mysore gentility.

As if to correspond to the lowliness of the protagonists, the policeman Umesh is not a high-ranking official. We are never certain why he is casually eliminating members of the gang—who appear to pose no threat to anyone except each other—and the only explanation is that he is maintaining 'law and order'. There is perhaps a clue in a brief shot before a minor liquidation when the assistant commissioner is seen talking on a mobile phone from a high rise and we see a more glamorous part of Bangalore sprawling below. This is perhaps interpretable as the machinery of the state being pressed into ruthless maintenance of 'law and order' for the glory of the Bangalore more visible to the outside world. The title of the film is also significant here because *duniya* is the Hindi and not the Kannada word for 'world'. There is evidently an equation made between Bangalore and the cruel world but, more importantly, the use of the *national* language to denote the world suggests the defeat of local claims upon the Karnataka's capital city.[12]

Another aspect of *Duniya* is its repeated references to the Rajkumar film *Sakshatkara* (1971), which is from the same group as *Kasturi Nivasa* (1970) and *Bangarada Manushya* (1972) that I have examined earlier. One sees the reference to the film as a lament over how the constituents of princely Mysore could have been reduced to such circumstances.[13] Where *Sakshatkara* was not specifically about Kannada speakers—these were the virtues that all humanity should possess—*Duniya*, by confining its characters to a space inhabited by a sub-class, suggests that the constituents of the region cannot claim to speak for humanity and this can be attributed to the injury done to their self-image by Bangalore.

The Anatomy of the Migrant

Bangalore now acquires an importance in Kannada cinema as never before but the city acquired global importance after 2000, which could not but have severe local repercussions—because of the economic gap that opened up between it and the rest of the region. The motif of the migrant in Bangalore, which is hardly new to Kannada cinema,[14] becomes stronger in the new millennium even when the films do not belong in the category dealt with in the last section—films like *Shruthi* and *Ganeshana Maduve*. Films like *Majestic*, *Jogi*, and *Duniya* deal with an underclass living on the edges of legality but there are other films like Prem's *Excuse Me* (2003) and Nagathihalli Chandrashekar's *Amrutha Dhare* (2005) in which the protagonists are affluent but the motif of the migrant seems important and still with the sense that he/she lives in temporary quarters. *Excuse Me* has approximately the same theme as *Cyrano de Bergerac*—the heroine (Ramya) falls in love with a young man because of his music and erroneously associates the music with his friend, who has fallen in love with her. Interestingly enough, both boys are from the same village and are staying in the house of a rich uncle in Bangalore while the girl is an entrenched Bangalorean. The entrenched Bangalorean is represented in the film as someone who lives in her own house. Migrants to Bangalore, apparently, can be distinguished by their living in rented quarters and *Shruthi* made us familiar with this motif. Since there is no returning from Bangalore despite being oppressed by it, these migrants are without loyalty to any territory—whether their homes or their place of domicile.

Amrutha Dhare does not specify where its protagonists hail from but the young man could be a Bangalorean (but disinherited by his father). The film is about a young couple struggling to acquire their own home in Bangalore—and placed in the position of migrants. The man sells it secretly when the woman becomes terminally ill and is therefore without a home.

It must be emphasized here that all 'migrants' in Kannada cinema do not come from the same economic mould. As already discussed with regard to films like *Belli Moda* (1966), there is a rich, sophisticated rural category of plantation owners in Kannada cinema who, in the cinema after 2000, are treated as Bangaloreans with ancestral property outside as in Yogaraj Bhat's *Galipata* (2008). But, going by the evidence of this film, these people are not 'culpable' for being Bangaloreans because they spurn the city, are intent on recovering their cultural heritage and connecting with the local populace—without, of course, surrendering their city privileges.[15]

Another aspect of the migrants in Kannada cinema is that they are not from across Karnataka but only from the areas which come under former princely Mysore. The Mandya in the 'Mandya Mangamma's colony' in *Durgi* is situated between Bangalore and Mysore, and in traditional 'old Mysore'. When a new community is imagined after 2000, it continues to be an exclusive one rather than an inclusive one connoted by the Kannada language. The name 'Sandalwood' associated with the Kannada film industry is also indicative of old Mysore rather than Karnataka as a whole. It would appear, therefore, that despite the demise of imagined Mysore, the constituency of Kannada cinema remains exclusive.

With the mythology of the migrant-as-underworld-don gaining momentum, the figure represented by the likes of Daasa, Jogi, and Shivalingu has gained unexpected durability and is used for purposes not envisaged by the earlier films. In Guru Deshpande's *Varasdhara* (2008), for instance, an underworld don takes on terrorists in Bangalore. Underworld figures have glamour everywhere—if *The Godfather* (1972) and Hindi films like *Satya* (1998) and *Company* (2002) are any indication—and the apparent reason is that they wield informal power. In fact, in films like Ram Gopal Varma's *Sarkar* (2005) the crime angle is virtually absent—so exclusively does the film focus on the power and influence side. The Kannada films, on the other hand, are not about informal power and the eponymous hero of *Appu*, though only a student, employs it more convincingly than the dreaded 'dons' in *Majestic* and *Jogi*. There is perhaps a clue to be found to the unusual status of the underworld don in Kannada cinema in a later gangster film K.M. Chaitanya's *Aa Dinagalu* (2007), which is a strikingly candid film, based on the memoirs of a former underworld figure, Agni Sridhar, who is now editing a Kannada tabloid.

Aa Dinagalu tells the inside story of an actual gang war in Bangalore in the 1980s. The gangster involved in the actual happenings is Kothwal Ramachandra, who had become *numero uno* in the absence of M.P. Jairaj, who was spending a ten-year term in jail for murder. Also involved are various minor hoodlums and the story revolves around Sridhar (Atul Kulkarni) and two others who conspire and kill Kothwal Ramachandra (Sharath Lohitashwa) when he is in their company, for which they get outside support from Jairaj (Ashish Vidyarthi). An important character in the story, perhaps a fictional one, provides the film with its romantic interest. Chetan, a Konkani-speaking Brahmin, is in love with Mallika who is from the Vokkaliga caste. Chetan's father (Girish Karnad), a minor industrialist, therefore, pays Kothwal Ramachandra to break up the romance. Chetan is upset by this and joins Sridhar and two others to liquidate Kothwal Ramachandra, who trusts them. The film concludes with the assailants jailed briefly but let off for lack of evidence.

Since the film is based on the memoirs of a don, one would expect it to provide us with a glamorized and self-justifying picture of the underworld, dons as possessors of limitless power. But there is a perceptible gap between the terrifying demeanour/ reputation of the dreaded hoodlum Kothwal Ramachandra and the docile way in which he responds to the minor industrialist—and allows himself to be shooed away. The story is told from Sridhar's viewpoint but it is Kothwal Ramachandra who is the protagonist and the film treats him with respect although his killing is the film's theme. This respect acknowledges Kothwal's mettle and suggests that his docility before the industrialist is not timidity but adherence to a social code.

There are different tales about Kothwal Ramachandra but one is that he was from Shimoga where he plied an autorickshaw.[16] Kothwal is perhaps admired because, despite being a migrant, he ruled Bangalore's underworld. He indicates to Chetan in the film that the underworld does not meddle in the affairs of respectable people like him. But the manner of his submission to Chetan's father makes us wonder if there could be other reasons as well. Both Kothwal and the industrialist appear conscious of their respective stations *within a hierarchy*. It is perhaps this aspect that makes 'respectable people' immune to underworld dons. This may be a specifically Mysore attitude because we see nothing comparable in Hindi films like *Satya* and *Kaminey*.[17] Seen in this context, the migrant's inability to rise above the low level described in *Majestic* and *Duniya* can be read as reverence for hierarchy. Bangalore is a cosmopolitan city; hierarchy is perhaps more fluid when the individual backgrounds of the populace are as indeterminate as they are in a cosmopolitan city but the migrant, because of persisting social habits, declines to take advantage of it.

I have been, all along, examining hierarchy only as filmic convention but it has now acquired the contours of a covert social stricture. It is only within their hierarchical station that the migrant protagonists in these films exhibit gallantry, but this limited gallantry is still enough for them to be heroic. This overriding consideration of hierarchy points to another important feature which is the lack of 'anti-outsider' rhetoric in Kannada cinema. Very rarely is the non-Kannadiga lampooned and/or made the villain. In *Appu*, one of the protagonist's adversaries is a Hindi speaking north Indian and the young man in *Amrutha Dhare* sells his home to a Marwari financier, but the rhetoric is stronger when filmmakers from Maharashtra rant against north Indians as in *Ankush* (1985). The difficulties faced by migrants are, instead, largely blamed on the state—a motif that goes back to *Shruthi* (1990). While there are, as I have explained, other reasons also for the state being made to shoulder the blame, I would like to argue that Kannada cinema finds it difficult to hierarchically locate the 'outsider' in relation to the constituents of the region, the term 'hierarchy' being used here as traditionally understood by Kannada cinema. Since a 'community' is difficult to envisage without hierarchical positions for all its members, Bangalore cannot represent a community. A way of circumventing this is to propose a self-contained community of migrants who respect and obey hierarchy and for whom hierarchical positions can be found.[18]

It is perhaps also appropriate to now draw the attention of the reader to the gradual transformation in the hierarchical status of the protagonist in Kannada cinema which, I have proposed, is related to the self-image of the region. In the 1970s, Rajkumar played the Brahmin in films like *Kasturi Nivasa* and *Bangarada Manushya*. The actor tried to keep the self-image alive till as late as *Akasmika* perhaps to counter the low self-esteem reflected by the vulgarity in the period. The protagonist of *Yajamana* played by Vishnuvardhan in 1990 can be understood as belonging to the landed class, that is, Vokkaliga caste, and he also speaks the Kannada associated with the peasantry. The portrayal of Shankar in *Yajamana* is apparently an effort to find a new self-image for the region—especially as a reaction to Bangalore's onslaught. Madesha in *Jogi* is of tribal origin and, as already suggested, the protagonist of *Duniya*, being a stonecutter, can be taken to be a Dalit. If my contention that the male protagonist reflects the self-image of the region is allowed, there is apparently a lowering of the self-image if gathered in terms of its hierarchical status.

The Local and the National in Global Bangalore

The new economy companies in Bangalore became visible slowly because even in 1991 only 2619 people out of over 3,80,000 workers were employed in the hardware and software fields. Information Technology (IT) and IT-enabled services accounted for 60,000 jobs in the late 1990s, but this has increased several-fold since then with medical transcription, back offices, and call centres expanding. Here again, language is the key and the opportunities offered by the new economy to those with English-medium education are only too evident. N.R. Narayana Murthy, a doyen of the IT industry, made a plea for a massive expansion of English education to wrest the opportunities offered by the global market. This was contested by the writer U.R. Ananthamurthy, a spokesman for Kannada, who called for measures to protect the beleaguered Kannada language and culture.[19] There are popular estimates that only 10 per cent of the jobs in the new economy companies are now held by Kannada speakers[20] because the companies recruit from all over India. Since the new economy companies pay their employees substantially higher wages, the spending power of the non-Kannada segment in Bangalore makes it very visible. Another reason for the disaffection of Kannada speakers is, perhaps indirectly, Bangalore's expansion. The entry of the private builder into the housing market led to housing sites and layouts gradually making way for apartment blocks/complexes.[21] This has not only resulted in the original families of bungalow-owners making over their properties to developers, but also farmers on the periphery of Bangalore having disposed of their land—only to find land prices sky-rocketing. Those now occupying the apartments where the ancestral houses/land of the local people once stood are new entrants to Bangalore with visibly more purchasing power. With Bangalore contributing to India's global image there is, in effect, a perceptible gap developing between those 'contributing to the nation' and those whose associations may be termed 'local'. A film that apparently registers this widening gap acutely is one of the highest grossing films that Kannada cinema has ever seen— Yogaraj Bhat's *Mungaru Maley* (2006).

Mungaru Maley is different from most of the other films discussed in this chapter because it contains very little violence and has a well-to-do protagonist. It begins with Preetham (Ganesh) catching sight of Nandini (Pooja Gandhi) outside a Bangalore shopping mall and being so smitten that he steps accidentally into a manhole. Nandini helps him out but she departs, also leaving behind a jewelled watch. The rest of the film is about Preetham and his mother in Kodagu, where she is visiting a friend—the wife of a decorated Kodava army officer and coffee planter named Subbaiah (Ananth Nag). Nandini is Subbaiah's daughter and Preetham gradually learns many facts. Preetham is in Kodagu with his mother to attend her wedding to a junior army officer who once saved Subbaiah's life. Preetham intends to leave but the girl teases him, coaxing him to remain behind, and press his suit. Preetham returns, the girl gradually returns his love, and consents to elope with him. Still, events make Preetham eventually realize that Nandini is not for him. After letting the girl understand this and saving the actual bridegroom from the villain, he leaves finally for Bangalore.

At first glance *Mungaru Maley* does not appear to have much to do with Bangalore city, but the first cause out of which the action emerges is Preetham's spotting Nandini outside a cantonment mall. The 'first cause' is crucial in the relay of the meaning in Indian popular cinema[22] and the meaning in both *Majestic* and *Duniya* materializes out of the protagonists' first encounter with the monstrousness of Bangalore city. But the cultural identities of the protagonists in *Mungaru Maley* still need to be recognized before we interpret the first cause.

Preetham may be identified as a well-to-do constituent of the region and his domineering father is a businessman—with connections in the government because policemen recognize him respectfully. Preetham is looked upon as a wastrel by his father and Preetham in turn, resents him. Nandini, on the other hand, is a Kodava and the daughter of a *national* hero. Kodavas have not generally been identified with Kannada speakers perhaps because they have been highly anglicized, often connecting directly with the nation. Two of India's greatest generals have been Kodava but they are rarely celebrated as local heroes—*Muthina Hara* (1990) was also about the Kodava as a national hero. It can therefore be argued that Nandini's identity, despite her speaking Kannada, is pan-Indian just as Preetham's is regional. The pan-Indian and the regional identities are not mutually exclusive but intersect, which does not mean that there is no tension between them. If this is conceded, the first cause is interpretable as the constituent of the region's love/desire being awakened by a woman with a pan-Indian identity in a space straddling two worlds—the region and global India (a shopping mall is the most visible sign of the 'global' in Bangalore).

An aspect of *Mungaru Male* which is intriguing is why the film is a 'tragedy' or why circumstances could not have been arranged so that Preetham marries Nandini—because there is no class barrier separating them. I will argue that the gap between them is 'unbridgeable' because of the social distance it allegorizes, a gap not between individuals but between the identities they represent. It is perhaps because the disparity between the regional and the pan-Indian identity in Bangalore is perceived to be so large that *Mungaru Male* is conceived as a tragedy.

Preetham has a pet rabbit which he names Devdas (after the icon of unrequited love). At the conclusion he tries to address the rabbit cheerfully on the notion of 'sacrifice' in love but the rodent expires abruptly and Preetham is heartbroken. The insertion of the animal into the story is strange but even stranger is an insipid 'joke' that assumes disproportionate importance. Preetham explains that 'Devdas' is wanted by the police for raping an elephant. The meaning is evidently the unfairness of a creature as mild and inoffensive as a rabbit being accused of an act so horrific. *Mungaru Male* is also implicit that the rabbit is Preetham's alter-ego and the death of the rabbit hurts him more than the loss of the heroine. It is significant that being mild and peace-loving is an important component of the constituents of the region's self-image.[23] If the rabbit's qualities are equated with theirs, the question is why the issue of 'rape' should be introduced but the issue of safety of women employees of new economy companies was current when the film was made because of a horrific rape and murder case which was then in the news.[24]

An aspect of the film that still needs reading is Preetham's oedipal conflict with his father. The father, although a businessman, is connected to the state through the incident of the policeman greeting him respectfully. It can be argued that the proximity between the father and the state and the estrangement between Preetham and his father covertly distances Preetham from the state. This discourse is perhaps comparable to that in *Majestic* and *Duniya* in which the state/state authority is the adversary of the respective protagonists.

As brought out frequently the mother is a recurring presence in Kannada cinema and has often represented the notion that confers her/his identity upon the constituent of the region. The tragedies in *Jogi* and *Duniya* arise because of Bangalore (as seductress) coming between the protagonist and his duty to his mother because the protagonist is distracted by Bangalore when his mother is dying. *Mungaru Male* is apparently different but it is Preetham's mother who puts the final seal of *disapproval* on his wooing of Nandini. On the evidence of these films one might say that the mother and Bangalore stand on opposite sides of the protagonist. 'Bangalore' is attractive but it is also either treacherous or inaccessible. Preetham suggests to his mother in *Mungaru Male* that she divorce his father and the sought for separation is perhaps between Bangalore and the region.[25]

The Supernatural and the Global

The remake in Kannada of a film made in another language is always difficult to interpret because the motifs originate in another milieu. At the same time it must be pertinent locally at least in a broad or abstract way and it is only this broad pertinence that I discovered in *Appu*. There are two films made in 2004 dealing with the supernatural which were originally made in other languages and at least one of which was phenomenally successful in Kannada. Sanjeevi's *Swetha Naga* is about a researcher in zoology—who is skeptical about the mythology around the cobra—who ventures into a forest. Madhu (Soundarya) finds certain sacred texts—the Nagashastra—with a tribe of snake worshippers but the manuscripts are watched over by a cobra said to be hundreds of years old. The tension in the story comes from the girl encountering an ascetic and the white snake which is his deity, she becoming a believer but unable to convince her prospective parents-in-law that her transformed state of receptiveness is not insanity. P. Vasu's *Apthamitra* (2004) is a ghost story about a road construction engineer Ramesh (Ramesh Arvind) who acquires a palace rumoured to be haunted. The palace once belonged to a king who had the dancer Nagavalli as his mistress. Nagavalli was burnt alive for being unfaithful. Although warned, Ramesh's sceptical wife Ganga (Soundarya) unlocks the haunted room in question and is possessed by the spirit of the dead Nagavalli. Doctor Vijay (Vishnuvardhan) is a psychiatrist who finds the means to cure Ganga with the help of an occultist (Avinash).

Before we go on to examine aspects of these two films it is pertinent to say that mainstream Hindi cinema has rarely dealt with the supernatural in this way. Popular cinema has been loosely termed 'fantastic' but, by and large, mainstream Hindi films do not find correspondence in the definition of fantasy generally cited[26] which concentrates on the response generated by the 'fantastic' events in the story. In this light, fantasy must be considered not just one mode but three. 'Fantasy' creates a situation in which the reader/audience experiences feelings of hesitation and awe provoked by strange, improbable events. If the implausibility of the events can be explained rationally or psychologically (for example, as a dream, hallucination), then the term 'uncanny' is applied. In stories like *Lord of the Rings*, in which an alternative world or reality is created, the term 'marvellous' is considered most appropriate to describe the work.

With the exception of films dealing with reincarnation (*Om Shanti Om*, 2007), mainstream Hindi 'fantasies' like *Mahal* (1949) and *Bees Saal Baad* (1962) are in the realm of the 'uncanny' because of the rational explanation offered. The issue of 'superstition' became central with the reform movements of the nineteenth and early twentieth century and the modern ideal was duly incorporated into the Nehruvian idea of the nation. When Kannada art cinema, in its first decade, tries to be pan-Indian, it specifically targets superstition and religious exploitation as in *Chomana Dudi* and *Ghatashraddha*. Reincarnation is a 'superstition' not disallowed perhaps because it is the one of the cornerstones of Hindu religious belief. When one looks for ghost stories in Hindi cinema, therefore, one looks *outside the mainstream* to films like those by the Ramsay brothers, *Purana Mandir* (1984), for example. This is because, unlike the mainstream Hindi film which addresses a national audience, 'B' category Hindi cinema—like Kannada cinema—addresses sections living on the margins. This is why 'B' category cinema does not show in the city multiplexes but in the smaller towns—and in Chandni Chowk rather than New Delhi.

The two Kannada films of 2004 are both 'fantastic' in as much as their supernatural side is sustained and not subsequently superseded by a rational explanation for the strange happenings. If one were to look for common motifs in the two films, both are about 'rationalists' who come face to face with the unexplainable and find themselves transformed despite themselves. More importantly perhaps, their marital lives or prospects of marriage are severely endangered by those who doubt that supernatural causes are behind their transformation. In *Apthamitra*, Ganga (possessed by Nagavalli) tries to seduce a married man—who Nagavalli's spirit has taken to be her former lover from 150 years before—but Ramesh will not believe that it is not Ganga who is acting this way but Nagavalli, through her. In *Swetha Naga*, Madhu is engaged to be married but her prospective in-laws hastily call off the marriage when they see her in her transformed state.

The narrative motif involving marriage ties or pairing thrown into crisis has not been employed often by Kannada cinema. When employed, it is related to a threat of some sort faced by the region which might endanger traditional values associated with it. In the late 1950s, *Rayara Sose* employs the motif to problematize the threat of wealth prevailing over the traditional notion of hierarchy. I explained in Chapter 2 how *Keralida Simha* and *Sahasa Simha* used the motif in the early 1980s when the nation state was beleaguered. In the late 1970s, *Na Ninna Bidalare*, which is also 'fantastic' by the accepted definition, threw marriage into crisis to signify the threat to endogamy from the cosmopolitan city. *Apthamitra* and *Swetha Naga* locate the threat to the family in skepticism and science although they make a token gesture towards pseudo-science (for example, parapsychology in *Apthamitra*). While on their own they may be considered regressive, they have other contextual implications.

The blaming of science for threatening the family might have been equated with the threat of the 'modern'—which sometimes finds reflection in 'luddite' alarm in Hindi cinema of the 1950s[27]—if

Kannada cinema had not consistently demonstrated its immunity to the threat. In *Apthamitra* the occultist is described as having demonstrated his powers all over the world and he acknowledges that he knew of Doctor Vijay when in the United States, because his book on parapsychology was recommended to him by an American professor. Since Hindi cinema responded to the 'global' with alarm in the early years of the new millennium just as it responded to the 'modern' in the 1950s,[28] it can be argued that it is the 'global' which is the threat in *Apthamitra* rather than the 'modern'. Significantly, the 'global' in Hindi cinema is also seen to endanger marital ties in films like *Jism* (2002), *Jurm* (2005), and *Aitraaz* (2004), but the motifs are not supernatural but pertain to the adulterous woman, who acquires her behavioural vocabulary in a global milieu. There is a sense to be had in the two kinds of cinema, of Hindi film audiences being closer to the everyday effects of globalization than their regional counterparts, to whom globalization is relatively distant because it threatens in more exceptional circumstances.

Another factor that may be important in *Apthamitra* is that Ganga, when possessed by Nagavalli's spirit, speaks Telugu—just as Regan speaks tongues other than English when possessed in *The Exorcist*. Telugu is a language familiar to those who speak Kannada but here it becomes sinister. Regional language films today frequently include characters from other regions or states. In the Malayalam film *Chattambi Nadu* (2009), Mammooty plays Veerendra Malayya who is apparently from Bellary in Karnataka. Recent Telugu cinema also frequently has villains from Bihar.[29] There is an effort to render the Telugu language exotic in *Apthamitra*, and this is perhaps comparable to international cinema after 2000—like Tarantino's *Inglourious Basterds* (2009) in which, too, the other language is made exotic and yet sinister. Pundits of globalization predicted that while globalization would bring nations closer, the result of the increasing intensity of contact and communication between the nation-states and other agencies would also produce a clashing of cultures, which could lead to heightened attempts to draw boundaries between the home country and the others.[30] India being home to so many languages, globalization may have led to a comparable 'intra-national' phenomenon. Globalization is the result of capital, production, and labour being endowed with unprecedented mobility[31] and this is happening within India as well. The process may be leading to a situation where different language-based cultures within India are coming closer but there is also significant resistance, that include attempts to erect cultural boundaries. A fair proportion of Kannada speakers understand Telugu but in *Apthamitra* there is an attempt to turn Telugu into an exotic yet threatening cultural object. In Sudeep's *My Autograph* (2006), which is also a remake, the same 'attraction-repulsion syndrome' finds expression when the male protagonist (Sudeep) is in Kerala where he loves a local girl, whom he can understand only through an interpreter but who returns his love. He is, however, not allowed to marry the girl and is even physically hurt by the locals.

Actors and Directors

One useful way of dividing Kannada cinema into two eras would be to look at the films after Rajkumar's departure from the screen differently. The star, as explained in this book, dominated the Kannada film from the mid 1950s onwards and embodied a cultural space—after it had become politically defunct but still needed to be imagined in order to give a people their regional identity. After Mysore fades from memory, his *Akasmika* (1993) still attempts to invoke its values, and the film stands as a bulwark against the trends contemporary to it.

Vishnuvardhan, who passed away in 2009, was the most important male star after Rajkumar. It can be argued that since the nation is nearly as important to Kannada film audiences as the region, in the period when Rajkumar's presence still dominated the milieu, Vishnuvardhan sometimes represents the national component in the identity of the constituent of the region. In films like *Muthina Hara* (1990) and *Nishabda* (1998), his role as soldier suggests this. Comparing Rajkumar's *Keralida Simha* (1981) and Vishnuvardhan's *Sahasa Simha* (1982), while both play police officers, the one played by Rajkumar is homegrown while the one in *Sahasa Simha* is associated with Bombay and the nation.

It is difficult to assert that any of the other male stars have played key roles in the development of Kannada cinema although Shankar Nag, Ambarish, Srinath, and Ravichandran have had their fan followings. From the 1990s onwards two talented stars with distinctive contributions have been Upendra and Jaggesh, both of whom capitalized on Kannada cinema's low and abusive tendencies of the 1990s, which I have already speculated about. The new millennium perhaps belongs to Shivaraj Kumar, Puneeth Rajkumar, and Ganesh as stars, and Ramesh Arvind as an actor, although it is too early to say what they represent. In any case, with no stable regional identity replacing the one associated with the defunct Mysore, the possibility of a towering male star emerging in Kannada cinema appears slight.

In writing about the rise of new Telugu stars after N.T. Rama Rao abruptly quit cinema and entered politics, S.V. Srinivas proposes that representational techniques identified with established stars began to be deployed to shore up the fortunes of relative newcomers and to create new stars.[32] Rajkumar dominated Kannada cinema even more than N.T. Rama Rao did Telugu cinema but his exit was far from abrupt. It could in fact be asserted that while his image depended on recollections of Mysore, Mysore faded away sooner than he did. His last film as hero, *Akasmika*, as I have repeatedly argued, was almost a tragic attempt to uphold a cultural space all but forgotten.

As regards heroines in Kannada cinema the situation is somewhat different because no female film star lasts longer than a few films today. As I have already argued, the wife or romantic heroine in Kannada cinema has embodied, in a sense, the constituents of the region. As long as the region was synonymous with Mysore as it was recollected, women film stars like Pandari Bai, Leelavathi, B. Saroja Devi, Jayanthi, Kalpana, and Arathi could embody its constituents. It is significant here that female stars like Saroja Devi, Kalpana, and Arathi—with stronger personas—emerged after 1956 when Mysore, being defunct as a political entity, needed to be 'brought to life' in the imagination of the region's constituents—to give them an identity and a self-image. After the 1980s, however, with imagined Mysore moribund, the feminine presences grow weaker and weaker. Malasri, the tomboy-turned-submissive-wife in *Nanjundi Kalyana* (1989), may appear the exception but her repertoire today excludes romance and conjugality. Many heroines today are from Punjab, Gujarat, or Bengal, as though the constituents of the region have an indeterminate identity.

Coming to the directors, Kannada cinema started with a few important directors like R. Nagendra Rao (*Vijayanagarada Veeraputra*), H.L.N. Simha (*Bedara Kannappa*), B.R. Panthulu

(*School Master*), M.R. Vittal (*Nandadeepa*), and B.S. Ranga (*Amarashilpi Jakanachari*), and the important directors in the middle period include G.V. Iyer (*Bhoodana*), Hunsur Krishnamurthy (*Satya Harishchandra*). Directors outside the mainstream in the 1960s include N. Lakshminarayan (*Naandi*), whose films have been regarded as precursors to Kannada art cinema.[33] Lakshminarayan used Rajkumar but still made films in which his star appeal was subdued as in *Uyyale* (1970). Also of importance here is M.V. Krishna Swamy, whose *Subba Sastry* (1966) is based on the Kannada play *Ashadabuthi* by A.N. Murthy Rao, which is an adaptation of Moliere's *Tartuffe*. I have not examined these directors' work because their importance lies elsewhere rather than in the construction of the regional identity. Krishna Swamy, for instance, worked with Roberto Rosselini and later played a big part in the film society movement in Bangalore in the early years, where Kannada art cinema may have originated.

Rajkumar dominated Kannada cinema from the late 1950s onwards but it is only in the 1970s that his presence begins to dictate the content of a film. The notion of the actor as 'parallel text' has been used to study the way major stars like Amitabh Bachchan influence the text.[34] Rajkumar was more important to Kannada cinema than Amitabh Bachchan has been to the Hindi mainstream film because his presence defined the self-image of the region. Since Rajkumar's presence dictates the content, the directors of his films have little or no 'authorial role', and filmmakers like Siddalingaiah have a greater say in films in which he is absent—like *Bhoothayyana Maga Ayyu* (1974). Puttanna Kanagal's importance to Kannada cinema lies in his films drawing audiences on the strength of his directorial presence—when Kannada cinema was virtually synonymous with Rajkumar. After Rajkumar's retirement from the screen, the only exceptional directorial presence may have been Upendra (*A*), who flourished briefly until his kind of cinema lost favour.

Kannada art cinema after *Samskara*, as already explained in Chapter 2, has not played a part in the construction of the regional identity but has tried to be a national cinema. The best known art film director in Kannada today is Girish Kasaravalli, whose *Ghatashraddha* (1977) has been written about. *Thayi Saheba* (1997), perhaps his most celebrated film, is informed by theoretical discourses in the cultural space of the nation and is a reexamination of the freedom from a feminist and post-colonial perspective.[35] Other filmmakers outside the mainstream who have been recently active are T.S. Nagabharana who also directed *Akasmika*, litterateur Baragur Ramachandrappa (*Shanti*, 2004), and Kavitha Lankesh. To give the reader a rough idea of the pre-occupations of Kannada art cinema today, Kavitha Lankesh's *Deveeri* (1999) deals with the migrant like many Kannada films after 2000. Where this film differs is in its emphasis on produc-ing an authentic picture of slum life. The woman protagonist is played by Nandita Das[36] and the story is told from the viewpoint of a little boy, Deveeri's younger brother. Although this is not specified the girl is apparently being drawn into the flesh trade and the film is—like *Kaadu* and *Ghatashraddha*—entirely about the child's awakening to this 'social reality'. The use of low Kannada is also not with the intention of being irreverent as in *Tarle Nan Maga* but an effort to be authetic. The film might equally have been set in a city other than Bangalore, an observation that cannot be made about *Duniya*. In *Deveeri* and a subsequent film, *Bimba* (2004), Kavitha Lankesh also attempts an exposé of the film industry, as if to distance herself from its doings and goings-on. This is different from Upendra's approach in *A* when he deals with its sordidness as an insider/participant might—because he shares responsibility for it.

Conclusion

Shrinking Constituency

There are various ways in which an inquiry such as this one can be concluded and while one would be to predict the direction that Kannada cinema might take, another would be to speculate about the 'psyche' of the constituent of the region. I began the enquiry into Kannada language cinema with the assumption that this cinema addressed the people of Karnataka. With the linguistic reorganization of the states, Kannada is the language spoken in Karnataka and that was the basis of the assumption. In the course of the inquiry, however, it has been gradually revealed that Kannada cinema has had as its constituency the people of princely Mysore and that, after the creation of greater Mysore in 1956, it continued to address only the same constituency. While it made attempts to include the entire 'Kannada nation' in its address and extend its reach, these attempts of Kannada cinema were sporadic—for example, *Sri Krishnadevaraya*, *Akasmika*—and largely from Rajkumar.

To take a view on how Kannada cinema regards Karnataka today, one could say that the state is segmented into three partly overlapping territories, and while the first territory ('the region') is the geographic space once constituting princely Mysore, the second is apparently Bangalore. Kannada cinema today regards as its major constituency those with their roots in the first territory but economically dependent on Bangalore. The third territory is constituted by the Kannada-speaking areas excluded by the first two, a territory that Kannada cinema generally declines to address. The 'region', which we might have taken to be Karnataka, appears to be shrinking steadily. Kannada films are, today, not even about those living in the rural areas and small towns of 'old' Mysore—if they are without affinities and associations in Bangalore. If we recollect, there was hope in films like *Bedara Kannappa* that with the integration of the poorer Kannada speaking areas with Mysore, they would gain a community. Judging entirely by the evidence of Kannada cinema, this has not happened. The 'community' has actually depleted with films in the past few years identifying migrants in Bangalore as the category to be addressed. It is difficult to see the direction taken by Kannada cinema as viable in the long term because the 'migrant' is not a permanent category. The film industry is apparently also under threat because of declining receipts.[1] The Karnataka Film Chamber of Commerce (KFCC) has responded by attempting to neutralize competition from other language films. It has laid down norms under which non-Kannada films may be exhibited in the state and a recent casualty was Rakesh Roshan's *Kites* (2010), which was initially 'banned' by the KFCC for violating the norms.[2] The agitating done periodically by the film industry is in the name of 'Kannada culture' but, as already suggested in this inquiry, Kannada cinema addresses only a sub-region and not the Kannada-speaking areas as a whole. If some Kannada cinema is shown in the Kannada-speaking areas outside the 'region', that is because there is an audience there which connects with the region—economically or through other associations—and not because the region has been extended to include their space. There have, however, been one or two unusual films which are conspicuously set outside the territory once constituting Mysore and Shankar Nag's *Minchina Ota* (1980), which is inspired by *Butch Cassidy and the Sundance Kid* (1969) and set in Dharwad, may serve as a model for a Kannada cinema not rooted in Mysore.

Mysoreans, Bangaloreans, Kannadigas, Indians

Judging from the covert segmentation of Karnataka by Kannada cinema it would appear that those who speak Kannada as a principal language ('Kannadigas') can be subdivided into three categories:

A. Those from the 'region' as defined by the cinema, that is, from the areas that once constituted princely Mysore. This category, which has all but forgotten the princely state, still honours its former codes, especially its deference to traditional hierarchy. This would include a category of migrants in Bangalore who are originally from the region.

B. Entrenched Bangaloreans who are cosmopolitan in spirit and 'sophisticated' and in whose service the state is now largely functioning (for example, the male protagonist of *Mungaru Maley*). Entrenched Bangaloreans are to be distinguished from a separate pan-Indian category associated with Bangalore which, unlike 'B', had never had any connections with Mysore. This would include some who speak Kannada as a principal language (for example, the heroine of *Mungaru Maley*) but also others who speak it hesitantly or not at all.[3]

C. Those Kannadigas from outside the 'Mysore' areas whom Kannada cinema appears to regard as outside its purview. Since Kannada cinema has never dealt with this category in its stories except peripherally and only occasionally, we may presume that to those from the region, the category 'C' Kannadiga is an uncertain quantity because they rarely interface with them.

Princely Mysore once regarded itself as a 'nation within a nation' and it would seem that the region's constituents still regard themselves in the same way. The unbridgeable gap between the male protagonist and the girl in *Mungaru Maley* is, therefore, actually comparable to the one between the protagonist of the Hindi film *Rang De Basanti* (2006) and the British girl, whom he can never marry because she is from outside the nation.[4] Since it is former Mysore and not Karnataka that is the 'nation within the nation', Kannadigas from outside the region have the same status as non-Kannadigas, that is, they are 'Indian' rather than from within the region and are excluded from the 'community'. The association of Belgaum and Hubli with India in *Bangarada Manushya* and *Akasmika* respectively also suggests this. The position of the non-Mysore Kannadiga may appear similar to those from Telengana in Telugu cinema but while Telenaganites complain that their images are distorted,[5] the non-Mysore

Kannadiga is not represented at all. To describe the constituents of the region as a 'community' should not be taken to mean that they share an object of loyalty or have a common purpose. The community is exclusive, which does not mean that it is cohesive. In the low-life films like *Duniya* and *Jogi* the bloody conflict is entirely within the community. In *America! America!*, there is no community of Indians or Kannadigas in America but only of immigrants from the region. This suggests that even after sixty years of Independence, the Indian nation has not penetrated the region enough to weaken the distinction between its constituents and other Indians in Kannada cinema—even those who speak Kannada. It may be remarked here that Tamil films have often been remade successfully in Hindi,[6] which is not true of Kannada cinema. This is arguably because the space of Tamil cinema (once part of British India) is more 'penetrated by the Indian nation' than is the 'region' and the nation is inscribed in Tamil cinema—even when Tamil politics has taken an adversarial position vis-à-vis the centre. As I have argued earlier, the Indian nation in Kannada cinema is synonymous with its authority—usually in the shape of the policeman—and this is different from a Tamil film like *Roja* or *Bombay* in which the nation is signified in ways comparable to Hindi cinema.[7]

During my study, I have demonstrated how Kannada cinema tries to discard its attributes to align itself with 'national' preoccupations. Progressively abandoned as film motifs after 1956 are those from mythology and local history, as well as those pertaining to endogamy and the sacred joint family. The discarding of these motifs has been associated with the fading of Mysore and princely rule from public memory. While the changes in Kannada cinema can also be attributed to the pull of the nation, the cinema of the new millennium makes us aware of how certain notions are still 'inviolable'. Despite its transformation, Kannada cinema continues to respect the notion of hierarchy as a *moral principle*, and the relationship between the hero and the heroine still allegorizes the exemplary one between the monarch and his subjects, although 'king' is now replaced by 'region'. The hierarchical position of the film hero within the story has declined from the 1970s and this corresponds to the lowering of the region's self-image. The abusive Kannada of the 1990s leaves Kannada cinema but low Kannada is still favoured in accordance with this decline.

Kannada cinema's partiality for 'low life' should not be taken to mean that the audiences whose concerns it addresses come from the same social segments that its films are about. That would be like imagining that the films about the rich in Hindi cinema are only consumed by the rich. If consuming popular cinema involves 'projection' of some kind, it is evidently possible to project oneself into characters from outside one's own social class. Kannada cinema addresses the constituents of the region, a category that dominates the political class[8] and the cultural establishment in Karnataka. Kannada cinema's vision of low life touching a chord in the constituents of the region suggests that—whether high or low—they are able to see themselves in its heroes and this would not have been possible if 'low life' did not have some significance for them. Since this significance is only in relation to Bangalore we need to look specifically at the regional identity in Bangalore and engage in some speculation.

The Regional Identity in Bangalore

Bangalore as an economic space perhaps has greater importance in Karnataka than Chennai has in Tamil Nadu or Hyderabad has in Andhra Pradesh. As against a total of three cities in Karnataka with a population of over 5 lakh, Tamil Nadu and Andhra Pradesh have five cities each.[9] Alternative commercial centres away from Bangalore are hard to identify in Karnataka because of the concentration of industrial activity around the state capital. The population of Bangalore grew from 17 lakh in 1971 to 51 lakh in 2001[10] but is roughly estimated at around 75 lakh in 2009, an increase of 47 per cent in eight years. In the previous decade, the population of Karnataka grew by 17.51 per cent[11] while that of Bangalore grew only by 23.5 per cent. Perhaps more importantly, the population of Karnataka increased from 53 million to around 64 million between 2001 and 2009[12] and the share of Bangalore in Karnataka's population increased from around 9.6 per cent in 2001 to around 11.72 per cent in the eight-year period, suggesting a sharp upward shift in the economic dependence of the state upon the city. It is apparent that Bangalore's importance in the region has grown monstrously in the new millennium and it is only this fact that finds reflection in Kannada cinema.

If Kannada cinema after 2000 has been dominated by violence, there has also been violence in fan activity within Bangalore. The film industry has a curious relationship with Bangalore and any agitation prmoted by it leads to violence in the city. Although it was once involved in larger matters as in the Gokak agitation, the film industry has recently been concerned only with film related issues. The largest disturbance caused by them was perhaps in July-August 2000 when Rajkumar was kidnapped by the notorious poacher and sandalwood smuggler Veerappan and life in the city came to a standstill for three whole days, disturbances continuing for the entire 108 days of the star's captivity. That these disturbances are often in support of 'causes' with no remedy is indicated by the widespread violence sparked off by Rajkumar's death (by natural causes) on 12 April 2006 when public transport and police vehicles were torched and a police constable murdered. Vishnuvardhan's death from a heart attack on 30 December 2009 also saw violence[13] and several public transport buses were burnt. It is convenient to assert that the disturbances were orchestrated, but the nature of the violence witnessed on television[14] suggests that the constituency of Kannada film enthusiasts is united by an impulsive rage. That the violence is confined to Bangalore and does not spill over to the other cities suggests that the object of the anger is specifically Bangalore. Explanations have not been offered hitherto for the recurrent outbursts of anger by Kannada film fans but since fan violence[15] and film motifs are articulated responses from the same constituency, the film researcher could understand the one by interpreting the other—and the film motifs have already been interpreted.

Judging from our experience of Kannada cinema after 2000 it would appear that the region, which has always been ambivalent about Bangalore, has found itself increasingly drawn to dealing with/in the city. Bangalore, which once mediated between the region and the nation, is now inclining towards the nation in the regional psyche.[16] Since my interpretation of Kannada cinema suggests that the region retains many of the characteristics of a 'nation within the nation' because the Indian nation has not fully penetrated it, Bangalore city is perhaps providing a violent cultural interface between the two. The process underway could be the crunching of the regional identity by the subsuming nation—armed in Bangalore by economic power the like of which the region has not seen. The local administration—dominated by politicians from the region—should rightly have have cushioned its impact[17] but the region's corruption has made it deeply susceptible to economic influences.[18] While Bangalore is the major revenue earner in Karnataka, a larger proportion of whatever is earned in the state capital should perhaps be spent to develop the other areas outside, but Bangalore is evidently using up too much of the revenue it is generating. It is perhaps this complicated scenario that sees constituents of the region becoming increasingly antagonistic towards the state—the antagonism even leading to the murder of the police constable on the day of Rajkumar's death.

Resisting the Nation

Judging from our experience of Kannada cinema, it does not appear that linguistic reorganization was successful in creating a single Kannada nation out of the different Kannada-speaking areas brought together. This would require deeper study but the vestiges of Mysore still appear to dominate the 'Kannada community' and the asymmetry in the constitution of the 'Kannada identity' was perhaps accentuated by Bangalore being made the capital of the Kannada state instead of a more appropriate city—like Davanagere or Hubli—which was more centrally located in the Kannada-speaking territory.

The cultural remains of the original princely state perhaps reside in Mysore city, in its palaces and its annual Dasara procession, but there is little evidence that the former Mysore still touches a sentimental chord in the region. In spite of the discouraging situation apparently prevailing with regard to the strength of the region in the local consciousness, the regional identity still resists subsumption by the nation. If such resistance had not been offered, Kannada cinema, like Hindi cinema, might perhaps have been celebrating wealth and consumption-based lifestyles—in Bangalore rather than Mumbai—instead of dealing with those living on the margins as it has been doing in the past few years.

Mainstream Hindi cinema may still be an 'all-Indian' cinema but it is hardly democratic in its reach. It is evident that since the 1990s its constitution is becoming increasingly asymmetric. I may not even be contradicted if I remark that the non-resident is more important to Hindi cinema than India's rural population or those who live in the small towns. It is in this context that 'minority cinemas' becomes important, because judging from Kannada cinema's role since 1947, they are intermittently engaged in resisting the nation. The national identity has tended to sub-sume other identities within India and it is only proper that it is resisted. At the same time it is evident that within Karnataka itself, Mysore has tended to exercise hegemonic cultural influence over the other Kannada-speaking areas.[19] Perhaps the time is ripe for other kinds of cinema in Kannada to appear and resist the region's hegemony in the same way that Kannada cinema is resisting the nation.

Notes

Introduction

1. In fact, it will be difficult to name more than a few art filmmakers whose films have not largely been adaptations of modern literature. Satyajit Ray, Bimal Roy, Mani Kaul, Kumar Shahani, Buddhadeb Dasgupta, and Girish Kasaravalli are among the filmmakers who have been most comfortable adapting modern literature.
2. A 'literary' influence upon popular cinema could however be the cheap literature—romantic or fantastic—produced in Urdu and Hindi. For a study of this literature see Pritchett (1985).
3. Lutze (1985a), p. 39.
4. Under the direct influence of Prime Minister Indira Gandhi, the FFC initiated 'New Indian Cinema' by financing Mani Kaul's *Uski Roti* (1969) and Mrinal Sen's *Bhuvan Shome* (1969). See Rajadhyaksha and Willemen (1995), pp. 150–1. The first Kannada art film was Pattabhirama Reddy's *Samskara* (1970). While this film was not funded by FFC and appeared to address local issues, the art films that followed may be regarded as having been inspired by the pan-national art film movement. This is supported by recent Kannada art cinema getting recognition at the national level but receiving substantially less local attention.
5. For a rudimentary account of the notion of co-authorship, see Real (1996), pp. 268–70.
6. This follows from Sudhir Kakar's remarks: 'The prospect of financial gain, like the opportunity for sexual liaison, does wonderful things for increasing the perception of the needs and desires of those who hold the key to these gratifications ... [Filmmakers] must intuitively

appeal to those concerns of the audience which are shared' (1980: 13).

7. Raghavendra (2008), pp. 228–30.

8. Ibid., pp. 24–68.

9. See Bordwell (1996), pp. 26–30. With specific reference to study of society in Karnataka it has been noted that Marxists, for instance, have underestimated local factors like caste when they cannot be easily approximated to class. Marxist studies have over time tended to concentrate on describing Indian reality rather than on predicting the course of change—that is, tended towards empiricism. See Pani (1998), pp. 64–84.

10. *Karnataka State Gazeteer* (1983), p. 6.

11. With Bangalore as the centre of film production. See Ramakrishnaiah (1992), pp. 2–4.

12. Raghavendra (2008), p. 22.

13. It has been argued that 'all-India' was a market created by colonial capital and subsequently taken over by the Indian bourgeoisie. If the print media has adopted English as the practical language for 'all-India' communication, the propagation of a peculiarly neutral, aseptic, non-literary brand of Hindi in the audiovisual media (radio, cinema, television) goes some direction in flattening out local nuance and difference. See Chatterjee (1997), p. 152.

14. Lutze (1985b), p. 5. Mainstream Hindi cinema has perhaps the same relationship to the regional cinemas as classical literature (and myth) in India has to 'folklore'. A.K. Ramanujan notes how folklore 'domesticates' classical literature when it draws from it. He cites a folk version of the Ramayana in which Rama blows his nose and his mucus drops into the Ganges River and considers this impossible in the Sanskrit text. He also cites instances where the menstrual blood of goddesses features in folk narratives. See Ramanujan (1986), pp. 65–6.

15. Karnataka has no regional political party and the national political parties have also ruled the state. In contrast, the strength of the DMK and the AIADMK in Tamil Nadu and the TDP in Andhra Pradesh points to politics in Andhra and Tamil Nadu embarking independently with less reliance upon political dispensations from the centre. If a relationship is inferred between a local political choice and local identity, one might suppose that the regional/local Tamil and Telugu identities are more likely to resist the subsuming tendency of the national identity.

16. Manor (1977a) and Hettne (1978).

17. The chieftains were called *polegar*s, local power-holders who were normally in charge of 20 villages—a political unit known as *pollam*. See Hettne (1978), pp. 30–1.

18. Nagar was stronghold of the former Dewan Rama Rao's family who were Brahmins. Conflict apparently broke out when Krishna Rao, a nephew of Rama Rao, was replaced by Vira Raj Urs as *foujdar* (commandant) of the Nagar division, Urs being of the same caste as the maharaja and a Kshatriya. This suggests that a Brahmin–Kshatriya cleavage could have contributed to the insurrection of 1830. See Hettne (1978), pp. 32–3.

19. According to the census the Arasus numbered less than 1,000 around this time. *Census of India, 1891*, XXV (4), p. 80, cited in Iyer (1928, II), pp. 47–73.

20. According to the census of 1931, Brahmins constituted 3.8 per cent of the population, Veerashaivas 12 per cent, and Vokkaligas 20.4 per cent. The category later to be termed 'scheduled castes' constituted 15.1 per cent of the population and Muslims 5.8 per cent. See *Census of India, 1931*, XXV (2), p. 230.

21. Björn Hettne (1978), pp. 28–9.

22. Ibid., p. 44.

23. Ibid., p. 37.

24. This may be partly responsible for the position of Karnataka as the most corrupt state in south India. Study conducted by Centre for Media Studies, Delhi, June 2005. See http://www.cmsindia.org/cms/events/corruption.pdf

25. *Census of India, 1931*, XXV (2), p. 230. The Veerashaivas are not a caste but a sect arising out of the Bhakti movement in the twelfth century and founded by a religious reformer.

26. *Census of India, 1951*, I (2b), pp. 2–13. This is as a percentage of total population engaged in agriculture.

27. *Census of India, 1941*, XXIII (4), pp. 24–5.

28. *The Mysore Gazette* (1937), I, pp. 251–2.

29. Manor (1977a), pp. 40–4.

30. Hettne (1978), pp. 70–8.

31. Ibid., p. 140.

32. Raghavendra (2008), pp. 24–68.

33. Lutze (1985b), p. 5.

34. Prasad (1999), pp. 50–1.

35. Borges (1999), 'From Allegories to Novels', pp. 339–40.

36. Mishra (2002), pp. 5–6. Mishra regards the epics as the origins of discursivity in Bollywood and this is equally true of the Kannada films just discussed. The Ramayana and the Mahabharata are crucial, Mishra argues, because they are precursor texts that govern the formation of Indian popular cinema.

37. Chatterjee (1993), pp. 5–6.

38. Since we use the term 'modern' in Indian cinema in different contexts, the first modern (to which Phalke responded) was mediated

by colonialism while the second (in the 1950s) was mediated by Nehruvian nationalism and the independent nation.

39. Rajadhyaksha (1987), p. 67.
40. Kapur (1987), p. 82.
41. The mythological element in *Gunasagari* is, specifically, Lord Shiva appearing in the shape of a bear and intervening in the action.
42. Sudraka, *The Little Clay Cart* (trans. Revilo Pendleton Oliver), in Wells (1964), pp. 122–3.
43. Nandy (1980), pp. 22–40.
44. A queen apart from being the king's wife is also his subject.
45. Barthes (1973), 'Myth Today', p. 143.
46. An example is the Telugu film *Ramudu Bheemudu* (1964) which allegorized the subdued India after the Chinese debacle and provided recompense through the aggressive twin brother being remade as *Ram Aur Shyam* (1967) and *Seeta Aur Geeta* (1972). This tendency can be attributed to Indian aesthetics/dramatics being primarily concerned with the capture of the 'immutable'. See Raghavendra (2008), pp. 158–60.
47. Caste becomes important in the 1980s in films like *Qayamat Se Qayamat Tak* (1988) and J.P. Dutta's *Ghulami* (1985), *Batwara* (1989), and *Hathyar* (1989). See Raghavendra (2008), pp. 224–7.
48. See Randorguy's blog, *The Kannada Cinema Pioneer—Nagendra Rao*, http://www.galatta.com/community/blog_entry.php?user=randorguy&blogentry_id=5032.
49. From the Monier-Williams' Sanskrit-English Dictionary (1979).
50. Dumont (1970), p. 259.
51. For an inquiry into how genealogy is made to figure in Hindi cinema see Mishra (1985), pp. 133–46.
52. See, for instance, Lannoy (1971),

> It has often been said that India has no indigenous ethical system that it has concentrated more on the mystical apprehension of an ultimate reality which transcends good and evil than on differentiating between good and evil acts. At best, so this theory runs, the pluralistic society of India has evolved a pluralistic religious system in which the sole ethical featured shared in common by all its elements is that of moral relativism. (p. 294)

> The perceived 'moral relativism' of Indian society is apparently founded on caste but since caste distinctions are officially taboo in India, birth and lineage become acceptable substitutes in cinema.

53. The wicked zamindars of the 1950s, the moneylender Sukhilala from *Aurat* (1940) and its remake *Mother India* (1957), for instance, appear to be departures. They seem to owe to the reformism and the reformism of the 1930s and the political radicalism of the 1950s, rather than to the code of dharma.

54. Nandy (1980), p. 22. See also, Nandy (1983), p. 25.
55. A. Philip Lutgendorf observes this shot composition and editing strategy in *Jai Santoshi Maa* (1975). See Lutgendorf (2002), p. 28. Also see Raghavendra (2008), p. 64.
56. This is the central hypotheses of scholars like Chakravarty (1998) and Prasad (1999).
57. Raghavendra (2008), pp. 102–27.
58. Manor (1977a), p. 1.
59. Chakravarty (1998), p. 99.
60. Manor (1977a), pp. 81–2.
61. For an account of the agitation for a Kannada-speaking state, see Weiner (1967), pp. 239–55.
62. Muthanna (1980), p. 89.
63. It is not accidental that all the chief ministers after the reorganization and up to 1973 were Veerashaivas.
64. Diwakar (1968), pp. 950–9.
65. See Jameson (1987).
66. The most exhaustively informative work on Kannada cinema is its first encyclopaedia—Vijaya and Subba Rao (2001). Copies of this encyclopaedia are hard to come by; other helpful works are Puttaswamy (2009), which appears to owe quite a lot to this encyclopaedia, and also an earlier work, Mudaliar (1998).

Chapter 1

1. Kothari (1964), pp. 1162–4.
2. The person was S. Chennaiah—who had been of assistance to the non-Brahmin associations in the 1930 and to the Congress after the 1937 merger. See Manor (1977a), p. 165.
3. Ibid., pp. 169–71.
4. Ibid., pp. 177–80.
5. Ibid.
6. Wood and Hammond (1975), p. 146.
7. Hettne (1978), pp. 341–2.
8. Rajadhyaksha and Willemen (1995), p. 329.
9. Asuras are not demons in the Christian sense but simply the opposite of what the gods represent. They are associated with the non-Aryan cults in the Vedas.
10. This relationship of quasi-equality between man and god may actually be closer to Brahminical or Vedic Hinduism because it was the later bhakti movement which emphasized the notion of the personal inadequacy of the worshipper and introduced an element of self-abasement into devotion. See Lannoy (1971), p. 206.
11. See, for instance, Vasudevan (2000), pp. 99–121.

12. *Bhakta Kanakadasa* (1960) also uses the motif of the son of a chieftain who becomes abruptly devout after being miraculously saved in battle. The film is being true to a legend here but Kanakadasa's family is resented by a deposed former chieftain who later understands his former adversary's true nature and becomes his follower. Also interesting here is that the motif of the deposed chieftain finds correspondence in Nijalingappa being replaced by B.D. Jatti in 1958 after there was dissension within the Congress although Nijalingappa became chief minister once again in 1962.

13. See Manor (1977a), 'The Formation of a United opposition to princely Autocracy: 1936–37', pp. 95–104.

14. In Hindu society the caste that exercised power (the Kshatriyas) was not the uppermost caste. The uppermost caste (the Brahmins) did not exercise power directly. It would therefore appear that the Hindu notion of hierarchy is different from the hierarchy imposed by wealth and access to power. The motif of the wise but poor Brahmin in fables ('*badabrahmana*' in Kannada) derives from a notion of hierarchy in which status is independent of wealth and power. See Dumont (2002), pp. 1–20.

15. For instance, the doctor disguises himself as a holy man and advises the moneylender on his conduct. This lampooning of holy men by the doctor is indication that he is an agent of modernity.

16. See Raghavendra (2008), pp. 129–32.

17. While Ranganna, Gundappa, and Nagappa are names with caste associations, the weakening of caste is suggested by the names given to the children—Gopi, Ravi, Vasu, Radha, and Gowri, which have no such associations.

18. Hettne (1978), 'Industrialise or Perish: The Growth of a Development Strategy', pp. 223–333.

19. See, for instance, see Heath (1977), p. 38.

20. Gavaskar (2003), p. 1114.

21. The characteristics betokening this escapism are identified as: films shot in picturesque hill-stations (instead of the grimy streets of Bombay) as in *Gumraah* (1963); foreign locales as in *Sangam* (1964); glamorous cabarets with Helen as in *Teesri Manzil* (1966); gadgets and sliding doors as in *Jewel Thief* (1967). See Raghavendra (2008), pp. 152–72.

22. Brooks (1985), pp. 11–12.

23. Ibid., p. 5.

24. An example of a schoolteacher as such an emblem in Hindi cinema is *Shri 420* (1955), although it is a woman who is a schoolteacher.

25. Although this aspect has invited no attention, the film bears a resemblance to B.V. Karanth's Kannada realist classic *Chomana Dudi*

(1975), based on a novella of the same name by Shivarama Karanth which was written in the 1930s.

26. Guha (2007), p. 219.

27. For instance, there is a film, N. Lakshminarayana's *Naandi* (1964) which resists such interpretation because it uses the idiom of realism and corresponds to Kannada 'middle cinema'. Laksminarayana later adapted Satyajit Ray's *Charulata* and he may be seen as a precursor of Kannada art cinema, which actually began with *Samskara* (1970). See Chakravarthy (2001), p. 9.

28. The only temple in the village is constructed by Lakshmipathy from the money got by cheating Dasanna.

29. As we saw even domestic melodramas like *Gunasagari* incorporate a mythological element in the shape of the bear which protects the heroine. The first 'social' in Kannada cinema was apparently H.L.N. Simha's *Samsara Nauka* (1936) but in the absence of available prints we cannot assert that it did not contain mythological elements.

30. I refer here to the term 'Camp' as defined by Susan Sontag (1983), pp. 105–20. Among other things, 'Camp sees everything in quotation marks. It's not a lamp but a "lamp", not a woman, but a "woman". To perceive Camp in objects and persons is to Being-as-playing-a-Role. It is the farthest extension, in sensibility, of the metaphor of life as theatre' (p. 109).

31. The protagonist in these Hindi films (who often has a mother and sometimes a sister) has rarely a brother—played by another key actor—which might have indicated the acceptance of the joint family as a convention. When a film shows differences between brothers as in *Gunga Jumna* (1961) or *Upkaar* (1968), this difference is problematized and merits interpretation.

32. Raghavendra (2008), pp. 150–60.

33. Rajadhyaksha and Willemen (1995), pp. 172–3.

34. Foreign trips are a way of bypassing the nation after 1961. With Kannada cinema not having the budgets of films like *Sangam* (1964), *Nandadeepa* (1963) deals with the sojourn as an absence.

35. See Raghavendra (2008), pp. 165–9.

36. Uberoi (2002), p. 327.

37. See, for instance, Shah (1996), pp. 537–42.

38. India held nearly 1,180 sq km of Pakistan while Pakistan had captured only 545 sq km of Indian territory. For a contemporary assessment see 'Silent Guns, Wary Combatants', *Time Magazine* (1 October 1965).

39. The fact that both films were made by B.R. Pathulu can also be used to explain the similarity in the films as owing to the director's personal outlook or beliefs. The reader's attention should however

be drawn to *School Master* having several aspects in common with *Rayara Sose* although that film was not made by Panthulu.

40. Bangalore's first industrial suburb Rajajinagar was built in the early 1960s. See Nair (2005), p. 89.

41. Since the idea of protagonist marrying his friend's sister is first mooted by her parents, we may presume that the hero and heroine belong to the same caste. Later, the hero's mother refers to the heroine's family as that of a '*shanbog*' (village accountant), traditionally a post occupied by Brahmins.

42. Srinivas (1976), p. 5.

43. See Janaki Nair (2005), p. 17.

44. Prasad (1999), p. 69.

45. The nationalist movement in Mysore was largely urban and student driven, and the film is hardly being truthful. The male protagonist of the film (Rajkumar) acquires his nationalist zeal as a student in Mysore but he carries on agitation as a peasant and eventually gives up his life in the struggle.

46. From Patel's death in December 1950 till his illness in 1962 Nehru enjoyed monolithic power. But power abhors a vacuum. So when Nehru was declining physically, in the early 1960s a rival centre of power developed. This was called the Syndicate and it comprised Kamaraj Nadar, Sanjiva Reddy, and S. Nijalingappa, the chief ministers of Madras, Andhra Pradesh, and Mysore respectively, as also Atulya Ghosh and S.K. Patil, party bosses of Bengal and Bombay ... But this ... Syndicate came to wield considerable power in the last years of Nehru's life and it was this Syndicate that helped Shastri to be Prime Minister in 1964 ... (Ghose 1993: 337).

47. Wood and Hammond (1975), p. 148.

48. The man on the flight by the protagonist is identified as 'Rao Bahadur Narasinga Rao' (Aswath), suggesting a wealthy local Brahmin wearing the title bestowed by the princely state.

49. Khilnani (1997), p. 42.

50. 'I read Amitabh as a "sub-text" which destabilizes the "positive" continuities we have detected in filmic discourse. But the "sub-text" becomes a fully-fledged parallel text and displaces the filmic text itself: the actor becomes the film.' See Mishra (1985), pp. 142–5.

51. Chakravarthy (2001), pp. 8–10. It may be inaccurate to regard them as 'phases' because they often exist concurrently. The last mythological films were made in the 1980s.

52. Nagaraj (2006), p. 105.

53. The most important study is perhaps Pandian (1992).

54. For an examination of the atheism in *Parasakhti*, see, Raghavendra (2009b), '*Parasakthi*: Agnosticism and the Ideological Hero', pp. 47–55.

55. N.T. Rama Rao's TDP was perceived as 'Hindu revivalism' because it took the side of Telugu against the elite Urdu of the Nizam.

   [Unlike in the north] in the south Urdu was always a minority and elite language. In Andhra Pradesh there are only 7 per cent who speak Urdu compared to 87 per cent who claim Telugu as their mother tongue ... Hindu revivalism is not directly related to Muslims; nevertheless, it makes life uncomfortable for them. In Andhra Pradesh the revival is a combination of various factors. In part it is a reassertion of Telugu language and culture; in part a political statement against the domination of Delhi represented by the Congress—the historical revolt of the south against the north. The man who symbolizes the revival is N.T. Rama Rao, the Chief Minister of Andhra Pradesh (Ahmed 1988: 168).

56. Kothari (1964), pp. 1166–7.
57. See Manor (1977a), p. 168.
58. Nagaraj (2006), p. 91.
59. See Raghavendra (2008), pp. 117–24.
60. Language itself could, of course, have been a political issue if Kannada had found itself an adversary. But it could be 'political' only in the Kannada-speaking areas outside princely Mysore which had been neglected and not in princely Mysore where it had been the dominant language—and there was no issue it could align itself against.
61. Gandhism is perhaps the only political philosophy that will find few opponents in India. Here is a description of the aims of the first Congress government:

   The ministers in the first cabinet took office with a nebulous mixture of ... Gandhian and socialist visions and utopian expectations. They sought to maintain the Congress consensus by soothing the grievances of all the disparate interests in the state and when they discovered that their consensus contained mutually antagonistic interests, they reacted with confusion and ineptitude which angered all parties concerned (Manor 1977a: 168).

62. This echoes remarks made about Rajkumar by his admirers. For instance, see http://www.screenindia.com/old/20001208/rehap.htm. The president of KFCC, K.C.N. Chandrashekar describes him as 'Ajathashatru, the one who has no enemies'.
63. Exceptions may be the films in which he plays double roles as in *Emme Thammanna*.
64. For instance, Ganapathy (2006). The title, *Kannada Muthina Kathe Rajkumar*, translates as 'the story of the Kannada pearl, Rajkumar'. The reference is evidently to a Rajkumar film *Ondu Muthina Kathe* (1987) ('the story of a pearl') with is based on a novella *The Pearl* by John Steinbeck.

Chapter 2

1. There was also no discourse in *Vijayanagarada Veeraputra* associating Krishnadevaraya with Kannada.

2. The nation has a subdued presence in Hindi cinema after the Chinese debacle because it is no longer able to function as a moral signpost as it did in the films of 1950s like *Mother India*. See Raghavendra (2008), pp. 152–66.

3. Ibid., pp. 108–10.

4. See, for instance, 'Kannadigas are at the Root of Kannada's problem', 19 April 2007, http://churumuri.wordpress.com. Access date 22/2/2011.

5. Hindi cinema of the 1950s is much more ambivalent towards the Nehruvian modern (than Kannada cinema is towards the Mysore modern) and this manifests itself in the way it views the city. For an understanding of the city in Nehru's scheme and the mixed results of urban development see Khilnani (1997), pp. 107–49.

6. Nair (2005), pp. 89–90.

7. Ravi in *Kasturi Nivasa* is perhaps also in the position of Satyajit Ray's zamindar in *Jalsaghar* (1958). The difference is that Ravi, being the moral centre of the film, embodies the film's viewpoint in a way that the zamindar from Ray's film does not.

8. Rajadhyaksha and Willemen (1995), p. 378.

9. Gaeffke (Utrecht) (1973), pp. 69–70.

10. Other instances are also cited in Robinson (1989).

11. Rajadhyaksha (2009), pp. 161–1.

12. For an account of the FFC and its policy, see Prasad (1999), p. 121.

13. In West Bengal, Satyajit Ray, Ritwik Ghatak, Bimal Roy, and Mrinal Sen had already made films outside the mainstream and the Malayalam art film arrived much later. Another kind of pan-Indian art cinema came out of the *Film and Television Institute of India* (FTII) with directors like Mani Kaul and Kumar Shahani, who were students of Ritwik Ghatak. Overall, the Bengali influence in the earliest art cinema is impossible to ignore. Kannada cinema appears the one striking exception around 1970. The later Kannada art cinema, from B.V. Karanth's *Chomana Dudi* (1975) to the films of Girish Kasaravalli, are perhaps also more pan-Indian than specifically Kannada. Many were financed by NFDC and were not seen widely in Karnataka but earned plaudits outside. These later Kannada art films, it can be argued, have not contributed to the construction of the Kannada identity as *Samskara* clearly did.

14. K.V. Puttappa's novel *Kanooru Subbamma Heggadathi* (1936) was made into a film in 1997 by Girish Karnad and K. Shivaram Karanth's *Chomana Dudi* (1931) was made into a film by B.V. Karanth in 1975.

15. Rajadhyaksha and Willemen (1995), p. 378.

16. See Ramanujan (1976), pp. 139–48.

17. See Abrams (1999), p. 167.

18. As an illustration Govind Nihalani's *Ardh Satya* (1983), which is about a policeman Anant Velankar—who has to seek the assistance of a gangster Rama Setty but strangles him when he proves too obnoxious—has motifs in common with films like *Tezaab* (1988) and *Pratighaat* (1987). Valicha, a critic writing about *Ardh Satya*: '(Rama Setty's strangling by police officer Anant Velankar) seems to have a meaning that one fails to perceive. In the older kind of film, it might have meant the triumph of good over evil. But here we can that it has no such message.' Valicha (1988), p. 107.

19. Ingmar Bergman's early films—*The Seventh Seal* and *Wild Strawberries*—are apparent examples, as is, perhaps, Carl Dreyer's *Ordet* (1955). Variations of this character-type are also to be found in the novels of Graham Greene. Belief need not necessarily be in religion and it could also be in an ideology—communism, for instance.

20. The films I refer to those like V. Shantaram's *Duniya Na Mane* (1937) which employs the motif of the strong woman in male dominated society.

21. For a useful account of the director's preoccupations and an analysis of a later film, see Yusufi (1988), pp. 50–2.

22. Prasad (1999), p. 86.

23. There is a greater similarity between Kalpana in these films and Nargis in films like *Awaara*. But there is an ugly element of sexism in the Hindi films because the woman makes gestures of submission. They are not 'feminist' in the way Puttanna's films can be regarded.

24. It is apparently only when Mysore has felt closest to the Indian nation—in the late 1950s after linguistic reorganization with films like *School Master* or in the years up to 1968 in *Bangarada Hoovu* and *Jedara Bale* that the feelings towards Bangalore are wholeheartedly positive.

25. Nataraj and Nataraj (1982), pp. 1503–6.

26. Manor (1977b), p. 1867.

27. The proprietor of a flour mill is a businessman rather than an industrialist, with the emphasis on procurement and sale of food products and the possibility of black-market activity—which is what Veerabhadraiah's brother-in-law briefly does. Ravi in *Kasturi Nivasa* is an industrialist rather than a businessman because he owns a match factory that processes forest produce. The 'sowkars' in *Nagara Haavu* are farmers trading in wholesale grain market.

28. Manor (1977b), pp. 1867–8.

29. Pani (1998), pp. 64–84. See also Damle (1989) and Pani (1983).

30. Manor (1980).
31. Ibid., pp. 203–5.
32. Ibid., p. 211.
33. Natraj and Nataraj (1982), p. 1505. Also see Manor (1980), pp. 201–2. There were apparently reports of shock among villagers in 1980 that their votes for Mrs Gandhi (and her 'hand' emblem) had caused Urs to resign.
34. Raghavendra (2008), p. 120.
35. There are two aspects of caste, a distinction that tends to be glossed over. The first is *varna* which is the broadly theoretical division of castes into four—Brahmin (priests), Kshatriya (warriors), Vaishya (merchants), and Shudra (peasants). Then there is *jati* which is the caste group at the local level. In *Samskara*, Putta belongs to the Maleru jati. In practice, it is usually difficult to assign varnas to jatis at the local level. In the Kannada films discussed hitherto, Malla Setty in *Gunasagari* is apparently a Vaishya because of the suffix 'Setty' it includes. Vokkaligas are Shudras and Iyengars (Alamelu in *Nagara Haavu*) and Madhwas (Praneshacharya in *Samskara*) are Brahmins. It is difficult to find a jati which corresponds to the 'Kshatriya' in Karnataka although the Arasus (the former Royal family and Devaraj Urs) have made a claim to belonging to the caste. Each Hindu has a jati but the vast majority of them cannot be accommodated within the varna categories. The Dalits (former untouchables) who figure in *Bhoothayyana Maga Ayyu* and in the later film *Chomana Dudi* are people outside the four varnas. 'Caste Hindus' are all those who can be accommodated within the four varnas.
36. Nataraj and Nataraj (1982), p. 1505.
37. Singh (2008), p. 51.
38. Even during the Emergency, Karnataka was spared most of the excesses of north India largely due to Urs keeping the Sanjay caucus at bay. The Congress, therefore, did not do badly in Karnataka in 1977 because of the Emergency—as happened at the national level. Manor (1980), pp. 201. Also see Manor (1978).
39. Apart from the crackdown on smuggling in the period and the enactment of a special law, the Conservation of Foreign Exchange and Prevention of Smuggling Activities Act (COFEPOSA), smuggling was associated with 'western behaviour' because smugglers cross the boundaries between East and West. See Pfleiderer (1985), p. 127. There was perhaps also an immediate reason for the negative connotations in 'western behaviour' and this is Mrs Gandhi's rhetoric being 'anti-American' in the 1970s because of her association with the political left.
40. Rajadhyaksha (2009), p. 248. Although this was articulated later in the 1970s there was an implicit understanding of what kind of

off-beat cinema was 'most suited to India' with Satyajit Ray as an unconscious model.

41. The major conflict is 'slight' in the sense that it has no underlying political basis and is simply brought about by the initial rudeness of Shivaganga's henchman to the seniors of Koppalu.

42. Nagaraj (1983), p. 11. Cited by Jayadev (1992), p. 29.

43. Jayadev (1992), pp. 23–9.

44. Its anti-Christian viewpoint is another aspect that has invited adverse comment.

45. Many of the champions of New Cinema also took this position. Here is Kumar Shahani, one of the early beneficiaries of FFC finance on the failings of popular cinema: 'Gratuitous violence, a life dependent on miracles (whether gods or superhumans), change of heart in evil men, and the abuse of women as servile of sexual and social exploitation are the cultural products of lumpen consciousness. Whatever the ostensible or overt themes of these films, their disorganized and anarchic form itself can subvert all hope of determination.' See Binford (1987), p. 148.

46. See Raghavendra (2009b), 'Introduction: Indistinct Shape, Composite Form', pp. xxvii–xxx.

47. *Chomana Dudi* includes a veiled attack on conversion and the abortionists in *Ghatashraddha* are Christian.

48. Vidyashankar (1992), pp. 17–20.

49. There is some significant literature in Kannada on film adaptations of Kannada literature. See, for instance, Ramachandrappa (1998). Also useful may be Prakash and Puttaswamy (1995). The latter book is concerned with the writing of Gnanapeeth Award winners, which has, by and large, not found its way into popular cinema.

50. Anderson (1983), p. 14.

51. Girish Karnad's subsequent films include *Kanooru Heggadathi* (2000), which is based on a novel by K.V. Puttappa (KuVemPu); and Girish Kasaravalli's films have always been literary adaptations.

Chapter 3

1. Roland Barthes (1973), 'Myth Today', p. 143.

2. See Schatz (1999), p. 647. As Schatz notes, 'The Western hero, regardless of his social or legal standing, is necessarily an agent of civilization in the savage frontier.'

3. Fehrenbach (1995), p. 150.

4. Heider (1991), pp. 39–57.

5. Shadi (1996), pp. 84–129.

6. See Raghavendra (2008), pp. 66–8.

7. Prasad (1999), pp. 48–9.

8. Hollywood 'genre films' are usually made by 'specialists' in the sense that certain filmmakers are associated with certain genres, Ford and Peckinpah with the western, Vincente Minnelli with the musical, and so on. This is not the case in Kannada cinema with Dorairaj-Bhagwan making *Kasturi Nivasa* and the CID 999 films. B.R. Panthulu made *School Master* as well as *Shri Krishnadevaraya*. This lends credence to my argument.

9. The films are not sequels. For an explanation for the absence of sequels in popular cinema, see Raghavendra (2008), pp. 33–41.

10. The film brings also back the comic subplot having no effect upon the story. This motif, as I have already explained, is a nod to the traditional notion of hierarchy—not to be found in most of the later films of the 1970s. Overall, this film brings back more than one former Mysore motif which had all but disappeared from Kannada cinema in 1979.

11. There are several definitions of the joint family and the most widely accepted one is a family in which siblings and their spouses live together under the same roof. For our purpose the sacred Hindu joint family of Kannada cinema is one with a living patriarch/matriarch and two or more siblings—or a married son. Ramanna (Ambarish), I would suggest, is present only to imply a joint family in *Ranganayaki* because he plays no other role in the narrative except to be a nominal 'brother' to the heroine.

12. Khilnani (1997), pp. 51–2.

13. The new political entrants considered themselves—and acted as—members of groups and communities, rather than liberal individuals. These collective identities in some cases began viciously to attack one another: in regions like Bihar, upper castes, their power threatened by the destruction of the vote banks they had controlled waged wars on those below them. Violence between society and the state also escalated ... India's political parties are a good index of the diversity (of the social identities they represent).... Democracy quickened the attraction of these social identities in various, often contradictory ways. The potentialities of religion, language and caste inspired parties to devise strategies that respectively appealed to the Hindu religion, the Hindi language or lower-caste status, in order to mobilize for power at the Centre. Regional politics also came violently alive, and very differently from the way it had in the 1950s. The claims of regional autonomy Nehru faced were reactions against the legacies of British rule, which had bequeathed the Indian state administrative territories containing different linguistic groups now discontented by their opportunities. The regional demands of the 1980s, by contrast, were explicitly directed against the central state,

which since the late 1960s had meddled in regional affairs, repeatedly invoking President's Rule and undermining the federal division of powers (Khilnani 1997: 50).

14. Karnataka sending twenty-seven Congress MPs to the Seventh Lok Sabha in 1980 should have perhaps brought the region much closer to the nation—or, rather, allowed for a happy 'union' of the two. The fact that the nation was beleaguered by divisive forces suggests that the union, if possible at all, could only be an unhappy one. Interestingly, Telugu cinema displays the same motif—Dasari Narayana Rao's *Premabhishekam*, (1980) and Andhra Pradesh had also overwhelmingly voted for the Congress in the same Seventh Lok Sabha election.

15. For a comprehensive account of politics in the state in the Urs period and after, see Srinivas (1984), pp. 69–75.

16. For an in-depth analysis of the Gokak agitation, see Harikumar (1982).

17. Srinivas (1984), pp. 69–75.

18. Raghavendra (2008), pp. 36–9, 156–8.

19. Scholes (1985), pp. 390–405.

20. Jayamanne (1992), pp. 145–53.

21. Raghavendra (2008), pp. 250–2.

22. Many of the Hindi films of the 1980s deal with caste or regional identity. In J.P. Dutta's *Ghulami*, a policeman declares that he is a Thakur first and a policeman afterwards. *Qayamat Se Qayamat Tak* revolves around two feuding Kshatriya families and *Ek Duuje Ke Liye* (1982) is about love between a north Indian and a south Indian being doomed.

23. Hierarchy and jati represent the two aspects of the caste system—one as theoretical categories and the other directly observed divisions. See Dumont (1998), pp. 72–9.

24. Two pertinent films are *Rajnigandha* (1975) in which the woman works for her PhD, and *Abhimaan* (1973) in which the man and his wife are singers, with the man becoming jealous at his wife's success.

25. By 'consideration' I mean that the courtesan is not physically abused in any way although the relationship is a cold, loveless, and commercial one.

26. For a revealing analysis of this see Nandy (1980), pp. 22–5.

27. *Samskara* is perhaps also vulnerable to the charge of objectifying its feminine characters under the pretext of asserting that the sex appeal of low caste women is greater than those from the Brahmin caste. *Kaadu*, *Chomana Dudi*, and *Ghatashraddha* are also films in which the woman's place is an unimportant one, even when she has

nominally the most important adult role—as in *Ghatashraddha*. One needs only to compare the portrayal of women in these films with that of Sarbojaya in *Pather Panchali* to understand it.

Chapter 4

1. 'Love' in western cinema is often subjected to psychoanalytical reading, largely that 'romance' exorcizes fears about interpersonal conflict, namely, the woman's latent fear of the hurt that men may cause them in relationships. See Radway (1987), p. 48. In Indian popular cinema (Kannada as much as Hindi), heterosexual relationships do not pass through the same stages of development—involving interpersonal conflict. Difficulties, when they arise, are caused by external agencies (the family, society, destiny, etc.) and not by interpersonal conflict between the lovers. We cannot, therefore, read Indian film romances as engaged in the exorcism of latent emotional fears and this makes psychoanalytic interpretations unproductive. As I have argued elsewhere, 'love' in Indian cinema is, rather, a device to bring the narrative to closure. See Raghavendra (2008), pp. 37–8.

2. http://www.rediff.com/news/jan/06cauvel.htm. Also see Anand (2004).

3. Raghavendra (2009a), pp. 15–17.

4. As instances, in the protagonists' adulation of their father, in 'true love' and in the brothers' loyalty to each other.

5. The protagonist is perhaps superior to his parents because he favours 'love' over money. But 'love' has such lustful connotations in the film that it is hardly a moral force.

6. While the father was not the moral centre of the story, he was still a respected figure. In Hindi cinema, the father could be hated as in *Awaara* (1951) but never despised as he is in this film because he is still respected. See Vasudevan (2000b), p. 110.

7. See, for instance, Subba Rao (1991). Also see Pinto (1992), p. 1837.

8. See Gould (1997).

9. Pinto (1992), pp. 1837–8.

10. For instance, N. Ponnappa's cartoons in the series 'Offside', *Times of India* (Bangalore edition), specifically showed P.V. Narasimha Rao being weighed against suitcases by Bangarappa. Politicians featured as types in political cartoons. H.D. Deve Gowda, as another instance, was represented as boorish rather than corrupt in the same series and his son H.D. Kumaraswamy, who also became chief minister through his efforts, as his loutish and spoilt child.

11. The vamp is perhaps first seen in Hindi cinema in the figure of the club dancer in the 1950s, for instance in *Baazi* (1951). The club

dancer can be interpreted at representing the threatening aspects of Nehruvian modernity. As already argued Nehruvian modernity represented no threat to Kannada cinema because modernity had already been ushered into Mysore in the 1920s through the efforts of statesmen like Visveswaraiya.

12. An exception here may be Puttanna Kanagal's *Manasa Sarovara* (1982), but its low view of women is usually attributed to the director's personal life.

13. See Raghavendra (2006).

14. Blogs are useful spaces here. For instance, the following provide a rough idea of the self-image of the Kannadiga. While the 'Kannadiga' is any person whose mother tongue is Kannada, we cannot be certain the region is the whole of Karnataka: http://www.ourkarnataka. com/issues/response_sameer_solution.htm; http://ibnlive.in.com/ blogs/views/kannada-vs-tamil-english-vs-hindi/1029-23.html (post 29 March 2006).

15. It is generally held that during Hegde's period in office (1983–8) both H.D. Deve Gowda and S.R. Bommai, who replaced him as chief minister, conspired to unseat him. Hegde, at that time, had his eye on New Delhi and this also contributed to the decline of governance in the state. See Natraj (1995), pp. 84–5.

16. See Pinto (1994), pp. 1511–12.

17. One of them is called 'Razor Manju' which is the kind of name that underworld figures are given.

18. Nair (2005), pp. 256–7.

19. Heitzman (2004), pp. 28–9.

20. *Census of India*, 1971. See also Kamath (1982), p. 439.

21. The occasion was a seventy-seven-day public sector strike when there was an attempt to divide the workers over the language issue. Nair (2005), pp. 255–7.

22. The only instance I recall is Belgaum in *Bangarada Manushya*, but that film does not invoke an emblem of Belgaum city in the same deliberate way. In *Akasmika*, there is a song sequence near the Kittur Chennamma statue in the well-known centre of Hubli city.

23. To the question of why Clara is introduced there is apparently no answer. Since Indira is the real heroine and she reappears, the male protagonist needs to be kept in an agitated state so he does not forget her meanwhile. I propose that the film hits upon the former alcoholic Clara as a way of keeping his interest (and our own) in Indira alive.

24. The film is not entirely innocent here because it is also using the three friends to titillate. On the one hand is the film's sincere castigation of the objectification of women and on the other is its urge to titillate by exploiting the notion and drawing some benefit for itself.

25. 'Narasimha Murthy' is as Brahmin as 'Thimmaraju' and 'Kataiah' are non-Brahmin in their associations. The caste associations of 'Vyasaraya' are perhaps more indeterminate.

26. While Upendra is perhaps the only filmmaker to constantly create the sense that anything can be 'seen', the sense that anything can be 'heard' is received in many other films with deliberately offensive dialogue, as for instance *Chaitrada Premanjali*.

27. Heitzman (2004), p. 165.

28. Nair (2005), p. 262.

29. Benjamin and Bhuvaneswari (2000), cited in Nair (2005), pp. 261–2.

30. Nair (2005), pp. 257–61.

31. Khilnani (1997), p. 95.

32. See, for instance, Bharucha (1995), pp. 801–4.

33. Raghavendra (2008), pp. 236–81.

34. There is a huge amount of abusive Kannada in Upendra's subsequent film, *Upendra* (1999), but the film was not a success. Upendra's later films as director are more civil.

35. The 'decadence' of the Nehruvian modern may have been inferred by Kannada cinema because of the image of the club dancer, gambler, etc., in Hindi films of the 1950s. For a description of these motifs see Vasudevan (2000b), p. 115.

36. We get a clue about such 'communities' from *Mother India*, in which the village is a microcosm of the nation. At the same time, the village also exists separately within the nation because the elderly Radha inaugurates a dam at a function presided over by statesmen. 'Communities', while being microcosms of larger entities, also exist as its constituents. The larger entity is also, in a sense, their ultimate arbiter.

37. See Manor (1996), pp. 2675–8.

Chapter 5

1. The statues of Queen Victoria, Edward VII, and Sir Mark Cubbon have stayed on in Cubbon Park, which is located at one end of Mahatma Gandhi Road (the former South Parade), the nerve centre of Cantonment. Their continued presence has been seen as one more instance of the large heartedness of Kannadigas by humorist A.N. Murthy Rao. See Nair (2005), pp. 295–6.

2. For an account, see Parthasarathy (2005), pp. 199–230.

3. Leahy (2006), p. 24.

4. N.R. Narayana Murthy, founder-chairman of Infosys Technologies, Bangalore's premier IT industry, became a controversial figure because of his views on the need for English education. He is a Kannada speaker who studied in Mysore. Much of the controversy

around him is registered in blogs. For instance, see http://ibnlive.
in.com/blogs/dpsatish/237/1409/narayana-murthy-as-prez-would-be-
a-shame.html posted 10 April, 2007.

5. Nair (2005), pp. 111–12, 246–7.
6. Ibid., pp. 334–5.
7. Ibid., p. 336.
8. For an assessment see Pani (2006), pp. 238–56.
9. Politics is perhaps more relevant to the marginalized than to the elite—which is less dependent on the political classes. Every act of 'withdrawal' by the state is also a step by which the electorate is made to relinquish its claims upon politics. The upwardly mobile urban classes are those with the least use for politics, which is perhaps why they are notoriously indifferent to elections.
10. The other options for the 'community'—'human beings', 'Indians', 'people from Karnataka', 'Kannada speakers', and 'Bangaloreans'—are evidently ruled out. It must also be remarked that the community is not denoted as Kannadiga and Jogi's gang even includes a Sikh. The community is perhaps simply 'us', with 'us' being connoted as Kannadigas.
11. The impossibility of the romance with the born and bred Bangalorean also substantiates this. Out of the other three films cited earlier, only in *Kitty* is the romance is taken to happy conclusion, the girl being from the same village as the male protagonist—sharing his status as a migrant, as it were.
12. Of course words make their way from one language to another and 'duniya' is one such word used sometimes in Kannada. But the privileging of a Hindi word in the title of the film should also be given attention.
13. U.R. Ananthamurthy laments the 'mindboggling tolerance of Kannadigas'. See 'Do not sacrifice Karnataka's Interests', *The Hindu* (16 February 2002). In the last chapter I tried to show how the overly tolerant woman had some correspondence with the self-image of the region's constituents. My inquiry into Kannada cinema suggests that 'tolerance' is not an attribute of 'Kannadigas'—all those who speak Kannada—but only of those from former princely Mysore.
14. Interestingly, it is difficult to recall a Kannada film in which someone is a migrant in Mysore or any other city rather than Bangalore.
15. It is somewhat ironic to see three young men driving in a SUV into a five star hotel, using the swimming pool and talking about their aversion for the city as they do in this film. But an aversion for Bangalore is apparently mandatory in Kannada cinema today.
16. This is the story told in Prem's *Kariya* (2003) in which there is an allusion to Kothwal Ramachandra.

17. *Appu*, exceptionally, violates hierarchy (the protagonist's treatment of the IPS officer) but the film evidently incorporates motifs carried forward from an original made in another language.

18. Since the population of Bangalore has increased from around 17 million in 1971 to 70 million in 2007, a majority of those who live in Bangalore are apparently migrants. See http://wgbis.ces.iisc.ernet.in/energy/water/paper/bangalore/index.htm

19. Nair (2005), pp. 265–6.

20. For instance see Venkatesh (2003). The author is a Kannada speaker, working in the IT industry. This is ironic but actual knowledge of Kannada is perhaps much wider than is revealed through mother-tongue counts because most people are multi-lingual. This means that it is not so much knowledge of Kannada as the identity conferred by the mother tongue that is important. See Nair (2005), p. 264.

21. Nair (2005), p. 132.

22. See Raghavendra (2008), p. 48. As an instance of the importance of the first cause in popular cinema, Vijay having 'Mera baap chor hai' tattooed on his forearm in *Deewar* (1975) determines the course of the story.

23. See, for instance, 'Kannadigas are at the Root of Kannada's problem' (19 April 2007), posted in http://churumuri.wordpress.com. This is how the writer describes Kannadigas: 'Soft. Mild. Docile. Laidback. … Not aggressive. Not ambitious … Lacking in drive …' Also see responses on the same site. As I have tried to bring out in the course of this book these are less the qualities attributed to 'Kannadigas' than to people from the areas under former princely Mysore. As I have argued at length in Chapter 4, the same aspect also finds different kind of representation in the motif of the tolerant and submissive woman in Kannada cinema.

24. See 'BPO employee rape and murder causes furore in Bangalore', Yahoo Indian News (2 January 2006). http://www.pinoyexchange.com/forums/showthread.php?t=252303. Access date 22/2/2011. The alleged rapist-murderer was a taxi driver and local.

25. A frequent complaint voiced against recent governments of Karnataka is that they give disproportionate attention to Bangalore. S.M. Krishna paid the price for it when, despite his efforts in Bangalore, the Congress was reduced to a coalition partner in the state in 2004. For an analysis see Assadi (2004), pp. 4221–8.

26. Todorov (1975), pp. 24–40.

27. The film I have in mind is B.R. Chopra's *Naya Daur* (1957), which deals with the village and the city and the issue of mechanization. At the climax of the film a bullock cart triumphs in a race with a bus.

28. Raghavendra (2008), pp. 294–5.

29. Prakash (2009).
30. Featherstone (1996), p. 60.
31. Dirlik (1996), p. 30.
32. Srinivas (2009), pp. 78–9.
33. See Chakravarthy (2001), pp. 9–10. There is also a D.Litt dissertation in Kannada, Seetharam (2001).
34. 'I read Amitabh as a "sub-text" which destabilizes the "positive" continuities we have detected in filmic discourse. But the "sub-text" becomes a fully-fledged parallel text and displaces the filmic text itself: the actor becomes the film.' Mishra (1985), p. 143. Also see 'The Actor as Parallel Text: Amitabh Bachchan', Mishra (2002), pp. 125–56.
35. See Chakravarthy (1998), pp. 16–30.
36. The use of Nandita Das in this film and in *Nalu Pennungal* (2007) by Adoor Gopalakrishnan, as well as Naseeruddin Shah and Deepti Naval in Girish Kasaravalli's *Mane* (1989), suggest that regional language art cinema in India is usually 'national' in its aspirations—rather than regional. It supports my decision not to interpret the films as local artifacts.

Conclusion

1. Data pertaining to film receipts is extrely difficult to come by but some information is available with regard to entertainment tax collections. Assuming 100 points for the tax collections of 1995–6, the index of collections in the subsequent years is as follows: 1996–7: 75.20; 1997–8: 103.01; 1998–9: 103.58; 1999–2000: 98.02; 2000–1: 111.15; 2001–2: 107.59; 2002–3: 100.44; 2003–4: 101.80; 2004–5: 99.21; 2005–6: 100.50; 2006–7: 123.14; 2007–8: 156.18; and 2008–9: 170.64. The data shows a significant improvement in collections in the last three years but this could be because of the increased prices of tickets on account of the multiplex boom. Overall, the data suggests stagnation of a high order if not an actual decline. Index is constructed from information provided in the unpublished PhD dissertation, B.Y. Krishnamurthy (2010).
2. See http://entertainment.oneindia.in/kannada/top-stories/2010/kites-kfcc-banned-210510.html. Only 21 prints of a non-Kannada film may be released across the state. See also, http://www.businessofcinema.com/news.php?newsid=16278.
3. Since the cinema is in Kannada, it would be difficult to include non-Kannada speaking characters. But the Tamil/Hindi ruffians in Bangalore in *AK 47* may be understood to represent them as does the English-speaking party crowd in *Yajamana*.
4. Raghavendra (2006), pp. 1503–5.

5. For instance, see 'The Distorted Portrayal of Telengana in Telugu Films', posted on the blog *'Simply Telangana'* on 15 January 2010. See http://www.simplytelangana.com/2010/01/15/the-distorted-portrayal-of-telangana-in-andhra-films/.

6. Apart from Mani Rathnam, whose *Roja* was phenomenally successful in both languages, and Sridhar (*Dil Ek Mandir*, 1963), even a propagandist DMK film like *Malaikallan* (1954) was successfully remade as *Azad* (1955).

7. *Roja* is more written about than *Bombay*. For *Roja*, see Niranjana (1994), pp. 79–82. For *Bombay*, see Vasudevan (2000), pp. 187–8.

8. Out of the twenty individuals who have been chief ministers of Mysore/Karnataka after 1947, only eight have been from outside the old Mysore.

9. For population figures relating to 2001, see http://www.citypopulation.de/India.

10. *Census of India: Census Data 2001—India at a glance*, Office of the Registrar General and Census Commissioner, India. http://www.censusindia.gov.in/Census_Data_2001/India_at_glance/religion.aspx, retrieved 26 November 2008.

11. http://www.mohfw.nic.in/NRHM/state%20Files/karnataka.htm. Access date 18/2/2011.

12. This is according to Karnataka Health Secretary, I.M. Perumal. See 'Official Favours Tough Birth Control Law', *The Hindu* (12 July 2009).

13. See 'Madness in Bangalore following Vishnuvardhan's death' in *MSN News*, http://news.in.msn.com/national/article.aspx?cp-documentid=3505247.

14. The incident I have in mind here is of a ragged and decrepit woman seen trying to damage a police vehicle with a stone during the violence after Rajkumar's death.

15. S.V. Srinivas has some useful views on fan violence but his work is related to fans of individual film stars while my inquiry is into the constituency of Kannada cinema as a whole. See Srinivas (2009), pp. 56–8.

16. There is also frequent talk that Bangalore should be administered as a union territory (for instance see http://bpradeepnair.blogspot.com/2004/11/bangalore-as-union-territory.html) If anything, the controversy around the notion recognizes the position that Bangalore has vis-à-vis the region and the expressed desire largely of those from outside the region to free it from local politics. See Sreenivasaraju (2008), p. 288.

17. Many migrants settle in slums and slum improvement might hold the key. But Bangalore is situated close to the border with both Tamil Nadu and Andhra Pradesh and there are migrants from the

other states as well in the slums. A government programme for slum improvement in the early 1990s fixed a cut off date for qualifying older slums for 'improvement' and younger slums for 'clearance'. The programme was called off when it was discovered that the Tamil slums would qualify for development while the Kannada slums would be cleared. See Nair (2005), p. 262.

18. To recapitulate, corruption was a huge problem in Mysore and this has increased proportionately. See the study conducted by Centre for Media Studies, Delhi in June 2005, http://www.cmsindia.org/cms/events/corruption.pdf. The latest 'developmental project' initiated by the BJP government involves the acquisition of 10,00,000 acres and create a 'land bank' for industrialists. A large chunk of this is in the region close to Bangalore and will mean more dispossessed people from the region. See Sreenivasaraju (2010).

19. There is already a Konkani and a Tulu cinema in Karnataka—made in the most prosperous region outside former Mysore, that is, Dakshin Kannada district. This Konkani cinema, while also being different from the Konkani cinema coming from Goa, is vastly different from Kannada cinema, culturally. Konkani cinema caters to a different language identity within Karnataka but there is no cinema yet that addresses the identities of the people of Hubli, Bidar, Gulbarga, Raichur, or Belgaum.

Bibliography

Abrams, M.H. 1999. *A Glossary of Literary Terms* (Indian Edition). New Delhi: Thomson-Heinle.

Ahmed, Akbar S. 1988. *Discovering Islam: Making Sense of Muslim History and Society*. London: Routledge.

Anand, P.B. 2004. *Water and Identity: An Analysis of the Cauvery River Water Dispute*, Bradford Centre for International Development (BCID), BCID Research Paper 3 (July), University of Bradford, http://www.brad.ac.uk/acad/bcid/research/papers/Paper3.pdf . Access date 22/2/2011.

Anderson, Benedict. 1983. *Imagined Communities: Reflections on the Origin and Spread of Nationalism*. London: Verso.

Assadi, Muzaffar. 2004. 'Karnataka Elections: Shifts, New Trends and the Congress Defeat', *Economic and Political Weekly*, Vol. XXXIX, No. 38 (18–24 September), pp. 4221–8.

Barthes, Roland. 1973. 'Myth Today', *Mythologies*. London: Paladin.

Bharucha, Rustom. 1995. 'Utopia in Bollywood: "Hum Aapke Hain Koun!"', *Economic and Political Weekly*, Vol. XXX, No. 15 (15 April), pp. 801–4.

Binford, Mira Reym. 1987. 'The Two Cinemas of India', in John D.H. Dowling (ed.), *Film and Politics in the Third World*. New York: Praeger, p. 148.

Bordwell, David. 1996. 'Contemporary Film Studies and the Vicissitudes of Grand Theory', in David Bordwell and Noël Carroll (eds), *Post-Theory: Reconstructing Film Studies*. Madison: The University of Wisconsin Press, pp. 3–36.

Borges, Jorge Luis. 1999. *Selected Non-Fictions*. New York: Penguin Books.

Brooks, Peter. 1985. *The Melodramatic Imagination: Balzac, Henry James, Melodrama and the Mode of Excess*. New York: Columbia University Press.

Chakravarthy, N. Manu. 1998. 'Negotiating Individual Freedom and Historical Necessity: The Feminist Cultural Politics of *Thayi Saheba*', *Deep Focus*, Vol. VIII, No. 1&2, pp. 16–30.

———. 2001. 'Of Icons and the Spirit of the Times', *Deep Focus*, Vol. IX, No. 1, pp. 5–10.

Chakravarty, Sumita S. 1998. *National Identity in Indian Popular Cinema*. New Delhi: Oxford University Press.

Chatterjee, Partha. 1993. *The Nation and its Fragments*. Princeton, NJ: Princeton University Press.

———. 1997. *A Possible India*. New Delhi: Oxford University Press.

Damle, C.B. 1989. 'Land Reform Legislation in Karnataka: Myth of Success', *Economic and Political Weekly*, Vol. XXIV, No. 33 (19 August), pp. 1896–1905.

Dirlik, Arif. 1996. 'The Global in the Local', in Rob Wilson and Wimal Dissanayake (eds), *Global Local: Cultural Production and the Transnational Imaginary*. Durham: Duke University Press, pp. 24–30.

Diwkar, R.R. (ed.). 1968. *Karnataka Through the Ages: From Prehistoric Times to the day of the Independence of India*. Government of Mysore.

Dumont, Louis. 1970. *Homo Hierarchicus: The Caste System and its Implications*. New Delhi: Oxford University Press.

Featherstone, Mike. 1996. 'Localism, Globalism, Cultural Identity', in Rob Wilson and Wimal Dissanayake (eds), *Global Local: Cultural Production and the Transnational Imaginary*. Durham: Duke University Press, p. 60.

Fehrenbach, Heide. 1995. *Cinema in Democratizing Germany*. Chapel Hill, NC: University of North Carolina Press.

Gaeffke, Utrecht. 1973. 'Vibhutibhushan Banerji's *Pather Panchali*', in The Cultural Department of the Embassy of the Federal Republic of Germany in India (ed.), *German Scholars in India*, Vol. I. Varanasi: The Chowkhamba Sanskrit Series Office, pp. 69–70.

Ganapathy, B. 2006. *Kannada Muthina Kathe Rajkumar*. Bangalore: Cinema Sahithya Prakashana.

Gavaskar, Mahesh. 2003. 'Land, Language and Politics: Apropos, 70th Kannada Sahitya Sammelan', *Economic and Political Weekly*, Vol. 38, Nos 12/13 (22–29 March), pp. 1113–16.

Ghosh, Sankar. 1993. *Jawaharlal Nehru: A Biography*. Bombay: Allied Publishers.

Gould, Harold A. 1997. 'General Elections 1996: Karnataka, Decline and Fall of the Congress Machine', *Economic and Political Weekly*, Vol. XXXII, No. 37 (13 September), pp. 2335–49.

Government of India. 1893. *Census of India, 1891*, XXV, four parts. Bangalore: Government of Mysore.

———. 1954. *Census of India, 1951*. Delhi.

———. 1932. *Census of India, 1931*, XXV, two parts. Bangalore: Government of Mysore.

———. 1942. *Census of India, 1941*, XXIII, two parts. Bangalore: Government of Mysore.

Government of Karnataka. 1982. *Karnataka State Gazetteer*, Bangalore: Government of Karnataka.

Government of Mysore. 1937, *The Mysore Gazette1908–1947*. Bangalore: Government of Mysore (10 June).

Guha, Ramachandra. 2007. *India after Gandhi: The History of the World's Largest Democracy*. New York: Harper-Collins.

Harikumar, K.N. 1982. 'Language and democracy', *Deccan Herald* (April 5).

Heath, Stephen. 1977. 'Contexts', *Edinburgh Magazine*, Vol. 2, p. 38.

Heider, Karl G. 1991. *Indonesian Cinema: National Culture on the Screen*. Honolulu: University of Hawaii Press.

Heitzman, James. 2004. *Network City: Planning the Information Society in Bangalore*. New Delhi: Oxford University Press.

Hettne, Björn. 1978. *The Political Economy of Indirect Rule: Mysore 1881–1947*. London: Curzon Press.

Iyer, Ananthakrishna. 1928. *The Mysore Tribes and Castes*, Vol. II. Bangalore: Mysore University.

Jameson, Frederic. 1987. 'Third World Literature in the Age of Multinational Capitalism', in C. Koelb and V. Lokke (eds), *The Current in Criticism*. West Lafayette, Indiana: Purdue University Press, pp. 65–88.

Jayadev, M.U. 1992. 'Cultural Determinants and Textual Indeterminancy: Deconstructing *Dudi*', *Deep Focus*, Vol. IV, No.1, pp. 23–9.

Jayamanne, L. 1992. 'Sri Lankan Family Melodrama: A Cinema of Primitive Attractions', *Screen*, 33(2), pp. 145–53.

Kakar, Sudhir. 1980. 'The Ties that Bind: Family Relationships in the Mythology of Hindi Cinema', *India International Centre, Quarterly Special Issue*, Vol. 8, No. 1 (March), pp. 11–20.

Kamath, U. Suryanath (ed.). 1982. *Karnataka State Gazeteer, Part 1*. Bangalore: Government of Karnataka.

Kapur, Geeta. 1987. 'Mythic Material in Indian Cinema', *Journal of Arts and Ideas*, No. 14–15 (July-December), pp. 79–107.

Khilnani, Sunil. 1997. *The Idea of India*. New Delhi: Penguin.

Kothari, Rajni. 1964. 'The Congress "System" in India, *Asian Survey*, Vol. 4, No. 12 (December), pp. 1162–4.

Krishnamurthy, B.Y. 2010. *Kannada Chalanachitraranga Ithihasa, Pravruthi Mathu Samasye: Ondu Sukshana Avalokana*. Unpublished PhD thesis, Mangalore University.

Lannoy, Richard. 1971. *The Speaking Tree: A Study of Indian Culture and Society*. New York: Oxford University Press.

Leahy, Joe. 2006. 'India's IT Groups Start to Move to "Near Sourcing"', *Financial Times* (2 November), p. 24.

Lutgendorf, Philip A. 2002. '"Made for Satisfaction" Goddess: *Jai Santoshi Maa*'. Revisited, Part 2, *Manushi*, No. 131 (July-August), pp. 24–37.

Lutze, Lothar. 1985a. 'Interview with Raj Khosla', in Beatrix Pfleiderer and Lothar Lutze (eds), *The Hindi Film: Agent and Re-agent of Cultural Change*. New Delhi: Manohar, p. 39.

———. 1985b. 'From Bharata to Bombay: Change and Continuity in Hindi Film Aesthetics', in Beatrix Pfleiderer and Lothar Lutze (eds), *The Hindi Film: Agent and Re-agent of Cultural Change*. New Delhi: Manohar, p. 8.

Manor, James. 1977a. *Political Change in an Indian State: Mysore 1917–1955*. New Delhi: Manohar.

———. 1977b. 'Structural Changes in Karnataka Politics', *Economic and Political Weekly*, Vol. XII, No. 44 (29 October), pp. 1865–9.

———. 1978. 'Where Congress Survived: Five states in the Indian General Election of 1977', *Asian Survey* (August), pp. 785–803.

———. 1980. 'Pragmatic Progressives in Regional Politics: The Case of Devaraj Urs', *Economic and Political Weekly*, Vol. XV, No. 5–7, Annual Number (February), pp. 201–13.

———. 1996. 'Understanding Deve Gowda', *Economic and Political Weekly*, Vol. XXXI, No. 39 (28 September), pp. 2675–8.

Mishra, Vijay. 1985. 'Towards a Theoretical Critique of Bombay Cinema', *Screen*, 26 (3–4), pp. 133–46.

———. 2002. *Bollywood Cinema: Temples of Desire*. London and New York: Routledge.

Mudaliar, Gangadhar. 1998. *Kannada Cinema Ithihasada Putagalalli*. Bangalore: Kannada Pusthaka Pradhikara.

Muthanna, M. 1980. *History of Modern Karnataka*. New Delhi: Sterling.

Nagaraj, D.R. 1983 'Karanth and the Kannada Novelistic Tradition', in G.S. Shivarudrappa (ed.), *Karanth as Novelist* (in Kannada). Bangalore: Prasaranga, pp. 11–13.

———. 2006. 'The Comic Collapse of Authority: an Essay on the Fears of the Public Spectator', in Vinay Lal and Ashis Nandy (eds), *Finger Printing Popular Culture: The Mythic and the Iconic in Indian Cinema*. New Delhi: Oxford University Press, pp. 87–120.

Nair, Janaki. 2005. *The Promise of the Metropolis: Bangalore's Twentieth Century*. New Delhi: Oxford University Press.

Nandy, Ashis. 1980. *At the Edge of Psychology*. New Delhi: Oxford University Press.

Nandy, Ashis. 1983. *The Intimate Enemy: Loss and Recovery of Self under Colonialism*. New Delhi: Oxford University Press.

Nataraj, Lalitha and V.K. Nataraj. 1982. 'Limits of Populism: Devaraj Urs and Karnataka Politics', *Economic and Political Weekly*, Vol. XVII, No. 37 (11 September), pp. 1503–6.

Nataraj, V.K. 1995. 'Karnataka: Elections and After', *Economic and Political Weekly*, Vol. XXX, No. 2 (14 January), pp. 84–5.

Niranjana, Tejaswini. 1994. 'Integrating whose nation? Tourists and Terrorists in *Roja'*, *Economic and Political Weekly*, Vol. XXIX, No. 3 (15 January), pp. 79–82.

Pandian, M.S.S. 1992. *The Image Trap: MG Ramachandran in Film and Politics*. Delhi: Sage.

Pani, Narendar. 1983. *Reforms to Pre-empt Change: Land Legislation in Karnataka*. New Delhi: Concept Publishing Company.

———. 1998. 'Political Economy of Karnataka, 1950–1995: An Overview', *Journal of Social and Economic Development*, Vol. I, No. I (January-June), pp. 64–84.

———. 2006. 'Icons and Reform Politics in India: The Case of SM Krishna', *Asian Survey*, Vol. 46, No. 2 (March-April), pp. 238–56.

Parthasarathy, Balaji. 2005. 'The Political Economy of the Computer Software Industry in Bangalore', in Ashwani Seth and M. Vijaybaskar (eds), *ICTs and Indian Economic Development*. New Delhi: Sage, pp. 199–230.

Pfleiderer, Beatrix. 1985. 'An Emprical Study of Urban and Semi-Urban Audience Reaction to Hindi Films', in Beatrix Pfleiderer and Lothar Lutze (eds), *The Hindi Film: Agent and Re-agent of Cultural Change*. Delhi: Manohar Publications, p. 89.

Pinto, Ambrose. 1992. 'Institutionalised Corruption', *Economic and Political Weekly*, Vol. XXVII, No. 35 (29 August), pp. 1837–8.

———. 1994. 'Karnataka Cabinet Reshuffle: Unviable', *Economic and Political Weekly*, Vol. XXIX, No. 25 (18 June), pp. 1511–12.

Prakash, E. Sathya. 2009. ' "Bihar" in the Telugu Cinematic Imagination', *Phalanx*, No. 4 (February), posted on www.phalanx.in/pages/article_ i003_Bihar_in_the_telugu_cinematic_imagination.html.   Access date 22/2/2011.

Prasad, M. Madhava. 1999. *Ideology of the Hindi Film*. New Delhi: Oxford University Press.

Pritchett, F.W. 1985. *Marvelous Encounters: Folk Romance in Urdu and Hindi*. Delhi: Manohar.

Puttaswamy, K. 2009. *Cinemayana*. Bangalore: Hasiru Prakashana.

Radway, Janice. 1987. *Reading the Romance*. London: Verso.

Raghavendra, M.K. 2006. 'Globalism and Indian Nationalism', *Economic and Political Weekly*, Vol. XLI, No. 16 (22 April), pp. 1503–5.

Raghavendra, M.K. 2008. *Seduced by the Familiar: Narration and Meaning in Indian Popular Cinema*. New Delhi: Oxford University Press.

———. 2009a. 'Social Dystopia or Entrepreneurial Fantasy: The Significance of *Kaminey*', *Economic and Political Weekly*, Vol. XLIV, No. 38 (19 September), pp. 15–17.

———. 2009b. *50 Indian Film Classics*. New Delhi: Harper-Collins.

Rajadhyaksha, Ashish. 1987. 'The Phalke Era: Conflict of Traditional Form and Modern Technology', *Journal of Arts and Ideas*, No. 14–15 (July–December), pp. 47–108.

———. 2009. *Indian Cinema in the Time of Celluloid: From Bollywood to the Emergency*. New Delhi: Tulika.

Rajadhyaksha, Ashish and Paul Willemen. 1995. *Encyclopaedia of Indian Cinema*. New Delhi: Oxford University Press.

Ramakrishnaiah, M.V. and H.N. Narahari Rao. 1992. *A Glimpse of Kannada Cinema*. Bangalore: Suchitra Film Society.

Ramanujan, A.K. (trans.). 1976. *Samskara: A Rite for a Dead Man*. New Delhi: Oxford University Press.

———. 1986. 'Two Realms of Kannada Folklore', in Stuart Blackburn and A.K. Ramanujan (eds), *Another Harmony: New Essays on the Folklore of India*. New Delhi: Oxford University Press, pp. 41–75.

Real, Michael R. 1996. *Exploring Media Culture*. Thousand Oaks: Sage.

Robinson, Andrew. 1989. *Satyajit Ray: The Inner Eye*. Calcutta: Rupa and Co.

Schatz, Thomas. 1999. 'Film Genre and the Genre Film',in Leo Braudy and Marshall Cohen (eds), *Film Theory and Criticism: Introductory Readings*. New York: Oxford University Press, pp. 691–702.

Scholes, Robert. 1985. 'Narration and Narrativity in Film', in Gerald Mast and Marshall Cohen (eds), *Film Theory and Criticism*. New York: Oxford University Press, pp. 390–405.

Seetharam, C. 2001. *N. Lakshminarayan—Ondu Adhyayana*, unpublished D.Litt thesis. Hampi: Kannada University.

Shadi, Ali Abu. 1996. 'Genres in Egyptian Cinema', in Alia Arasoughly (ed.), *Screens of Life: Critical Film Writing from the Arab World*. Quebec: World Heritage Press, pp. 84–129.

Shah, A.M. 1996. 'Is the Joint Family Disintegrating?', *Economic and Political Weekly*, Vol. XXXI, No. 9, pp. 537–42.

Singh, Chiranjiv. 2008. 'New Shoots and Old Roots: The Cultural Backdrop of Bangalore', in Aditi De (ed.), *Multiple City: Writings on Bangalore*. New Delhi: Penguin, pp. 49–60.

Sontag, Susan. 1983. 'Notes on "Camp"', *Susan Sontag Reader*. Harmondsworth: Penguin, pp. 105–20.

Sreenivasaraju, Sugata. 2008. *Keeping Faith with the Mother Tongue: The Anxieties of a Local Culture*. Bangalore: Navakarnataka Publications.

Sreenivasaraju, Sugata. 2010. 'The Land Bank Ledger', *Outlook* (14 May).

Srinivas, M.N. 1984. 'M.N. Panini, Politics and Society in Karnataka', *Economic and Political Weekly*, Vol. XIX, No. 2 (14 January), pp. 69–75.

Srinivas, S.V. 2009. *Megastar: Chiranjeevi and Telugu Cinema after N.T. Rama Rao*. New Delhi: Oxford University Press.

Subba Rao, V.N. 1991. 'A Macabre Episode Indeed', *Deccan Herald* (9 April), p. 6.

Sudraka (trans. Revilo Pendleton Oliver). 1964. *The Little Clay Cart*, in Henry W. Wells (ed.), *Six Sanskrit Plays*. Bombay: Asia Publishing House.

The Hindu. 2002. 'Do not sacrifice Karnataka's Interests' (16 February).

———. 2009. 'Official Favours Tough Birth Control Law' (12 July).

Todorov, Tsvetan. 1975. *The Fantastic: A Structural Approach to a Literary Genre* (trans. Richard Howard). Ithaca, NY: Cornell University Press.

Uberoi, Patricia. 2002. 'Imagining the Family, An Ethnography of Viewing *Hum Aapke Hain Koun ...!*', in Rachel Dwyer and Christopher Pinney (eds), *Pleasure and the Nation: The History, Politics and Consumption of Public Culture in India*. New Delhi: Oxford University Press, pp. 309–50.

Valicha, Kishore. 1988. *The Moving Image: A Study of Indian Cinema*. Hyderabad: Orient Longman.

Vasudevan, Ravi. 2000a. '*Bombay* and its Public', in Rachel Dwyer and Christopher Pinney (eds), *Pleasure and the Nation: The History, Consumption and Politics of Public Culture in India*. New Delhi: Oxford University Press, pp. 186–211.

———. 2000b. 'Shifting Codes, Dissolving Identities: The Hindi Popular Film of the 1950s as Popular Culture', in Ravi Vasudevan (ed.), *Making Meaning in Indian Cinema*. New Delhi: Oxford University Press, pp. 99–121.

Venkatesh, M.S. 2003. 'Is it a sin to be born as a Kannadiga in Karnataka?', http://news.indiainfo.com, posted on 11 September.

Vidyashankar, N. 1992. 'The Kannada New Wave: A Cinema of Cultural Rootlessness', in M.V. Ramakrishnaiah and H.N. Narahari Rao (eds), *A Glimpse of Kannada Cinema*. Bangalore: Suchitra Film Society, pp. 17–20.

Vijaya, M.B. Singh and V.N. Subba Rao. 2001. *Kannada Chalanachitra Ithihasa, Prasaranga*. Hampi: Kannada University.

Weiner, Myron. 1967. *Party Building in a New Nation*. Chicago: Chicago University Press, pp. 239–55.

Williams, Monier. 1979. *Sanskrit-English Dictionary*. Delhi: Motilal Banarasidas.

Wood, Glynn and Robert Hammond. 1975. 'Electoral Politics in a Congress Dominant state, Mysore 1956-1972', in J.O. Field, F. Frankel, Mary F. Katzenstein, and M. Weiner (eds), *Studies in Electoral Politics in the Indian states*, Vol. IV. Delhi: Manohar.

Yusufi, Sandhya. 1988. 'Puttannna Kanagal: An Analysis', *Deep Focus*, Vol. 1, No. 2 (June), pp. 50–2.

Film Index

8½ 118

A 119–20, 126, 159–60
Aa Dinagalu 147–8
Aag xxxix
Aakrosh 69
Aar Paar 120
Agneepath 93
Aitraaz 156
AK 47 123–4, 126–7, 135
Akaler Sandhane 118
Akasmika 110, 113–17, 119, 126–9,
    149, 157–8, 160–61, 163, 185n22
Amar 9
Amarashilpi Jakannachari 24–5, 159
America! America! 99, 121–2, 126,
    164
American Graffiti 91
Amrutha Dhare 146, 149
Amruthavarshini 100, 121–2, 126
Anand (Hindi) 83
Anand 89–91, 93, 96, 98, 105, 139
Andaz xxxvi
Ankush 80, 93–4, 149
Anmol Ghadi xxviii, xxx
Anna Thangi xxxii, 10–11, 15, 21,
    26–7, 35, 60–1

Antha 79–81, 93, 97, 101–02, 127,
    133
Anubhava 88, 96, 107, 119
Appu 139–42, 147, 149, 153, 188n18
Apthamitra 154–7
Aradhana 63
Arjun 93–4
Auto Raja 77, 98
Awaara xxviii, xxxiv–xxxv, 9, 37, 63
Ayodhya ka Raja xxvi

Baa Nalie Madhuchadrakke 100,
    105, 107, 126–8
Baazi xxxvi, 12
Babruvahana 65, 75, 82, 127
Bandhana 88, 96, 108
Bandini 28
Bangarada Hoovu 31, 34, 37–8, 85
Bangarada Manushya 42, 58, 60,
    62, 108, 136–7, 145, 149, 163,
    185n22
Batwara 93
Bedara Kannappa xlii–xliii, xlv, 4–6,
    19, 22, 26, 35, 82, 84, 94, 127,
    158, 162
Beedhi Basavanna 30
Bees Saal Baad 154

Beladingala Bale 99, 111, 121–2, 126, 135
Bellimoda 50–1, 55, 77, 94, 97, 147
Betaab 90
Bhagyada Bagilu 30
Bhakta Kanakadasa xxix, 8
Bhakta Vijaya xlii, xliv–xlv, 4–6
Bhaktha Prahalada 38, 81–2, 92, 97, 100, 127
Bhale Jodi 41–2, 77
Bhoodana 19–21, 23, 27, 159
Bhoothayyana Maga Ayyu 58, 61–3, 94, 111, 132, 159, 180n35
Bhukailasa 4–6, 20–1, 35, 38
Bhuvan Shome 169n4
Bimba 160
Bombat Hendthi 104, 111, 123, 126
Bombay 123, 164
Border 101, 125
Butch Cassidy and the Sundance Kid 162

Chaitrada Premanjali 99, 105, 107, 110, 126, 186n25
Chandavaliya Thota 26–7, 29, 31, 35, 38, 60, 62–3, 137
Chandralekha xxix
Chattambi Nadu 156
Chiranjeevi xxx, 7–8
Chomana Dudi 67, 69–70, 132, 154, 180n35, 183n27
Chupke Chupke 139
Cleopatra 74
Company 147
Contempt 118
Coolie 94
Cyrano de Bergerac 146

Daari Thappida Maga 64
Damini 92, 101
Day for Night 118
Deewar 63, 133
Devdas xxiii, xxx, 32, 37
Deveeri 160
Dharmatma xxv
Dhool ka Phool xxxi, 7, 52
Diksha 70
Dil ek Mandir 10, 12
Dilwale Dulhaniya Le Jayenge 91, 125

Doni Sagali 110, 126
Duniya na Mane xxviii, 97
Duniya 142–6, 149, 150–1, 153, 160, 164
Durgi 142–3, 147

Ek Duuje Ke Liye 94
Emme Thammanna 29–30
Eradu Kanasu 58, 60
Excuse Me 146

Footpath xxxv

Gajendra 93
Galipata 147
Gandhada Gudi 58
Ganeshana Maduve 102–4, 107, 111, 113, 118, 122, 126, 129, 146
Geejagana Goodu 70
Geetha 82
Gejje Pooje 51–52, 56, 94, 96
Ghatashraddha 67, 70, 132, 154, 159–60, 181n47, 183n27
Ghayal 93–4
Ghulami 93
Goadalli CID 999, 61, 66, 127
Grahana 70
Grease 2, 89
Guide 28
Gumraah 52
Gunasagari xx–xxii, xxiv, xxvi, xxviii–xxxiii, xxxix–xl, xlv, 8–9, 27, 57, 172n43, 180n35

Halu Jenu 80, 83–4, 116, 133
Hannele Chiguridaga 30
Haqeeqat 25
Harishchandra xx–xxiv, xxvi, xxviii, xxxi, xxxix, xlii, xlv, 6, 9, 19, 21
Hombisilu 95
Hongkongnalli Agent Amar 94
Hrudaya Hadithu 111, 126
Hum Aapke Hain Koun ...! xxviii, xxx, 28, 92, 111, 124–5
Hum Dil De Chuke Sanam 125
Humayun xxxi

Immadi Pulakeshi 23
Inglourious Basterds 156

Jailor 32
Janmada Jodi 110, 117, 126
Jedara Bale 33, 35, 38, 61, 75, 85,
    135
Jism 156
Jogi 142–3, 147, 150, 153, 164
Joke Falls 139
Jurm 156

Kaadu Kudre 70
Kaadu 67–70, 160, 183n27
Kaagaz Ke Phool 118, 121
Kabhi Alvida na Kehna xxviii
Kaivara Mahathme 6, 8, 21
Kala Bazar 120
Kala Pani 29, 32
Kaminey 104, 149
Kanneshwar Rama 70
Kasturi Nivasa 42–5, 48–9, 52, 55,
    58, 74, 84, 94, 108, 128, 132, 145,
    149, 182n8
Kavirathna Kalidasa xlv, 82
Keralida Simha 79–80, 155, 157
Kismet 37
Kites 162
Kitti 142–3
Kittur Chanamma 15, 17, 19–20, 23
Kulagowrava 42

La Religieuse 70
Lagaan xxviii, 111, 125
Lord of the Rings 154

Mahakavi Kalidasa xlii, xliv–xlv,
    17, 82
Mahal 9, 43, 154
Mahishasura Mardhini 4–6, 21, 42,
    82, 131
Majestic 142–4, 146–7, 149, 151, 153
Malaya Marutha 92, 98
Manasa Sarovara 185n12
Manthralaya Mahathme 21–2, 35
Mayor Muthanna 34, 38
Mere Mehboob xxxi
Meri Awaaz Suno 93
Mili 83
Minchina Ota 162
Mohabbatein 125
Mother India xxviii, xxxvi, 12, 23,
    63, 133, 186n36

Mr. Rajkumar 42
Mungaru Maley 151–3, 163
Muthina Hara 100, 126–7, 152, 157
My Autograph 157

Na Ninna Bidalare 75–6, 90, 94, 133,
    155
Naalu Pennungal 189n36
Naandi 35, 159
Nagara Haavu 53, 55–6, 62, 78, 94,
    110–11, 180n35
Nammoora Mandara Hoove 118–9,
    122, 126
Nanda Gokula 56–8, 73, 75, 94
Nandadeepa 26–7, 30, 159
Nanjundi Kalyana 89–91, 96, 98,
    108, 158
Naseeb 94
Naya Daur xxxvi, 29, 37, 188n27
Nikaah xxxi
Nishabda 102, 126–7, 135, 157
Nishant 62
Nishkarsha 100, 111, 121–2, 126–7

Ohileshwara xlvi
Om Shanti Om 154
Operation Diamond Racket 61,
    66–7, 75, 85
Operation Jackpot 61

Pakeezah xxxi
Pallavi 70
Panchamaveda 99, 110, 126
Parasakthi xxxvi, 36, 176n54
Pather Panchali 46–7, 67, 184n27
Pattanakke Banda Patniyaru 76–7,
    90, 98, 135
Phaniyamma 70
Phool Aur Kaante 93, 101
Pratighaat 80, 93
Prem Pujari 85
Prem Rog 93
Premaloka 89–91, 98, 105, 133
Purana Mandir 155

Qayamat Se Qayamat Tak 93

Raja Harishchandra 21–2
Ram Aur Shyam 42
Ramudu Bheemudu 25

Ranadheera Kanteerava 15–17, 23, 35, 85
Rang De Basanti 108, 163
Ranganayaki 77–8, 100
Rayara Sose 8, 10–13, 18–19, 21, 26–7, 155
Roja xiii, 164, 190n6
Rowdy Ranganna 30

Sahasa Simha 79–81, 83–5, 90, 92, 94, 96, 99, 155, 157
Sakshatkara 42, 145
Saladin 74
Samskara 45–9, 67–70, 95, 132, 159, 169n4, 180n35
Sandhyaraga 32, 38
Sangam 25
Sangliana 93, 101
Sant Tukaram xliii, 21–2, 35, 38
Sarkar 147
Sarvamangala 32, 56
Sathya Harishchandra 21, 61, 159
Satya 125, 143–4, 147, 149
Satyam Shivam Sundaram xxxv
School Master xxxii, 8, 11–13, 15–16, 19–21, 26–7, 29, 37, 42, 44, 73, 84–5, 131, 159, 182n8
Shahenshah 93
Shahjehan xxxi
Shankar Guru 66–7, 76, 85
Shanti 160
Sharapanjara 51–2, 56, 94
Sheesh Mahal 43
Shh! 100, 118–19, 122, 126–8
Shiva Mechida Kannappa 82
Sholay 56
Shruthi 102, 111, 122, 126, 129, 139, 146, 149
Shwetha Naga 153, 155

Sodari xlvi
Sose Thanda Sowbhagya 76–8
SP Sangliana 2 101–02, 105, 111, 117, 122, 126–8, 135, 141
Sri Krishna Garudi 4
Sri Krishnadevaraya 41, 85, 98, 104, 161, 182n8
Subba Sastry 159

Tansen xxxi
Taqdeer 37
Tarle Nan Maga 103–04, 107, 111, 113, 115, 117–19, 121–3, 126–8, 134, 160
Tezaab 93
Thayi Saheba 159
The Exorcist 75, 156
The Godfather 147
The Life of Christ xxv
The Searchers 74
The Seventh Seal 45
The Ten Commandments 75
Trishul 90

Upkaar xxviii
Uski Roti 169n4
Utkarsha 100, 111, 122, 126–8
Uyaale 159

Vamsha Vriksha 49
Varasdhara 147
Vasanthasena xx, xxvi, xxvii–xxix, xxxi, xxxiii, xl, xlv, 20
Veera Sankalpa 24–5, 84
Vijayanagarada Veeraputra 15–17, 19–20, 23, 25, 41–2, 131, 158

Yajamana 136–9, 141, 149–50

General Index

Akali Dal 79
All India Congress Committee
    xxxvii–xxxviii, 33–4
Ambarish 55, 77, 80, 89, 157
Amrohi, Kamal 9
Ananthamurthy, U.R. 45, 47–8, 70–1,
    150
Anderson, Benedict 71
Andhra Pradesh xv, xlii, 165
Arasukumar, B.A. 31
Arathi 53, 55, 77, 95, 158
Arvind, Ramesh 119, 139, 154, 158
Ashadabuthi 159
Ashwath 4–5, 30, 44, 53, 57, 77
Asrani 56
Auden, W.H. 71
Avinash 154

Baboo, Dinesh 100, 102
Babu, S.V. Rajendra Singh 79, 88,
    100, 110
Bachchan, Amitabh 35, 159
Bai, Pandari xxxix, xlii, 4, 158
Balakrishna 4, 11, 22
Balayya, T.S. xxxix
Banerji, Vibhutibhushan 47

Bangalore, xiv, 31–4, 44, 53, 122
    cinematic representations 62,
        110–16, 123, 138–9
    regional identity 165
Bangalore Agenda Task Force (BATF)
    141
Bangarappa, S. 105–06
Barjatya, Sooraj 124
Barthes, Roland 74, 181n1
Barua, P.C. xxiii, 37
Benegal, Shyam 62
Bergman, Ingmar 45, 179n19
Bhagwat, Kusum 22
Bhagwatar, Honnappa xxxix, xliv
Bharathi 41
Bharatiya Janata Party (BJP) 101
Bhat, Yogaraj 147, 151
Bhave, K.P. xxx, 7
Bhave, Vinobha 19
Bhyrappa, S.L. 49, 71
Bindranwale, Jarnail Singh 79
Bommai, S.R. 87, 185n15

Cariappa, Gen. 100
Chaitanya, K.M. 147
Chandra, N. 80

Chandrashekar, Nagathihalli 99–100, 105, 146
Chatterjee, Partha xxiv
Congress (I) 86, 105
Congress (O) 54
Congress (R) 54–5, 67, 78
Congress Party 1–3, 33–4, 36, 40

Darshan 143
Das, Nandita 160, 189n36
Datanna 139
Dattaraj, G. 79
Desai, Sunil Kumar 99–100, 118–19
Deshpande, R.H. xli
Deshpande, Guru 147
Devi, B. Saroja 4, 17, 24, 158
Diderot, Denis 70
Dorairaj/Bhagwan 33
Dravida Munnetra Kazhagam (DMK) xxxvi–xxxvii, 36
Dutt, Guru 118
Dutta, J.P. 101, 183n22
Dwarakish 25, 102

Ekikarana Movement xli
Encyclopaedia of Indian Cinema 23

Fellini, Federico 118
Film and Television Institute of India (FTII) 178n13
Film Finance Corporation (FFC) xii, 68, 169n4, 181n45
Film genres
  Heimatfilme 74
  Kompeni 74
  Perjuangan 74
Ford, John 74

Gandhi, M.K. xxv, xxxviii
Gandhi, Indira 34, 40, 54–6, 60, 62, 65–8, 78–9, 85–7, 93, 132–3, 180n33
Gandhi, Pooja 151
Gandhi, Rajiv 87, 93, 105, 124
Gandhi, Sanjay 86
Ganesan, Shivaji 12, 36
Ganesh 151, 158
Gangadhar 81
Gayathri 77

Geetha 114
Geethapriya 95
Giri, V.V. 34
Godard, Jean-Luc 118
Gokak, V.K. 87
Gokak Committee Report 87
Gopalakrishnan, Adoor 189n36
Gowda, H.D. Deve 128, 184n10

Hanumanthiah, K. xlii, 2–3
Harijan xxxviii
Hegde, Ramakrishna 87, 106, 185n15
Hyderabad xiv

Indian cinema 15
  art xi
  Bhojpuri xii
  Caste in 93–7, 172n49
  Hindi xi–xv, xvii, xix–xxii, xxviii
    code of dharma xxxiii
    comparisons with 130–1, 134, 154, 167
    modernism 40, 178n5
    post-1947 xxxv
  Kannada xii–xiv, xvii, xx–xxiv, xxix
    anti-brahminism 36
    caste representations 31
    comic Brahmin xxxii
    heroic past 15
    Hindu hierarchy 9
    moral instruction xxxiii–xxxiv
    mythological 27
    New Wave 70–1
    post-1947 xxxv, xxxix
  Malayalam xii
  middle xi
  popular xi
  Tamil xii, xv
Indian National Congress xvii, xxiv
Indira, M.K. 51, 71
Information and Broadcasting Ministry 68
Ismail, Sir Mirza xxxviii, 14, 40
Iyengar, Gorur Ramaswamy 71
Iyer, G.V. xliii, 19–20, 22, 159

Jagadeesh, Jai 143
Jagannath, Puri 139

Jaggesh 103, 157
Jairaj, M.P. 148
Janata Party 79, 87, 105
Jayanthi 41, 89, 158
Jeetendra 93

Kakar, Sudhir 169n6
Kalpana 30–1, 50–1, 60, 158
Kambar, Chandrashekhar 70
Kanagal, Puttanna 42, 49, 52–4, 56,
    77, 97, 108
Kannada 150, 163
    adaptations from literature 133
    bowdlerization 109, 126–7
    Gokak agitation 85, 166
    Language agitation 87
    Pragathisheela movement 69
Kapoor, Raj xxxv, xxxix, 37–8
Karanth, B.V. 49, 67–9, 175n25
Karanth, K. Shivaram 47, 69, 71
Karanth, Prema 70
Karnad, Girish 45, 49, 67, 123, 148,
    179n14, 181n51
Karnataka xiv–xv, 59
    Population 165
Karnataka Film Chamber of
    Commerce (KFCC) 162
Karnataka Provincial Congress
    Committee (KPCC) xli
Karnataka Vidyavardhaka Sangha
    xli
Kasaravalli, Girish 67, 70, 133, 159,
    169n1, 189n36
Kashinath 88
Kaul, Arun 70
Kaul, Mani 169n1
Khan, Mehboob 9, 12
Khosla, Raj 32
Krishna, S.M. 139, 141
Krishnamurthy, Hunsur 4, 21, 24–5,
    65, 159
Krishnamurthy, P.H. 99
Kulkarni, Atul 148
Kumar, Dilip xxiii
Kumar, Kalyana 8, 19, 24, 50
Kumar, Rajendra 52
Kumar, Udaya 16, 19

Lakshmi 75, 80

Lakshminarayan, N. 159, 175n27
Land Reforms Act 59–60
Lankesh, P. 45, 70
Lankesh, Kavitha 133, 160
Leelavathi 4, 22, 51, 77, 89, 158
Lohitashwa, Sharath 148
Lokesh 61, 89
Lotman, J.M. xxii

Madhavi 83, 114
Mammooty 156
Manusmriti xxvii
Modi, Sohrab 32
Mricchakatika xxvi
Mudduraj 142
Mukherjee, Hrishikesh 83, 139
Murthy, N.R. Narayana 150
Mysore xi, xiv–xx, xxviii, xlvi–xlvii
    accession 1, 7
    caste xxxii, xli, 2, 54–57
    language 18
    marriages xxx
    modernism 14, 31–3, 40, 43–4
    post-1947 xxxvii
    renamed Karnataka 59, 64
    representation in cinema 31–4, 63
Mysore Congress xxxvii–xxxviii,
    xl–xli, 2–3, 8, 33

Nadkarni, Sundarrao 21
Nag, Ananth 75, 81, 102, 151
Nag, Shankar 77, 82, 101, 157, 162
Nagabharana, T.S. 70, 110, 114, 117,
    160
Nagaraj, D.R. 37
Namboodaripad, E.M.S. 62
Nanjundappa, P. 101
Narasimharaju xliii, 4, 9, 21
Narayan, S. 99, 105, 110
National Film Development
    Corporation (NFDC) xii, 178n13
Nihalani, Govind 69, 179n18
Nijalingappa 4, 33–4, 40, 55, 61, 85,
    174n12

Panthulu, B.R. xxxii, 8, 11, 15, 17,
    29–30, 37, 41, 158, 175n39,
    182n8
Patil, Ashok 139

Patil, Veerendra 54, 105–06
Pattabhi, Aroor xlii, xliv
Phalke, D.G. xxv
Prabhakar 89
Prasad, Vinaya 102
Prem 142, 146
Prema 119
Puneeth Rajkumar 139, 158
Puri, Amrish 67
Puri, Om 123
Puttappa, K.V. 47

Quit India Movement xxxviii

Raghavendra Rajkumar 90
Rajashekar, H.S. 111
Rajashekar, M.S. 89
Rajan, N.C. 15
Rajkumar xlii, xliv, 4–5, 10, 15, 17, 19, 21–3, 29, 31, 33–8, 41–2, 45, 57–60, 63, 65, 80–1–83, 87, 114, 116, 132–4, 136, 145, 157, 159, 161, 166–7
Ramachandra, H.S. Phani 102
Ramachandra, Kothwal 148, 187n16
Ramachandran, M.G. 35
Ramachandrappa, Baragur 160
Ramamurthy, R. 30
Ramanujan, A.K. 48, 170n14
Ranga, B.S. 4, 23, 42, 159
Ranga, T.S. 70
Rao, A.N. Krishna (ANaKru) 45, 71
Rao, A.N. Murthy 159
Rao, A.V. Seshagiri 76
Rao, Aluru Venkata xli, 18
Rao, R. Gundu, 78, 86–7, 106
Rao, N.T. Rama 36, 158
Rao, N. Omprakash 123
Rao, Nagendra xx, xxvi, xxxii, 15–16, 21, 158
Rao, P.N. Ramachandra 104
Rao, P.V. Narasimha 124, 142
Rao, Singeetham Srinivasa 80, 83, 89
Rao, T.R. Subba (TaRaSu) 28, 45, 53, 71
Rao, Vasudeva 69
Rathnam, Mani xiii, 190n6
Ravichandran, V. 88–9, 92, 157
Ravishankar 142
Rawail, H.S. xxx

Ray, Satyajit 47, 49, 67–8, 169n1
Reddy, K.C. 2
Reddy, Pattabhirama 45, 67, 169n4
Reddy, Sanjeeva 34
Reddy, Snehlatha 45
Rivette, Jacques 70
Roshan, Rakesh 162
Rosselini, Roberto 159
Roy, Bimal xxiii, 32, 169n1
Roy, Raja Ram Mohan xxxiii

S.K. Patil Film Enquiry Commission Report of 1951 68
Sab, Abdul Nazir 87
Saigal, K.L. xxiii
Sangliana, H.T. 101
Saritha 80
Sastry, K.R. Seetharama xlii, xliv, 10
Satya, P.N. 142
Sathyu, M.S. 70
Sen, Mrinal 118, 169n4
Seshadri 136
Shahani, Kumar 169n1, 181n45
Shankar, K. 4
Shankar, M.P. 61
Shantaram, V. xxv–xxvi, xxviii, 179n20
Shastri, Lal Bahadur 40
Shirur xx, xxvi
Shivarajkumar 89, 119, 123, 139, 158
Shivaram, Pekete 42, 64
Siddalingaiah 34, 42, 58
Simha, H.L.N. xx, xlii, 158
Simon, Joe 79, 94
Singh, Manmohan 124
Sino-Indian War 29, 42, 84
Somashekar, K. 66
Somashekar, V. 93
Soori 142
Soundarya 110, 153–4
Srinath 89, 157
Srinivas, M.N. 31
Srinivas, S.V. 158
Srinivas, Thoogudeepa 81, 115
Sriramulu, Potti xlii
Sudeep 157
Sudarshan 16
Sudharani 89
Sudraka xxvi, 172n44

Suhasini 88, 100
Swamy, M.V. Krishna 159
Swamy, Y.R. xxx, 8, 56

Tamil Nadu xv, 165
Tarantino, Quentin 156
Thakur, T.V. Singh xlvi, 6, 8, 21
Thimmaiah, Gen. 100
Triveni 45, 50, 52, 71
Truffaut, Francois 118

Umashri 88
Upendra 100, 118–22, 157, 159–60,
    186n26
Urban Land Ceiling Act 59
Urs, D. Devaraj 54–5, 58–62, 66, 78,
    85–7, 106, 132–3, 180n33

Vajramuni 114
Varma, Ram Gopal 147
Vasan, S.S. xxix
Vasu, P. 154
Veerappan 166
Verma, Raja Ravi xxv–xxvi
Vidyarthi, Ashish 148
Vijay 58, 75, 77, 144
Vishnuvardhan 53, 61, 76, 81, 88–9,
    95, 100, 150, 154, 157, 166
Vishwanath, P.H. 110
Visveswaraiya, M. xx, 14, 40, 43, 59,
    63, 132
Vittal, M.R. 27, 30, 159
Vivekananda xxxiii

Wadeyar, Maharaja Jayachamaraja 1